D0880928

The Effects of
Parental Dysfunction
on Children

The Effects of Parental Dysfunction on Children

Edited by

Robert J. McMahon
University of Washington
Seattle, Washington

and

Ray DeV. Peters
Queen's University
Kingston, Ontario

Kluwer Academic/Plenum Publishers
New York, Boston, Dordrecht, London, Moscow

ISBN 0-306-47252-X

©2002 Kluwer Academic / Plenum Publishers, New York
233 Spring Street, New York, New York 10013

http://www.kluweronline.com

10 9 8 7 6 5 4 3 2 1

A C.I.P. record for this book is available from the Library of Congress

Contributors

William R. Beardslee, Harvard Medical School, Boston, Massachusetts

Vivianne Bentley, Concordia University, Montreal, Quebec, Canada

Devon D. Brewer, University of Washington, Seattle, Washington

Heather Carmichael Olson, University of Washington, Seattle, Washington

Richard F. Catalano, University of Washington, Seattle, Washington

Jessica Cooperman, Concordia University, Montreal, Quebec, Canada

Mark R. Dadds, Griffith University, Brisbane, Queensland, Australia

W. Hobart Davies, University of Wisconsin-Milwaukee, Milwaukee, Wisconsin

Maurice A. Feldman, Queen's University, Kingston, Ontario, Canada

Hiram E. Fitzgerald, Michigan State University, East Lansing, Michigan

Charles B. Fleming, University of Washington, Seattle, Washington

Paul J. Frick, University of New Orleans, New Orleans, Louisiana

Randy R. Gainey, Old Dominion University, Norfolk, Virginia

Kevin P. Haggerty, University of Washington, Seattle, Washington

Lizbeth Hoke, Judge Baker Children's Center, Boston, Massachusetts

Jane E. Ledingham, University of Ottawa, Ottawa, Ontario, Canada

Bryan R. Loney, Florida State University, Tallahassee, Florida

Robert J. McMahon, University of Washington, Seattle, Washington

Kathleen Ries Merikangas, Yale University School of Medicine, New Haven, Connecticut

Ray DeV. Peters, Queen's University, Kingston, Ontario, Canada

Christina Saltaris, Concordia University, Montreal, Quebec, Canada

Alex E. Schwartzman, Concordia University, Montreal, Quebec, Canada

Lisa A. Serbin, Concordia University, Montreal, Quebec, Canada

Dale M. Stack, Concordia University, Montreal, Quebec, Canada

Susan Swatling, Judge Baker Children's Center, Boston, Massachusetts

Polly Van de Velde, Judge Baker Children's Center, Boston, Massachusetts

Eve M. Versage, Judge Baker Children's Center, Boston, Massachusetts

Elaine F. Walker, Emory University, Atlanta, Georgia

Robert A. Zucker, University of Michigan, Ann Arbor, Michigan

Preface

The 1998 Banff International Conference on Behavioural Science addressed the topic of the effects of parental behavioral and emotional dysfunctions on children in the family. Recent experience with interventions designed to promote the well being of children and to prevent mental health problems has identified particular challenges in families with dysfunctional parents. These families are often very difficult to engage in mental health promotion and prevention programs, and they may be especially recalcitrant to intervention. The focus of this volume is to explore the current level of knowledge regarding the processes by which a number of parental dysfunctions influence the developmental outcomes of children.

Renowned scientist-practitioners from the United States, Canada, and Australia participated in the conference, and subsequently contributed 10 chapters based on their presentations to this volume. The major topics addressed by the conference were those of children growing up in families in which the parents suffer from major psychosocial difficulties, including schizophrenia, depression, alcoholism, drug addiction, anxiety disorders, intellectual disabilities, and antisocial personality disorder. This volume is divided into two sections. In the first section, two chapters provide scholarly descriptions of developmental models for conceptualizing the various risk and protective factors (genetic, biological, and environmental) that play critical roles in the transmission of the effects of parental dysfunction to the development of the child. In the second section, the remaining eight chapters focus on specific parental dysfunctions and their effects on children in the family. These chapters cover descriptive psychopathology, implications for intervention (both treatment and prevention), and descriptions of intervention procedures.

Part 1, 'Conceptual Overview,' begins with a chapter by Elaine F. Walker, who introduces the volume by presenting a developmentally oriented conceptual model for examining the risk factors that affect the children of dysfunctional parents, with an emphasis on prenatal factors that comprise fetal neurodevelopment and postnatal events that serve to trigger the expression of vulnerabilities. To illustrate the importance of focusing on developmental pathways, Walker presents a multi-factor risk model to describe the epigenesis of vulnerability to schizophrenia, along with empirical evidence to support this model. In Chapter 2, Kathleen Ries Merikangas examines the role of familial factors in the development of dysfunction as well as potential mechanisms for familial aggregation, using substance use disorders as an example. She begins with a description of the goals and methods of genetic epidemiology. Using illustrative data from a high-risk study of substance use and anxiety disorders, Merikangas describes how genetic epidemiological methods can shed light on various methods of familial aggregation. She also presents implications for prevention and treatment.

Part 2, 'Parental Dysfunctions,' presents detailed expositions of specific parental dysfunctions and their effects on children in the family. In Chapter 3, Lisa A. Serbin and colleagues focus on the risk to offspring of parents from a prospective longitudinal study of individuals from inner-city Montreal with lower socioeconomic status backgrounds. The parents in this sample have been followed since they were elementary school children into parenthood. Within this sample of socially and economically disadvantaged young adults, intergenerational risk and prediction of problems in offspring were examined in relation to the parents' patterns of childhood aggression and social withdrawal. The complex, multiple challenges facing these individuals as they become parents are described. The focus of the chapter is on the prediction of adverse birth circumstances and parenting problems, which may predict risk and negative outcomes for a new generation of children. Implications of these findings for prevention and early intervention focusing on parents and their young children are also considered.

Two chapters focus on internalizing disorders. In Chapter 4, William R. Beardslee and colleagues describe their programmatic efforts to prevent depression in children through the promotion of resiliency. The Preventive Intervention Project works with families to prevent difficulties in children from homes in which there is parental affective illness by promoting resilient traits and modifying risk factors associated with parental affective illness. The chapter begins with a review of the risks associated with parental affective illness. Beardslee and colleagues then describe the theoretical framework and the content of this empirically validated, clinician-facilitated intervention.

It is well established that anxiety problems and disorders run in families. In Chapter 5, Mark R. Dadds reviews family processes implicated in the development, maintenance, and treatment of these problems in children and adolescents. Dadds focuses on how social learning processes may operate within variations in the quality of intimate relationships in the family to lead to anxiety disorders. He provides examples of how these processes can be contrasted and integrated at both clinical and theoretical levels.

Antisocial behavior causes great monetary and social costs to society. In Chapter 6, Paul J. Frick and Brian R. Loney examine heredity, observational learning, and disrupted socialization as possible mechanisms involved in the association between parent and child antisocial disorders. Based on their own programmatic research, they propose that parental antisocial behavior is linked primarily to a subgroup of children with conduct disorders who also demonstrate high rates of 'callous-unemotional' traits. Ineffective parenting practices, which have been closely tied to the development of child conduct disorders, are less strongly associated with conduct disorders in these children. Instead, Frick and Loney speculate that a temperamental predisposition (low fearful inhibitions) may be an important intergenerational link between parental and child antisocial behavior.

The next three chapters focus on parental alcohol and other substance use. In Chapter 7, Hiram E. Fitzgerald, W. Hobart Davies, and Robert A. Zucker first review the findings from a prospective longitudinal study of children at high risk for the later development of alcoholism with high antisocial coactions. The developmental sequence for the emergence of such coactions is regulated by familial aggressive behavior, negative affect, and alcohol abuse, embedded within a genetic vulnerability for such attributes, and shaped by parents who model disorganized and addictive behaviors. Fitzgerald and colleagues then describe a parenting and communication skills-based intervention designed to benefit children growing up in an alcoholic home. The program is a behavior management and communication skills-based intervention that has been used to promote prosocial behavioral development and empower parents to deal with the development of antisocial behavior beginning during the preschool years.

Heather Carmichael Olson then describes the most recent research available on the range of possible consequences for children born affected by exposure to alcohol because of maternal drinking during pregnancy. She begins with an overview of diagnosis and terminology, incidence, and causal factors and mechanisms for the disabilities experienced by these children. Carmichael-Olson then describes a number of salient issues for clinical practice. She places special emphasis on the importance of early assessment and intervention procedures to deal with children experiencing fetal alcohol syndrome and related conditions

Risk factors for substance abuse that have been identified indicate that children of substance abusers are likely to be exposed to elevated levels of several of these risk factors. In Chapter 9, Richard F. Catalano, Kevin P. Haggerty, and colleagues review the scientific findings of the Focus on Families (FOF) Project. This intervention employs group training and home-based services aimed at reducing family-related risk factors, enhancing protective factors, and reducing illicit drug use among parents and their children. A proposed agenda for future research on processes of change among high-risk families is also outlined.

The final chapter in this volume focuses on children of parents with intellectual disabilities. As society moves towards supporting full inclusion of people with disabilities, questions are raised about parenting rights and competencies, and the impact of parental disabilities on offspring. Maurice A. Feldman provides an overview of the current state of knowledge on the development of children raised by parents with intellectual disabilities. He also reviews what is known about the effectiveness of child-focused intervention projects, consisting of extensive day-care experiences with parent home-visiting. The chapter concludes with a review of research concerning the effectiveness of projects that focus on parents with intellectual disabilities.

THE BANFF CONFERENCES ON BEHAVIOURAL SCIENCE

This volume is one of a continuing series of publications sponsored by the Banff International Conferences on Behavioural Science. We are pleased to join Kluwer Academic/Plenum Press in bringing this volume to an audience of practitioners, investigators, and students. The publications arise from conferences held each spring since 1969 in Banff, Alberta, Canada, with papers representing the product of deliberations on themes and key issues. The conferences bring together outstanding behavioral scientists and professionals in a forum where they can present and discuss data related to emergent issues and topics. As a continuing event, the Banff International Conferences have served as an expressive 'early indicator' of the developing nature and composition of the behavioral sciences and scientific applications to human problems and issues.

Because distance, schedules, and restricted audience preclude wide attendance at the conferences, the resulting publications have equal status with the conferences proper. Each presenter at each Banff Conference wrote a chapter specifically for the present volume, separate from his or her presentation and discussion at the conference itself. Consequently, this volume is not a set of conference proceedings. Rather, it is an integrated volume of chapters contributed by leading researchers and practitioners who have had the unique opportunity of spending several days together presenting and discussing ideas prior to preparing their chapters.

Our 'conference of colleagues' format provides for formal and informal interactions among all participants through invited addresses, workshops, poster presentations, and conversation hours. When combined with sightseeing expeditions, cross country and downhill skiing, and other recreational activities in the spectacular Canadian Rockies, the conferences have generated great enthusiasm and satisfaction among participants. The Banff Centre, our venue for the Conferences for more than 30 years, has contributed immeasurably to the success of these meetings through its very comfortable accommodation, dining, and conference facilities. The following documents conference themes over the past 33 years.

1969	I	Ideal Mental Health Services
1970	II	Services and Programs for Exceptional Children and Youth
1971	III	Implementing Behavioural Programs for Schools and Clinics
1972	IV	Behaviour Change: Methodology, Concepts, and Practice
1973	V	Evaluation of Behavioural Programs in Community, Residential, and School Settings
1974	VI	Behaviour Modification and Families and Behavioural Approaches to Parenting

1975	VII	The Behavioural Management of Anxiety, Depression, and Pain
1976	VIII	Behavioural Self-Management Strategies, Techniques, and Outcomes
1977	IX	Behavioural Systems for the Developmentally Disabled
		A. School and Family Environments
		B. Institutional, Clinical, and Community Environments
1978	X	Behavioural Medicine: Changing Health Lifestyles
1979	XI	Violent Behaviour: Social Learning Approaches to Prediction, Management, and Treatment
1980	XII	Adherence, Compliance, and Generalization in Behavioural Medicine
1981	XIII	Essentials of Behavioural Treatments for Families
1982	XIV	Advances in Clinical Behaviour Therapy
1983	XV	Childhood Disorders: Behavioural-Developmental Approaches
1984	XVI	Education in '1984'
1985	XVII	Social Learning and Systems Approaches to Marriage and the Family
1986	XVIII	Health Enhancement, Disease Prevention, and Early Intervention: Biobehavioural Perspectives
1987	XIX	Early Intervention in the Coming Decade
1988	XX	Behaviour Disorders of Adolescence: Research, Intervention, and Policy in Clinical and School Settings
1989	XXI	Psychology, Sport, and Health Promotion
1990	XXII	Aggression and Violence Throughout the Lifespan
1991	XXIII	Addictive Behaviours Across the Lifespan: Prevention, Treatment, and Policy Issues
1992	XXIV	State of the Art in Cognitive/Behaviour Therapy
1993	XXV	Anxiety and Depression in Adults and Children
1994	XXVI	Prevention and Early Intervention: Child Disorders, Substance Abuse, and Delinquency
1995	XXVII	Child Abuse: New Directions in Prevention and Treatment Across the Lifespan
1996	XXVIII	Best Practice: Developing and Promoting Empirically Validated Interventions
1997	XXIX	Stress: Vulnerability and Resiliency
1998	XXX	Children of Disordered Parents
1999	XXXI	Suicide: Prediction, Prevention, and Intervention
2000	XXXII	Resilience: Children, Families, and Communities
2001	XXXIII	Emotional Self-Regulation: Development, Successes, and Failures
2002	XXXIV	Adolescent Substance Abuse: Innovative Approaches to Prevention and Treatment

We would like to acknowledge the expert guidance and support that we received from Mariclaire Cloutier, Siiri Lelumees, Anna Tobias, and Teresa Krauss at Kluwer Academic/Plenum Press and the assistance of Judi Amsel.

It has been a pleasure working with them. Special thanks go to our colleagues on the Planning Committee, Drs. Ken Craig and Keith Dobson. While preparing this volume, Bob McMahon was on the faculty of the University of Washington, and Ray Peters was on the faculty of Queen's University. The assistance and support of these institutions is gratefully acknowledged.

Robert J. McMahon
Ray DeV. Peters

Contents

The Effects of
Parental Dysfunction
on Children

PART 1

Conceptual Overview

CHAPTER 1

The Role of Endogenous and Exogenous Risk Factors in the Genesis of Schizophrenia

ELAINE F. WALKER

The children of parents with psychiatric disorders have been the focus of numerous clinical studies over the past three decades (Walker, 1991). The primary reason for interest in this population is that research with families has consistently shown these children to be at 'high-risk' for developing psychopathology. Behavioral genetic research indicates that this is due, at least in part, to the transmission of genetic vulnerabilities from parents to their offspring (Gottesman, 1991). Given this assumption, investigators have conducted prospective longitudinal studies of the offspring of mentally ill parents with the aim of identifying 'markers' of constitutional risk for pychopathology.

However, real world phenomena have posed some formidable challenges for researchers. In 1989, we published a paper entitled 'The nonorthogonal nature of risk factors' in the *Journal of Primary Prevention* (Walker, Downey, & Nightingale, 1989). The central thesis of this paper is that risk factors for psychological maladjustment are highly intercorrelated, making the task of identifying specific determinants of psychopathology more complex. The most obvious example is the correlation between genetic and family environment risk factors: Psychiatrically disturbed parents not only transmit genetic liabilities to some of their offspring, but they may also be unable to provide an optimal caregiving environment. Thus, genetic vulnerabilities are correlated with environmental adversity. In discussing this issue, we described several other sources of correlated risk factors.

In our 1989 article on the problem of confounded risk factors, the chief focus was on postnatal experiences. Since that time, however, experimental neuroscience research has revealed that a myriad of prenatal environmental factors influence fetal central nervous system (CNS) development, as well as postnatal functioning (Walker & Diforio, 1997). Although these experimental studies have been conducted on animals, the results of clinical research suggest that the same effects occur in humans. Taken together, these findings interject greater complexity into the discussion of confounded risk factors.

There are two key findings in the experimental literature that have particular relevance to our understanding of the development of children whose parents have psychiatric illnesses. First, prenatal maternal experiences, most notably maternal exposure to stress, can have significant effects on fetal neurodevelopment. Second, these neural changes can persist into the postnatal period and influence behavior, as well as sensitivity to external stressors. This body of findings suggests the possibility that the environmental risk factors impinging on children of parents with psychiatric disorders can begin in-utero. Thus, our implicit tendency to conceptualize environmental influences as events that occur during postnatal development may be shortsighted.

This chapter explores recent literature on the prenatal and postnatal determinants of behavioral development, with the goal of reconceptualizing the epigenetic process in schizophrenia. We begin by briefly examining the relation between parental psychiatric status and prenatal factors. This is followed by an overview of the prenatal factors that influence fetal neurodevelopment. The discussion then turns to some potential implications of these findings for research on the development of children with mentally ill parents. Finally, we discuss some clinical research findings, including those from our studies of children at risk for psychopathology, which shed light on the interactional processes that determine the developmental course of children whose parents have mental illness. Although the present chapter is primarily concerned with the determinants of schizophrenia, we should note that similar processes are probably operative in other psychiatric disorders.

THE ASSOCIATION BETWEEN PARENTAL PSYCHIATRIC STATUS AND PRENATAL FACTORS

Psychiatric disorders are often associated with deficits in socioemotional and cognitive functioning which, in turn, compromise the patient's social and economic well being. It is, therefore, not surprising that women with psychiatric illnesses experience a heightened rate of exposure to stressful events during pregnancy (Miller, 1997). For example, pregnant women with schizophrenia are more likely to have financial problems, to have a limited social network, to be unmarried and to report that their pregnancy is unwanted (Miller & Finnerty, 1996). Studies of pregnant women without psychiatric disorders have documented that being unmarried and having an unwanted pregnancy are both associated with heightened levels of self-reported stress (Berkman, 1969; Kuhn, 1982; Rosin, 1985).

Physical risk factors are also more common in the pregnancies of women with mental illness. For example, pregnant women with schizophrenia are more likely to be victims of physical and sexual abuse (Goodman, Rosenberg, Mueser, & Drake, 1997) and to use recreational drugs and alcohol (Miller, 1997). Finally, due to limited financial and social resources, women with psychiatric disorders get poorer prenatal care (Miller, 1997).

In sum, there are well-established associations between maternal psychiatric status and both socioemotional and physical complications of pregnancy. Although there is little empirical research on the biological offspring of men with psychiatric disorders, it is reasonable to assume that they are also exposed to greater prenatal risk. Certainly, women whose spouses have a major mental disorder are more likely to be subjected to stressful interpersonal events and financial problems than are women with healthy spouses.

THE EFFECT OF PRENATAL EVENTS ON FETAL NEURODEVELOPMENT

We now turn to the factors that compromise fetal neurodevelopment. Experimental research on animals has revealed that a broad range of prenatal factors has the potential for altering CNS structure and function. Some of these factors, particularly maternal exposure to stressful events, are among those shown to occur at an elevated rate in the pregnancies of women with schizophrenia.

Experimental studies of rodents and nonhuman primates have revealed that the hypothalamic-pituitary-adrenal (HPA) axis is altered in offspring whose mothers were exposed to prenatal stress (e.g., loud noise, social isolation, periodic physical restraint) (for a review, see Walker & Diforio, 1997). The HPA axis is one of the major brain systems that mediates the mammalian response to stress, and it governs the release of 'stress hormones' (primarily cortisol in primates and corticosterone in rodents) from the adrenal cortex. Rodents born to dams who were stressed in the prenatal period show heightened stress hormone release as neonates and during adulthood (Vallee, Mayo, Dellu, & LeMoal, 1997). The same effect has been demonstrated in studies of nonhuman primates (Uno, Eisele, Sakai, & DeJesus, 1994). Thus the mother's experiences during pregnancy can alter her offspring's postnatal neurophysiology, rendering the organism more sensitive to stressful postnatal events.

It appears that maternal release of stress hormones during pregnancy is largely responsible for this effect. When pregnant dams are injected with adrenal hormones during pregnancy, the same neurohormonal consequences are observed in offspring (Fameli, Kitraki, & Stylianopoulou, 1994). But, when secretion of adrenal hormones is suppressed during pregnancy, maternal exposure to stress has no measurable effect on offspring behavior or biological stress sensitivity (Barbazanges, Piazza, LeMoal, & Maccari, 1996).

The dysregulation of HPA function observed in prenatally stressed animals is mediated by damage to the hippocampus. Specifically, prenatally stressed rodents (Barbazanges, et al., 1996; Vaid, et al., 1997) and primates (Uno, et al., 1994) show hippocampal abnormalities, including reductions in the cellular density of glucocorticoid receptors (GRs) in the hippocampus. Because the hippocampus contains a relatively high density of GRs, it plays an important role in the provision of negative feedback to the HPA axis. Thus, a reduction in the density of hippocampal GRs compromises its function in 'dampening' the intensity of the organism's biological stress response.

We are not aware of any published reports on the effects of prenatal maternal stress on cortisol release or hippocampal morphology in human offspring. But it has been shown that exposure to psychosocial stressors is associated with HPA dysregulation in pregnant women (Wadhwa, Dunkel-Schetter, Chicz-Demet, & Porto, 1996). Further, as described below, behavioral studies of the children of women exposed to trauma during pregnancy suggest that prenatal stress disrupts human fetal neurodevelopment.

While the effects of prenatal stress on postnatal stress hormone release have been the most consistently documented, it is noteworthy that recent studies have also revealed a variety of other physical and behavioral consequences. Prenatally stressed rodents show behavioral abnormalities, such as heightened aversion to novelty, into adulthood (Poltyrev, Keshet, Kay, & Weinstock, 1996; Vallee, et al., 1997). Among primates, prenatal stress is linked with an increase in motor deficits (Schneider, 1992a,b), subtle physical abnormalities (Newell-Morris, Farenbruch, & Sackett, 1989) and social impairment (Clarke, Soto, Bergholz, & Schneider, 1996; Schneider, 1992a,b) in offspring. It is noteworthy that all of these abnormalities have also been observed in schizophrenia patients (Walker & Diforio, 1997).

The effects of prenatal exposure to alcohol and certain other drugs on postnatal cognitive and behavioral development in humans are well-documented (Loebstein & Korn, 1997). In addition, recent investigations have shown that prenatal alcohol exposure produces HPA dysregulation in rodent offspring (Ogilvie & Rivier, 1997; Osborn, Kim, Yu, Herbert, & Weinberg, 1996). Similar effects have been observed in human neonates (Ramsey, Bendersky, & Lewis, 1996).

THE EFFECTS OF POSTNATAL EXPERIENCES ON BRAIN FUNCTION

Although a discussion of the effects of postnatal experiences on brain development is beyond the scope of this chapter, it is noteworthy that there is a rapidly accumulating body of literature which documents the effects of environmental factors on the CNS. For example, chronic postnatal exposure to stress (e.g., aversive noise, social isolation, maternal deprivation) can have consequences similar to those observed in prenatally stressed animals (Friedman, Charney, & Deutch, 1995; Sapolsky, 1992). Specifically, postnatally stressed animals show elevated corticosterone release and hippocampal damage. Maternally deprived rat pups also manifest greater biological sensitivity to stress. It is, therefore, plausible that the socioemotional stress and deprivation experienced by some children of parents with mental illness has a detrimental effect on CNS development, contributing further to their vulnerability to psychopathology.

Conversely, postnatal stimulation can have beneficial physical effects. Neonatal rat pups who experience handling show reduced corticosterone response to stress (Vallee, et al., 1997). Numerous studies have shown that the provision of an enriched environment can enhance brain growth in animals (Rosenzweig & Bennett, 1996). More recent studies of human infants suggest that early environmental factors also influence human brain development (Holden, 1996; Johnson, 1997).

A MODEL OF THE RISK FACTORS IMPINGING ON THE CHILDREN OF PSYCHIATRICALLY DISTURBED PARENTS

The results of experimental research on animals clearly demonstrate that some of the prenatal risk factors that occur at an elevated rate in psychiatrically disturbed women can alter fetal neurodevelopment. Specifically, preclinical research has shown that offspring of mothers exposed to elevated stress hormones or alcohol during the prenatal period show neuroendocrine and other abnormalities that persist into adulthood. This suggests that there are two mechanisms through which maternal psychiatric disorder determines constitutional vulnerability to disturbance in offspring. The first, now well established, is through the transmission of genetic liabilities: As noted, both adoption and twin studies indicate that genetic factors play a role in heightening risk for psychiatric disorder among the offspring of mentally ill parents. The second likely mechanism, which is suggested by the findings reviewed above, is through the effects of prenatal factors, including maternal neuroendocrine activity, on fetal neurodevelopment.

Given the myriad of factors that have been shown to disrupt fetal neurodevelopment, we are compelled to reconceptualize the influence of environmental factors on behavior. Specifically, we must assume that maternal behavior and experiences can have implications for offspring development beginning at conception. In other words, the environmental influences that are relevant to psychopathology begin in the prenatal period.

Drawing on the research findings reviewed above, the schematic in Figure 1-1 illustrates some hypothesized causal pathways linking risk factors with psychiatric outcome. (In this model, the focus is on maternal mental

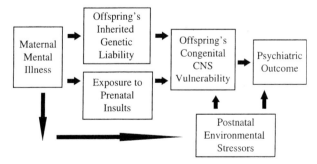

Figure 1-1 The pathways through which maternal psychiatric status influences psychiatric outcome in offspring.

illness, although as noted, offspring of men with mental illness may also be exposed to more prenatal risk factors). It is assumed that the mother's illness has the potential to influence the infant's congenital CNS vulnerability via two pathways: the transmission of genetic liabilities *and* exposure to prenatal insults that can disrupt fetal neurodevelopment. Thus the relation between maternal psychiatric disorder and the infant's vulnerability is presumed to be *mediated* by these two factors. In addition to their additive effects on congenital vulnerability, it is possible that there is an interactive effect of heredity and prenatal factors. In this regard, it has been suggested that genetic liability for schizophrenia may render the fetus more susceptible to prenatal insults (Eyler-Zorilla & Cannon, 1995; Walker & Diforio, 1997).

During postnatal development, the quality of the rearing environment comes into play. A nonoptimal environment has the potential to contribute further to the child's constitutional vulnerability. Also, implicit in this and other diathesis-stress models (Rosenthal, 1970) is the assumption that there is an interactive effect of constitutional vulnerability and postnatal environment factors, such that the vulnerable child is more sensitive to psychosocial stress. Thus, postnatal events have the potential to trigger the behavioral expression of vulnerabilities to psychiatric disorder.

The Longitudinal Effects of Prenatal and Postnatal Stress Exposure on Human Behavioral Outcomes

We now turn to the question of empirical support for this model. As mentioned, behavioral genetic paradigms have provided convincing evidence for the role of genetic factors in determining liabilities for mental disorders. Garnering empirical evidence on the effects of environmental stressors on human development is more difficult, however. All of the experimental research on prenatal and postnatal stressors is conducted with animal subjects. The clinical studies of human subjects are correlational in nature, and they do not involve the experimental controls required to demonstrate causal effects. Nonetheless, the results of these studies suggest that the same processes identified in research on animals are operative in human development.

There is now an extensive body of literature documenting the relation between physical complications of pregnancy and the child's later risk for mental illness. Specifically, it has been shown that maternal viral infections, toxemia and complications capable of producing hypoxia result in an elevated rate of schizophrenia in offspring (for a review, see Mednick & Hollister, 1995). As pointed out by Walker and Diforio (1997), animal studies have revealed that these same factors also disrupt the HPA axis and produce hippocampal damage in offspring. Thus, a common denominator linking a variety of prenatal complications with schizophrenia may be their effects on the biological regulation of the stress response.

To date, at least two studies of human subjects have shown that children whose mothers are exposed to stress during pregnancy are at heightened risk for schizophrenia. When compared to offspring of a comparison group, the offspring of women whose husbands died during the pregnancy were found to show an elevated rate of schizophrenia in adulthood (Huttunen, 1989). In the other report, the pregnant women were victims of a devastating flood that occurred in Europe (Selten, van Duursen, van der Graaf, Gispen-de Weid, & Kahn, 1997). Although information on the psychiatric status of these parents was not available, it is presumed that most were healthy.

A critical issue that remains to be addressed concerns the effects of prenatal maternal stress on the risk rate for psychopathology in the children of mentally ill parents. Of particular interest is the question of whether prenatal stressors interact with maternal psychiatric status in their effects on offspring. The extant data most pertinent to this question are the findings on physical complications of pregnancy. Some investigators (Eyler-Zorilla & Cannon, 1995) have reported an interactive effect of obstetrical complications and maternal mental illness on the psychiatric outcome of offspring. Thus, exposure to complications may have a greater effect on the offspring of schizophrenic women than on the offspring of normals.

Several lines of investigation indicate that the biological children of women with schizophrenia are more behaviorally sensitive to postnatal stress. In our studies of a Danish cohort, we found that high-risk children who experienced a period of institutional rearing, due to their mothers' episodes of schizophrenia, showed more severe disturbance later in life than did those who were cared for by relatives (Walker, Cudeck, Mednick, & Schulsinger, 1981). A subsequent study of another sample revealed an interactive effect of parental maltreatment *and* parental mental illness on rates of behavioral problems in children: High-risk children appeared to be more sensitive to the effects of exposure to parental maltreatment (Walker, Downey, & Bergman, 1989). Consistent with this report, studies of high-risk children who were adopted in infancy have shown that those exposed to nonoptimal rearing environments are more likely to develop psychiatric symptoms (Tienari, 1991).

The above findings suggest the prediction that biological children of mothers with schizophrenia will show an augmentation of the biological response to stress. Despite the centrality of this hypothesis to the diathesis-stress model, we are not aware of any published studies on stress hormone responses in high-risk children. Nonetheless, clinical research with adult schizophrenia patients indicates that they are characterized by an increase in baseline cortisol release, as well as a heightened cortisol response to pharmacologic challenge (for a comprehensive review, see Walker & Diforio, 1997).

In order to examine the role of biological sensitivity to stress in the development of psychotic symptoms, we recently initiated a prospective study of children who manifest behavioral signs of risk for schizophrenia; namely, Schizotypal Personality Disorder (SPD). The ultimate goal is to chart the developmental trajectories of these children through adolescence and into early adulthood. As described below, findings from the first assessment of these children lend support to the assumption that children at risk for schizophrenia are hypersensitive to environmental stressors.

The Emory Study of Children with Schizotypal Symptoms

Research has documented that SPD occurs at an elevated rate in the biological relatives of patients with schizophrenia (Raine & Mednick, 1995). The defining signs of SPD are excessive social anxiety, unusual perceptual experiences (e.g., strange bodily sensations), odd or magical beliefs (e.g., bizarre fantasies, superstitiousness), suspiciousness, inappropriate affect, and lack of close friends. These features parallel the prodromal signs of schizophrenia and have been shown to occur in preadolescents and adolescents. Thus, it appears that SPD is a 'subclinical' syndrome that progresses to schizophrenia in some individuals.

Three groups of children are participating in our longitudinal study: 20 who met DSM IV diagnostic criteria for SPD, 19 with other personality disorders (Other Disorders [OD] group), and 26 with no Axis II disorder (Normal Control [NC] group). None of the children met criteria for an Axis I disorder at the initial assessment. The mean ages for the SPD, OD and NC groups are 14.2 years, 14.7 years, and 13.9 years, respectively. The age range is from 11 to 18 years.

It was initially of interest to determine whether the SPD group manifested physical signs of vulnerability similar to those observed in adult patients with schizophrenia. First, when compared to the other two groups, the rate of minor physical anomalies of the head and upper extremities was elevated in the SPD children (Davis-Weinstein, Diforio, Schiffman, Walker, & Bonsall, 1999). Minor physical anomalies are subtle physical malformations that are known to be linked with abnormalities in prenatal development (Bell & Waldrop, 1989). Similar to schizophrenia patients (Green, Satz, & Christenson, 1994), the SPD subjects were characterized by a higher rate of abnormalities in dermatoglyphics; specifically, greater asymmetries in finger ridge counts (Davis-Weinstein, et al., 1999). Previous research has also linked these abnormalities with prenatal complications in human subjects (Schaumann & Alter, 1976), and recent studies of nonhuman primates indicate that maternal exposure to stress during pregnancy results in dermal asymmetries in offspring (Newell-Morris, et al., 1989). Finally, when compared to the other two groups, the SPD children manifested more involuntary movements during a videotaped interview (Walker, Lewis, Loewy, & Palyo, 1999). Excess involuntary movements have also been documented in schizophrenia patients, as well as infants who later develop schizophrenia (Walker, Savoie, & Davis, 1994). Taken together, these results provide support for the assumption that children with SPD have a constitutional vulnerability that is expressed in morphological and motoric abnormalities that parallel those observed in schizophrenia.

In order to examine activity of the HPA axis in the study participants, we obtained saliva samples for assay of cortisol at four predetermined points (hourly intervals) during the interview. Group comparisons revealed that the SPD children manifested higher mean cortisol levels, with the most pronounced group difference at the onset of the evaluation (Davis-Weinstein, et al., 1999). This is consistent with the hypothesis that children at risk for schizophrenia are more biologically reactive to stress. Further, consistent with the hypothesis that heightened baseline cortisol is partially determined by prenatal factors, cortisol levels were positively correlated with ratings of dermatoglyphic abnormalities. Our study of SPD targets the preadolescent/adolescent period because it is known to be characterized by significant changes in behavioral adjustment. Like some previous studies, our research revealed a significant positive correlation between age and cortisol level, suggesting that normal maturational processes are associated with an increase in HPA activity. This may reflect a normative pubertal increase in sensitivity to environmental stress. Whatever the case, these findings are consistent with the observation that the prodromal signs of schizophrenia usually arise in adolescence.

A Neural Diathesis-Stress Model

In a recent paper (Walker & Diforio, 1997), we proposed a 'neural diathesis-stress' model of schizophrenia that is intended to elucidate the neurophysiological processes that mediate the effects of stress on the expression of schizophrenia symptoms. The model is based, in part, on the findings described above. Specifically, the effects of HPA activation on other neural systems, particularly those that have been implicated in schizophrenia (e.g., the dopamine system and excitatory amino acids), are examined. Although discussion of the pertinent literature is beyond the scope of this chapter, it should be noted that the release of adrenal steroids enhances dopamine (DA) activity and can alter DA receptors. Thus, the worsening of schizophrenia symptoms in response to stress exposure may be due to the augmenting effects of cortisol on DA activity.

Implications for Future Research and Preventive Intervention

The multiplicity and complexity of the risk factors that impinge on children of parents with mental illness makes clinical research more difficult. Nonetheless, the pivotal questions in this area can be addressed in carefully designed empirical studies. Although our focus here has been on schizophrenia, we should emphasize that the same research questions and prevention implications apply to the children of parents with affective disorders (see Chapter 4).

One important question concerns the differential effects of prenatal and genetic factors on risk for schizophrenia, as well as other mental disorders. Through what neural mechanism do prenatal insults increase vulnerability for schizophrenia? Are prenatal insults sufficient, in the absence of a genetic liability, to produce vulnerability for schizophrenia? We must also explore, more systematically, the interactions among risk factors. Does the inherited vulnerability to schizophrenia render the fetus more sensitive to stressful prenatal events? Answers to these and other important questions will emanate from prospective studies of the prenatal and postnatal development of children whose biological parents suffer from psychiatric disorders.

To date, most longitudinal studies of high-risk children were initiated when the subjects were in late childhood, so data on the prenatal and neonatal periods were either not collected at all or were obtained retrospectively. In order to answer the questions posed above, a new generation of high-risk studies will be needed. These studies can take advantage of the plethora of contemporary medical technologies available for documenting fetal development and maternal well-being. Beginning in the prenatal period, they can monitor: (a) the mothers' neurochemical, environmental, and psychological status, and (b) the fetuses' physical and behavioral characteristics.

Prevention

The fact that a large proportion of female psychiatric patients report unwanted pregnancies points to the urgent need to provide family planning services for this population (Miller & Finnerty, 1996). Further, child-rearing is demanding, and recent studies indicate that, independent of marital status and social support, women with young children in the home show levels of cortisol release that exceed those of women without children (Luecken, et al., 1997). The demands of rearing young children may, therefore, exacerbate the psychiatric symptoms of parents and increase their risk of relapse. Thus, pregnancy prevention may be one facet of secondary prevention in the treatment of mothers with schizophrenia.

Given the assumptions of our model, there are also several clear-cut implications for primary preventive intervention. The first step would be the development of programs that insure the provision of high-quality prenatal care and socioemotional support to pregnant, mentally ill women. This could potentially serve to reduce the morbidity risk among their offspring. Such prenatal programs would be especially important if future research reveals that genetic risk for schizophrenia is associated with hypersensitivity to prenatal insults.

Assuming that some offspring of parents with psychiatric disorder are characterized by a heightened sensitivity to stress, the quality of the environment to which they are exposed takes on even greater importance. During the postnatal period, children and parents would undoubtedly benefit from social support programs aimed at buffering family members from excessive stress. The adolescent period may be an especially critical one in this regard, as pubertal development appears to be linked with heightened activity of the HPA axis.

ACKNOWLEDGMENTS

This work was supported by a Research Scientist Development Award (MH00876) to Dr. Walker from the National Institute of Mental Health.

REFERENCES

Barbazanges, A., Piazza, P. V., Le Moal, M., & Maccari, S. (1996). Maternal glucocorticoid secretion mediates long-term effects of prenatal stress. *Journal of Neuroscience, 16*, 3943–3949.

Bell, R. Q. & Waldrop, M. F. (1989). Achievement and cognitive correlates of minor physical anomalies in early development. In H. Bornstein & N. Krasnegor (Eds.), *Stability and continuity in mental development* (pp. 63–850). Hillsdale, NJ: Lawrence Erlbaum Associates.

Berkman, P. L. (1969). Spouseless motherhood, psychological stress, and physical morbidity. *Journal of Health and Social Behavior, 10*, 323–334.

Clarke, A. S., Soto, A., Bergholz, T., & Schneider, M. L. (1996). Maternal gestational stress alters adaptive and social behavior in adolescent rhesus monkey offspring. *Infant Behavior & Development, 19*, 451–461.

Davis-Weinstein, D., Diforio, D., Schiffman, J., Walker, E., & Bonsall, R. (1999). Minor physical anomalies, dermatoglyphic asymmetries and cortisol levels in adolescents with Schizotypal Personality Disorder. *American Journal of Psychiatry, 156*, 617–623.

Eyler-Zorrilla, L. T. & Cannon, T. D. (1995). Structural brain abnormalities in schizophrenia: Distribution, etiology, and implications. In S. A. Mednick & J. M. Hollister (Eds.), *Neural development and schizophrenia* (pp. 57–69). New York: Plenum Press.

Fameli, M., Kitraki, E., & Stylianopoulou, F. (1994). Effects of hyperactivity of the maternal hypothalamic-pituitary-adrenal (HPA) axis during pregnancy on the development of the HPA axis and brain monoamines of the offspring. *International Journal of Developmental Neuroscience, 12*, 651–659.

Friedman, M. J., Charrney, D. S., & Deutsch, A. Y. (Eds.). (1995). *Neurobiological and clinical consequences of stress: From normal adaptation to Post-Traumatic Stress Disorder.* Philadelphia: Lippincott-Raven Publishers.

Goodman, L. A., Rosenberg, S. D., Mueser, K. T., & Drake, R. E. (1997). Physical and sexual assault history in women with serious mental illness: Prevalence, correlates, treatment, and future research. *Schizophrenia Bulletin, 23*, 685–696.

Gottesman, I. I. (1991). *Schizophrenia genesis: The origins of madness.* New York: W. H. Freeman.

Green, M. F., Satz, P., & Christenson, C. (1994). Minor physical anomalies in schizophrenia patients, bipolar patients, and their siblings. *Schizophrenia Bulletin, 20*, 433–440.

Holden, C. (1996). Small refugees suffer the effects of early neglect. *Science, 274*(5290), 1076–1077.

Huttunen, M. O. (1989). Maternal stress during pregnancy and the behavior of the offspring. In S. Doxiadis & S. Stewart (Eds.), *Early influences shaping the individual* (pp.175–182). New York: Plenum Press.

Johnson, M. (1997). *Developmental cognitive neuroscience: An introduction.* Oxford, England: Blackwell.

Kuhn, J. C. (1982). Stress factors preceding postpartum psychosis: A case study of an unwed adolescent. *Maternal-Child Nursing Journal, 11*, 95–108.

Loebstein, R. & Koren, G. (1997). Pregnancy outcome and neurodevelopment of children exposed in utero to psychoactive drugs: The Motherisk experience. *Journal of Psychiatry and Neuroscience, 22*, 192–196.

Luecken, L. J., Suarez, E. C., Kuhn, C. M., Barefoot, J. C., Blumenthal, J. A., Siegler, I. C., & Williams, R. B. (1997). Stress in employed women: Impact of marital status and children at home on neurohormone output and home strain. *Psychosomatic Medicine, 59*, 352–359.

McNeil, T. F., Kaij, L., & Malmquist-Larsson, A. (1984). Women with nonorganic psychosis: Pregnancy's effect on mental health during pregnancy. *Acta Psychiatrica Scandinavica, 70*, 140–148.

Mednick, S. A. & Hollister, J. M. (1995). *Neural development and schizophrenia: Theory and research.* New York: Plenum Press.

Miller, L. J. (1997). Sexuality, reproduction, and family planning in women with schizophrenia. *Schizophrenia Bulletin, 23*, 623–636.

Miller, L. J. & Finnerty, M. (1996). Sexuality, pregnancy, and childbearing among women with schizophrenia-spectrum disorders. *Psychiatric Services, 47*, 502–505.

Newell-Morris, L. L., Fahrenbruch, C. E., & Sackett, G. P. (1989). Prenatal psychological stress, dermatoglyphic asymmetry and pregnancy outcome in the pigtailed macaque (macaca nemestina). *Biology of the Neonate, 56*, 61–75.

Ogilvie, K. M. & Rivier, C. (1997). Prenatal alcohol exposure results in hyperactivity of the hypo-thalamic-pituitary-adrenal axis of the offspring: Modulation of fostering at birth and postnatal handling. *Alcoholism, Clinical and Experimental Research, 21*, 424–429.

Osborn, J. A., Kim, C. K., Yu, W., Herbert, L., & Weinberg, J. (1996). Fetal ethanol exposure alters pituitary-adrenal sensitivity to dexamethasone suppression. *Psychoneuroendocrinology, 21*, 127–143.

Poltyrev, T., Keshet, G. I., Kay, G., & Weinstock, M. (1996). Role of experimental conditions in determining differences in exploratory behavior of prenatally stressed rats. *Developmental Psychobiology, 29*, 453–462.

Raine, A. & Mednick, S. A. (Eds.). (1995). *Schizotypal personality disorder*. London: Cambridge University Press.

Ramsay, D. S., Bendersky, M. I., & Lewis, M. (1996). Effect of prenatal alcohol and cigarette expo-sure on two- and six-month old infants' adrenocortical reactivity to stress. *Journal of Pediatric Psychology, 21*, 833–840.

Rosenthal, D. (1970). *Genetic theory and abnormal behavior*. New York: McGraw-Hill.

Rosenzweig, M. & Bennet, E. (1996). Psychobiology of plasticity: Effects of training and experience on brain and behavior. *Behavioural Brain Research, 78*, 57–65.

Rosin, A. (1985). Levels of stress between married and unmarried maternity patients as affected by wanted and unwanted pregnancy, age and number of children. *Dissertation Abstracts International, 46*(4-A), 885–886.

Sacker, A., Done, D. J., & Crow, T. J. (1996). Obstetric complications in children born to parents with schizophrenia: A meta-analysis of case-control studies. *Psychological Medicine, 26*, 279–287.

Sapolsky, R. (1992). *Stress, the aging brain, and the mechanisms of neuron death*. Cambridge: MIT Press.

Schaumann, B. & Alter, M. (1976). *Dermatoglyphics and medical disorders*. New York: Springer-Verlag.

Schneider, M. L. (1992a). The effect of mild stress during pregnancy on birth weight and neuro-motor maturation in Rhesus monkey infants (Macaca mulatta). *Infant Behavior and Development, 15*, 389–403.

Schneider, M. L. (1992b). Prenatal stress exposure alters postnatal behavioral expression under conditions of novelty challenge in rhesus monkey infants. *Developmental Psychobiology, 25*, 529–540.

Selten, J. P., van Duursen, R., van der Graaf, Y., Gispen-de Wied, C., & Kahn, R. S. (1997). Second trimester exposure to maternal stress is a possible factor for psychotic illness in the child. *Schizophrenia Research, 24*, 258.

Sorg, B. & Kalivas, P. (1995). Stress and neuronal sensitization. In M. Friedman, D. Charney, & A. Deutsch (Eds.), *Neurobiological and clinical consequences of stress: From normal adapta-tion to Post-Traumatic Stress Disorder* (pp. 83–102). Philadelphia: Lippincott-Raven Publishers.

Tienari, P. (1991). Interaction between genetic vulnerability and family environment. *Acta Psychiatrica Scandinavica, 84*, 460–465.

Uno, H., Eisele, S., Sakai, A., & DeJesus, O. (1994). Neurotoxicity of glucocorticoids in the primate brain. *Hormones and Behavior, 28*, 336–348.

Vaid, R. R., Yee, B. K., Shalev, U., Rawlins, J. N. P., Weiner, I., Feldon, J., & Totterdell, S. (1997). Neonatal nonhandling and in utero prenatal stress reduce the density of NADPH-diaphorasee-reactive neurons in the fascia dentata and Ammon's horn of rats. *Journal of Neuroscience, 17*, 5599–5609.

Vallee, M., Mayo, W., Dellu, F., & Le Moal, M. (1997). Prenatal stress induces high anxiety and postnatal handling induces low anxiety in adult offspring: Correlation with stress-induced corticosterone secretion. *Journal of Neuroscience, 17*, 2626–2636.

Wadhwa, P. D., Dunkel-Schetter, C., Chicz-DeMet, A., & Porto, M. (1996). Prenatal psychosocial fac-tors and the neuroendocrine axis in human pregnancy. *Psychosomatic Medicine, 58*, 432–446.

Walker, E. F. (Ed.). (1991). *Schizophrenia: A life-course developmental perspective.* New York: Academic Press.

Walker, E. F. (1994). The developmentally moderated expression of the neuropathology underlying schizophrenia. *Schizophrenia Bulletin, 20,* 453–480.

Walker, E. F. & Diforio, D. (1997). Schizophrenia: A neural diathesis-stress model. *Psychological Review, 104,* 667–685.

Walker, E. F., Cudek, R., Mednick, S. A., & Schulsinger, F. (1981). The effects of parental absence and institutionalization on the development of clinical symptoms in high-risk children. *Acta Psychiatrica Scandinavica, 63,* 95–109.

Walker, E. F., Downey, G., & Bergman, A. (1989). The effects of parental psychopathology and maltreatment on child behavior: A test of the diathesis-stress model. *Child Development, 60,* 15–24.

Walker, E. F., Downey, G., & Nightingale, N. (1989). The nonorthogonal nature of risk factors. *Journal of Primary Prevention, 9,* 15–24.

Walker, E. F., Savoie, T., & Davis, D. (1994). Neuromotor precursors of schizophrenia. *Schizophrenia Bulletin, 20,* 453–480.

Walker, E. F., Neumann, C., Baum, K. M., Davis, D., Diforio, D., & Bergman, A. (1996). Developmental pathways to schizophrenia: Moderating effects of stress. *Development and Psychopathology, 8,* 647–665.

Walker, E. F., Lewis, N., Loewy, R., & Palyo, S. (1999). Motor dysfunction and risk for schizophrenia. *Development and Psychopathology, 11,* 509–523.

CHAPTER 2

Familial Factors and Substance Use Disorders

KATHLEEN RIES MERIKANGAS

The most recent large-scale epidemiologic study of psychopathology in the United States indicates that nearly half of the population will experience a major psychiatric illness at some point over their lifetime (Kessler, et al., 1994). Moreover, alcohol abuse and dependence were the most frequently occurring of all disorders, affecting one in every 5 males and one in every 12 females. Drug use disorders, though less common, are highly prevalent and are often associated with alcoholism and other forms of psychopathology. There is also a particularly disturbing trend for substance use among adolescents, with the age of onset of substance dependence steadily decreasing. Substance use disorders (i.e., alcohol and drug use disorders) are often associated with intense suffering, physical and emotional illness, and social and occupational impairment. They have a dramatic impact on the family (particularly among children), important consequences for economic productivity, and high mortality stemming from alcohol- and drug-related accidents, homicide and suicide (e.g., Dawson & Grant, 1993; Lewinsohn, Rohde, & Seeley, 1995). In summary, substance use disorders are a major public health concern that warrants the aggressive pursuit of effective strategies for prevention.

This chapter examines the role of familial factors in the development of substance use disorders and the potential mechanisms for familial aggregation. The material is presented in the following five sections: (a) the goals and methods of the discipline of genetic epidemiology are described to provide background on the application of this approach to identifying genetic and environmental factors in the development of psychopathology; (b) sources of evidence of familial aggregation of substance abuse are reviewed; (c) mechanisms for familial transmission are reviewed; (d) illustrative data from our high-risk study of substance abuse and anxiety disorders are presented; and (e) the implications for prevention and treatment are discussed.

OVERVIEW OF GENETIC EPIDEMIOLOGY

Epidemiology is defined as the study of the distribution and determinants of diseases in human populations. Epidemiologic studies are concerned with the extent and types of illnesses in groups of people and with the factors that influence their distribution (Mausner & Kramer, 1984). Researchers in this domain are concerned with the role of both intrinsic and extrinsic factors, consisting of interactions that may occur between the host, the agent, and the environment (the classic triangle of epidemiology) to produce a disease state. In chronic disease epidemiology, the host is the individual, the agent is the specific casual factor (e.g., virus, drug, bacteria), and the environment is the relevant context in which the association between the host and the agent occur. An important goal of epidemiologic studies is to identify the etiology of a disease and thereby prevent or intervene in the progression of the disorder. In order to achieve this goal, epidemiologic studies generally proceed from descriptive studies which specify the amount and distribution of a disease within a population by person, place, and time (that is, descriptive epidemiology), to more focused studies of the determinants of disease in specific groups (that is, analytic epidemiology; Mausner & Kramer, 1984).

Although the goal of epidemiology is to study the interaction between the host, agent, and environment, epidemiologists have tended to neglect 'host' characteristics other than demographics (Kuller, 1979). However, increasing evidence reveals that environmental risk factors may either potentiate or protect against expression of underlying genetic and biological vulnerability factors. Furthermore, despite their history of independence, the fields of epidemiology and genetics share much common ground. Both are interested in determining the etiology of complex human disorders and predicting familial recurrence risks for such disorders. Synthesis of genetics and epidemiology is essential to understand the complex etiology of most human diseases. The advent of the field of genetic epidemiology has served to bridge the gap between the two fields (Morton, 1982). Genetic epidemiology is defined as the study of the distribution, risk factors, and inherited causes (both genetic and cultural) of disease in groups of relatives. The major study designs that have been employed to identify the role of familial/genetic factors in the etiology of diseases include family, high-risk, twin, and adoption studies as described below.

Family Studies

The observation that some disorders aggregate in families serves as prerequisite evidence suggesting a possible genetic component. The basic family study approach involves identifying individuals with a particular psychiatric disorder (the proband) and then determining the rates of disorder in the proband's relatives. These morbidity statistics can then be compared to the rates of disorder in families of unaffected individuals (controls). The common indicator of familial aggregation is the relative risk ratio, computed as the rate of disorder in families of affected persons divided by the corresponding rate in families of controls.

While family studies are an important starting point of genetic epidemiology, data from family studies cannot provide conclusive evidence regarding the role of genetic factors since cultural factors are also shared among families. Therefore, family studies may look beyond basic familial aggregation to examine specific patterns of transmission that more clearly identify the genetic influences. These specific patterns of transmission within families may vary according to whether the genes are dominant or recessive, autosomal or X-linked, or multifactorial (including nongenetic factors; Merikangas & Kupfer, 1995).

Although the family study design has typically been employed to elucidate the degree and mode of transmission of most disorders, there are numerous other purposes for the application of such data. The major advantage of studying diseases within families is that the assumption of etiologic homogeneity of the underlying factor eliminates the effects of heterogeneity which are present in comparisons between families. Family studies can therefore be employed to examine the validity of diagnostic categories by assessing the specificity of transmission of symptom patterns and disorders as compared to between-family designs (Tsuang, et al., 1996). Data from family studies may also provide evidence regarding etiologic or phenotypic heterogeneity. Phenotypic heterogeneity is suggested by variable expressivity of symptoms, whereas etiologic heterogeneity is demonstrated by homotypic expression of different etiologic factors between families. Moreover, the family study method permits assessment of associations between disorders by evaluating specific patterns of associations of two or more disorders within families. Controlled family studies have been employed to date in investigating the comorbidity of anxiety and depression (Merikangas, 1990), panic disorder and depression (Maier, Buller, & Hallmayer, 1988), alcoholism and depression (Merikangas, Leckman, Prusoff, Pauls, & Weissman, 1985), and simultaneous familial associations between anxiety, affective disorders and alcoholism (Maier & Merikangas, 1992; Merikangas, Risch, & Weissman, 1994; Merikangas, et al., 1998b).

High-Risk Studies

An important subtype of family study is the high-risk design, which investigates unaffected offspring of parents with major psychiatric disorders compared to those of controls. By focusing on individuals with the greatest probability of developing specific disorders, the high-risk design: (a) maximizes the potential case yield; (b) increases the power within the sample to observe hypothesized risk factor associations; (c) increases the likelihood of observing the effects of mediating and moderating variables when drawing comparisons between and within subgroups of individuals with and without the primary risk factor (e.g., children of alcoholics with or without accompanying risk factors); and (d) identifies early patterns of disease given the exposure (e.g., parental psychopathology).

Few of the high-risk studies to date, however, have studied the specificity of associations between vulnerability markers due to a lack of adequate controls. The inclusion of psychiatric comparison groups enables conclusions regarding the specificity of associations between a particular disorder and putative markers. For example, studies of offspring of parents with anxiety disorders have revealed a high degree of specificity of risk for anxiety disorders, but a lack of specificity with respect to depression (Beidel & Turner, 1997; Sylvester, Hyde, & Reichler, 1987; Turner & Beidel, 1988; Warner, Mufson, & Weissman, 1995b). That is, studies that employed a comparison group of parent probands with depressive disorders have shown that rates of anxiety disorders are also increased among the offspring of these parents (Beidel & Turner, 1997; Sylvester, Hyde, & Reichler, 1988; Turner, Beidel, & Costello, 1987; Warner, Kessler, Hughes, Anthony, & Nelson, 1995a). Conversely, offspring of parents with anxiety disorders and depression have elevated rates of depression when compared to those of controls (Sylvester, et al., 1988), or to offspring of anxiety disordered parents without depression (Biederman, Rosenbaum, Bolduc, Faraone, & Hirshfeld, 1991). Likewise, Warner, et al. (1995a) found that paternal alcoholism was a more potent predictor of depression in offspring than either maternal or paternal depression. In contrast, specificity of familial transmission was demonstrated by the results of our recent high-risk study that yielded different patterns of potentiated startle among offspring of parents with anxiety disorders compared to those of alcoholics and controls (Grillon, Dierker, & Merikangas, 1998). Such studies enable investigation of the specificity of familial factors as opposed to generalized impact of psychopathology in general.

Twin Studies

The twin study method compares concordance rates for monozygotic twins (who share the same genotype) with those of dizygotic twins (who share an average of 50 percent of their genes in common). To support a genetic etiology, the concordance rates for monozygotic twins should be significantly greater than dizygotic twins, and consistent with the concept of familial aggregation, the degree of concordance between co-twins of either type can also be used to provide information about the magnitude of genetic or environmental effects. However, the problem of confounding between genes and shared environment has also been raised against twin study paradigms. The possibility of environmental factors that may covary with zygosity is therefore an important consideration.

Although the traditional application of the twin design focuses of the estimation of the heritability (i.e., the proportion of variance attributable to genes) of a trait, there are several other research questions for which the twin study may be of value. Differences in concordance rates between monozygotic and dizygotic twins may be investigated at the level of symptoms or symptom clusters in order to study the validity of symptom complexes. Varying forms or degrees of expression of a particular disease in monozygotic twins may be an important source of evidence of the validity of the construct or disease entity. For example, Kendler, Neale, Kessler, Heath, and Eaves (1992) have employed the twin study design to investigate the validity of the diagnostic categories of depression. In addition, Kendler, et al. (1996) showed that monozygotic twins were not only more often concordant for depression than dizygotic twins, but that they were concordant for specific depression subtypes, underscoring the heterogeneity of these disorders and need for nosology that reflects these entities. Finally, twin studies are also a powerful source of information on sources of comorbidity between disorders (Kendler, Neale, Kessler, Heath, & Eaves, 1993).

Adoption Studies

Family and twin studies are genetically informative because they hold the environment 'constant' while examining the rates of disorder across different levels of genetic relationship. An alternative approach is to vary the environment while comparing individuals across degrees of genetic similarity. Adoption studies are part of this latter approach in that psychiatric similarity between an adoptee and his or her biological versus adoptive relatives is examined. An alternative design compares the biological relatives of affected adoptees with those of unaffected, or control adoptees. This approach is the most powerful for identifying genetic factors by minimizing the degree of familial aggregation that can be explained by same-environment confounds. The most powerful application of the adoption study is the cross-fostering study, which, in addition to the traditional adoption approach, examines adoptees *without* biologic risk reared in homes of affected parents. This permits assessment of *gene-environment* interaction (Wahlberg, et al., 1997).

However, adoption studies are also characterized by certain characteristics that may bias results. Biological parents of adopted children are known to have higher rates of psychopathology, alcoholism or criminality than other parents, and adopted children may themselves be at greater risk for psychiatric disorders (e.g., Bohman, 1978; Lipman, Offord, & Boyle, 1993). Although such criticisms may be valid reasons to carefully interpret the rates of disorder found in these studies, they do not negate the value of adoption studies to clarify genetic and environmental effects (in particular for disorders showing specificity of transmission).

After demonstration of familial aggregation and genetic heritability, genetic epidemiology is concerned with the interactive influences of genetic and environmental influences on particular disorders. The research designs of genetic epidemiology attempt to hold environmental factors constant while allowing genetic factors to vary (or the converse), employing paradigms such as comparisons between discordant monozygotic twins and cross-fostering studies. These research paradigms are all based upon the lack of one-to-one correspondence between the genotype and phenotype. One basic approach of genetic epidemiology is therefore to use within-family designs to minimize the probability of heterogeneity, assuming that the etiology of a disease is likely to be homogeneous within families. This design reduces or eliminates the danger of genetic heterogeneity which is likely to characterize the psychiatric disorders.

The two chief study paradigms for studying gene-environment interactions involve holding either the genetic background or the environment constant and evaluating systematic changes in the other (MacMahon, 1968; Susser, 1985). Examples of studies that hold genetic background constant while observing differential environmental exposures include: studies of discordant twins, migrant population studies, relatives exposed to a particular agent such as virus, twins reared separately, or the family set design, in which comparisons are made among families of similar structure living in distinct environments.

Examples of paradigms in which the environment is held constant and genetic factors are allowed to vary include: monozygotic twins of affected individuals compared to dizygotic twins and nontwin siblings; offspring of matings between relatives, compared to those of random matings; half-siblings compared to full siblings living in the same home; and first degree relatives of affected individuals. In both types of studies, observations can be made regarding time-space clustering of disease, which can provide information regarding environmental agents, or a characteristic age of onset and course, which may provide information on genetic factors. Application of the genetic-epidemiologic approach has yielded information on risk and etiologic factors for a number of disorders such as diabetes, hyperlipidemia, and coronary heart disease (King, Lee, Spinner, Thomson, & Wrensch, 1984).

Genetic epidemiology is one of the most powerful approaches for gaining understanding of the causes of psychopathology. The lack of integration of biological, genetic factors or indices thereof is a major limitation of risk factors research for emotional and behavioral disorders. Despite the lack of biologic and genetic markers, the genetic epidemiologic approach appears to be one of the most promising avenues to unravel the complex mechanisms through which genes may exert their influence. Indeed, Lee Robins' (1992) discussion of the future of psychiatric epidemiology concluded that the greatest hope for more definitive causal findings in psychiatry lies in genetic epidemiology.

FAMILIAL FACTORS IN SUBSTANCE USE DISORDERS

Family Studies

The familial aggregation of alcoholism and drug abuse has been well established (for comprehensive reviews of alcoholism see McGue, 1994, and Heath, et al., 1997; and for drug abuse, see Gordon, 1994). Controlled family studies of alcoholic probands reveal a three-fold increased risk of alcoholism and two-fold increased risk of drug abuse among the relatives of probands with alcoholism as compared to those of controls. Numerous family history studies and systematic family studies of substance abusers in treatment settings (Gfroerer,

1987; Hill, Cloninger, & Ayre, 1977; Meller, Rinehart, Cadoret, & Troughton, 1988; Merikangas, et al., 1998c; Mirin, Weiss, Griffin, & Michael, 1991; Mirin, Weiss, & Michael, 1988; Rounsaville, Tierney, Crits-Christoph, Weissman, & Kleber, 1982) reveal a significantly increased risk of both alcoholism and drug abuse among relatives when compared to population expectations. However, these findings are suggestive at best because of insufficient evidence from family studies that employ contemporary family study methodology to investigate the familial patterns of drug abuse. The optimal methodology includes an epidemiological sample of pure and comorbid probands recruited from both treatment and community settings, direct interviewing of available first-degree relatives, and a contemporaneous control group selected with similar methods.

To date, there are only two family studies of drug abusers in which relatives were interviewed directly (Mirin, et al., 1991; Rounsaville, et al., 1991). The first controlled family study of substance use disorders using contemporary family study data was recently published by Merikangas, et al. (1998c). In order to more accurately assess the risk of drug abuse in relatives, it is important to examine different generations or cohorts to take into account the availability of illicit substances across time periods. Family studies which investigated generational differences in the transmission of substance abuse revealed that drug use (Gfroerer, 1987) and abuse (Merikangas, Rounsaville, & Prusoff, 1992) are elevated among siblings of drug abusers, and that there is a direct relationship between parental drug use (Gfroerer, 1987) and abuse (Luthar, Anton, Merikangas, & Rounsaville, 1992; Merikangas, et al., 1992); and use and abuse in offspring. Furthermore, Merikangas, et al. (1992) showed that there is a strong association between rates of drug abuse in siblings of opioid abusers and the number of parents with substance abuse.

Genetic Factors: Twin Studies

There are an increasing number of twin studies that have provided evidence that genetic factors play a major role in the familial aggregation of substance use and abuse. Twin studies on the use of specific drugs have yielded evidence for significant heritability (h^2) of nicotine, caffeine, tranquilizer, and sedative use (Claridge, Ross, & Hume, 1978; Gurling, Grant, & Dangl, 1985; Pedersen, 1981). A twin study by Jang, Livesley, and Vernon (1995) revealed a moderate degree of heritability for the frequency of use and the tendency to use numerous illicit substances ($h^2 = .32$). Several twin studies have also provided evidence that genetic factors play a major role in the familial aggregation of substance use and abuse (Grove, et al., 1990; Jang, et al., 1995; Kendler & Prescott, 1998; Pickens, et al., 1991; Tsuang, et al., 1998). In the first twin study using diagnostic criteria for drug abuse and dependence, Pickens, et al. (1991) reported far greater heritability for alcohol dependence than for abuse (.60 vs. .38 for males; .42 vs. 0 for females) and a lower but significant degree of heritability for drug abuse or dependence (.30 for both males and females). In the largest twin study to date, Tsuang, et al. (1998) found that substance abuse in general was highly heritable, and that the contribution of genetic factors was more significant for frequent use or abuse than for non-problematic use.

One of the strongest sources of evidence regarding the role of genetic factors in the etiology of drug abuse derives from monozygotic twins reared apart. Grove, et al. (1990) examined the concordance for alcoholism, drug abuse, and Antisocial Personality Disorder among monozygotic twin pairs separated at birth. The heritability estimate of drug abuse of .45 far exceeded that of alcoholism of .11. Furthermore, drug abuse was strongly associated with Conduct Disorder in childhood and antisocial personality in adulthood. These findings suggest that genetic factors explain a large proportion of the variance in the development of drug abuse, and that a large proportion of the heritability of substance abuse in adulthood can be attributed to shared genetic factors which underlie the development of behavior problems in childhood (Grove, et al., 1990).

Although most twin studies of substance abuse have focused on alcoholism, there are two published studies that have investigated twin concordance for drug abuse or dependence in large series of twins (Jang, et al., 1995; Kendler & Prescott, 1988; Pickens, et al., 1991; Tsuang, et al., 1996, 1998). Pickens, et al. (1991) found that both male and female monozygotic twin pairs had a 1.5-fold increased risk of drug abuse compared to dizygotic pairs, but the heritability of drug abuse was only significant for males, possibly due to the low number of female pairs with substance abuse. Sex differences in the components of the genetic and environmental factors also emerged; the concordance for males could be attributed to both shared genes and environmental factors, whereas for females, the majority of variance was attributable to the unique environmental experiences of individual twins. Likewise, Jang, et al. (1995), Kendler and Prescott (1998), and Tsuang, et al. (1998) reported significant genetic contributions to drug abuse.

Adoption Studies

The optimal study paradigm for discriminating the role of genetic and environmental factors and their interaction in the development of a disorder is the cross-fostering study in which (1) adoptees with biologic vulnerability are reared in homes of non-drug abusing adoptive parents and (2) adoptees who lack a parental history of substance abuse are reared in homes of parents with substance abuse. Such studies can determine the effects of biologic vulnerability and environmental exposure to substance abuse and their mutual influence in the risk of substance abuse. The classic adoption studies of Cadoret and colleagues (Cadoret, 1992; Cadoret, Troughton, O' Gorman, & Heywood, 1986; Cadoret, Yates, Troughton, Woodworth, & Stewart, 1996) have been highly informative in elucidating the role of genetic factors in the development of drug use and abuse in a U.S. sample. The major results of their studies reveal that genetic factors play a far more important role in the transition from drug use to abuse than in drug use itself. Additionally, their work identifies two major biologic/genetic pathways to the development of drug abuse in adoptees: one which is driven by substance abuse in the biologic parent and is limited to drug abuse and dependence in the adoptee; and another which appears to be an expression of underlying aggression and related to criminality in the biologic parent (Cadoret, Yates, Troughton, Woodworth, & Stewart, 1995). These pathways to drug abuse were recently confirmed in a study of female adoptees by the same group of investigators (Cadoret, et al., 1996). Exposure to a sibling or peer with deviant behavior appears to contribute to the development of drug use, but not abuse. None of the adoption studies have thus far been able to detect a gene-environment interaction in the genesis of drug initiation or in the transition from use to abuse (Cadoret, 1992).

High-Risk Studies

Aside from pre-existing emotional and behavior disorders, a family history of alcoholism has been shown to be the most consistent risk factor for development of alcoholism in vulnerable youth (Chassin, Rogosch, & Barrera, 1991; Merikangas, Dierker, & Szatmari, 1998a; Sher, Walitzer, Wood, & Brent, 1991). Among high-risk studies that have focused on the young offspring of alcoholic parents, findings have generally supported an increase in risk for the development of alcohol use, drug use and related problems (West & Prinz, 1987). For example, Chassin, et al. (1991) found that parental alcoholism is a significant risk factor for child symptomatology and substance use among 10- to 15-year-old offspring, with the risk found to be stronger among those offspring of parents with current rather than remitted alcoholism. Similarly, several investigators (Hill, Steinhauer, & Zubin, 1992; Johnson, Leonard, & Jacob, 1989; Merikangas, et al., 1998a; Reich, Earls, Frankel, & Shayka, 1993) have reported an increased risk of substance-related problems among the offspring of alcoholic parents. Aside from genetic factors, there are numerous other mechanisms through which parents may convey an increased risk of substance abuse to their offspring including serving as negative role models for the use/abuse of drugs as well as using drugs as coping mechanisms (Brook, Whiteman, Gordon, & Cohen, 1986b). Moreover, adolescents with a family history of substance abuse are more likely to associate with deviant peers than those without familial loading (Kandel & Andrews, 1987). Despite abundant research seeking to identify premorbid vulnerability markers for alcoholism (especially in youth), however, there are to date no confirmed markers aside from family history that specifically predict its development. One major reason for the problems in developing successful models for alcoholism is that there are multiple pathways to the development of this disorder, with varying degrees of environmental and genetic contributions.

There is now substantial evidence that different risk factors may be involved in the different stages of development of alcoholism. Whereas individual demographic characteristics and peer influences strongly influence exposure and initial patterns of use of alcohol and drugs, family history of substance abuse and both familial and personal psychopathology play a more salient role in the transition to problematic alcohol use and dependence. For example, the adoption studies of Cadoret, et al. (1994) revealed that drug disorders in the biologic parent are associated far more strongly with drug abuse than with initial use of drugs. Likewise, twin (Lyons, et al., 1997; Pickens, et al., 1991) and family (Merikangas, et al., 1998b) study data confirm the greater impact of genetic and familial risk factors on the later stages of the alcohol trajectory.

There are fewer controlled studies of offspring of drug abusers than of alcoholics. Moss and colleagues reported that the pre-adolescent sons of fathers with substance abuse had elevated rates of externalizing problems and socialization problems (Moss, Majumder, & Vanyukov, 1994), increased rates of anxiety disorders (Moss, Mezzich, Yao, Gavaler, & Martin, 1995), and higher levels of aggression, inattention, and impulsivity (Martin, et al., 1994) than offspring of non-substance abusers. Similarly, Gabel and Shindledecker (1992) reported that sons of substance abusing parents had more Conduct Disorder in association with severe aggressive/destructive behavior than sons of non-substance abusing parents, while daughters of substance abusing parents were more likely to receive diagnoses of Attention-Deficit Hyperactivity Disorder and Conduct Disorder than the female offspring of non-substance abusing parents. Wilens, Biederman, Kiely, Bredin, and Spencer (1994) likewise reported significantly elevated scores on a dimensional symptom rating scale of psychopathology among the children of opioid dependent parents.

Summary

In summary, the results of family, high-risk, twin, and adoption studies of substance use disorders reveal that both alcoholism and drug abuse/dependence are familial and that genetic factors explain a substantial proportion of the variance in their etiology. In fact, family history of substance use disorders is the most potent and consistent risk factor for the development of substance use disorders in offspring. Factors associated with increased familial aggregation of substance use disorders include male gender, parental concordance, and comorbid psychopathology, particularly alcoholism and antisocial behavior. Substance dependence is far more heritable than either substance use or abuse, and genetic factors appear to be more important in the transmission of substance problems among males. The results regarding the role of genetic factors in the persistence, but not initiation, of certain substances confirm findings in animals (Marley, Witkin, & Goldberg, 1991). These findings are particularly interesting when all three sources of genetic evidence also suggest two independent pathways to substance use disorders: one in which shared etiologic factors influence the development of antisocial personality and substance use; and another which appears to underlie the development of substance dependence. However, there is a striking lack of controlled family studies of substance use disorders. These studies are critical for elucidating the role of genetic and environmental factors in the transmission of substance use disorders, validating phenotypic definitions of substance use/abuse/dependence, and identifying sources of heterogeneity in their etiology, particularly with respect to the role of comorbid psychiatric disorders and polysubstance abuse.

MECHANISMS FOR FAMILIAL TRANSMISSION

Family Factors Specific to Substance Abuse

There are several specific and non-specific environmental mechanisms through which parents may convey increased risk of substance abuse to their offspring. Table 2-1 lists the possible mechanisms through which families may enhance the risk of substance use and abuse in their offspring. Aside from transmission of genetic factors which determine the physiological effects of drugs and metabolism, the family may also enhance the risk of substance abuse through several factors specific to substance use as well as a broad range of non-specific factors that characterize homes of parents with dysfunction secondary to a psychiatric or somatic illness. Parents may directly influence the use and abuse of drugs in their offspring through (a) exposure to drugs in the prenatal phase of development, (b) providing negative role models in terms of general use/abuse of drugs or the use of drugs as a coping mechanism, or (c) enhancing the availability of drugs. In addition, substance abuse in both parents substantially elevates offspring risk.

Several investigators have examined the role of exposure to parental drug use and the risk of drug use among offspring of parents with substance abuse (e.g., Duncan, Duncan, Hops, & Stoolmiller, 1995). The use of drugs or alcohol as a coping strategy among parents may serve as a model for the development of maladaptive coping skills among offspring (Patterson, 1986). Several studies have found that in addition to exposure to parental drug use, parental attitudes towards drug use may also play a key role in the attitudes and behavior related

Table 2-1   Family environment and substance use disorders

Specific Factors
• Exposure to Drugs
• Modeling of Substance Use
• Increased Availability of Drugs

Non-Specific Factors
• Psychopathology
• Disrupted Family Structure
• Marital Discord
• Impaired Parenting
• Exposure to Stress
• Neglect/Deprivation
• Abuse

---

to drug use among offspring (Barnes & Welte, 1986; Brook, Whiteman, Gordon, & Cohen, 1986a). The effects of either direct modeling of parental substance use or the tendency to use substances as a coping mechanism have been shown to have far smaller effects on drug use in offspring than other parent influences, chiefly those involving the quality of the parent-child relationship and parental monitoring of the behavior of their adolescent offspring (Molina, Chassin, & Curran, 1994).

Non-Specific Family Factors

As listed in Table 2-1, non-specific factors through which parental substance abuse and its sequelae may influence offspring include psychopathology, disrupted family structure, exposure to marital discord, impairment in parenting behavior, exposure to high levels of both acute and chronic stress, social deprivation, and physical, sexual and emotional abuse. The high divorce rates among substance abusers may also be associated with an elevated risk of the development of substance abuse in offspring and deviant behavior in general due to the non-intact home and disrupted family structure. Such families have been found to have less stability (e.g., more moves), and thus require coping and adaptation strategies that may far exceed the ability of exposed youngsters (Peterson & Zill, 1986; Zimmerman, Coryell, & Pfohl, 1986). Clair and Genest (1987) reported that the families of alcoholic children were far more dysfunctional than those of controls. Furthermore, Smart, Chibucos, and Didier (1990) found that adolescents who came from dysfunctional families were especially vulnerable to substance use. Social stress emanating from the disruptive family environment of substance abusing parents has also been shown to increase drug use among exposed adolescents (Rhodes & Jason, 1990).

Several studies have shown that parental psychopathology may be an important mediator of familial risk. Sher, et al. (1991) proposed separate pathways from parental history of alcoholism to alcohol use and abuse in offspring; one pathway reveals a direct link between parental alcoholism influencing alcohol expectancies which lead to increased consumption of alcohol; the other pathway is comprised of parental alcoholism associated with behavioral undercontrol, resulting in a broad array of risk-taking behaviors, particularly alcohol and drug use. Other forms of psychopathology in youth were also associated with parental alcoholism, particularly anxiety and depression. This intriguing association between comorbidity in high-risk youth and family history of alcoholism was identified by Sher, et al. as being one of the key potential mediators of the development of alcoholism, leading to strong recommendations for further research to gain understanding of the mechanisms involved in the link between parental and child comorbidity. Likewise, Chassin and colleagues' (1991) study of younger offspring of alcoholics revealed that the link between parental alcoholism and externalizing symptoms in children was mediated by co-occurring parental psychopathology and parental stress. Similar to Sher, et al., they concluded that further research on the role of internalizing and externalizing symptoms and disorders was critical to further progress in our understanding of the pathways to the development of alcoholism. Therefore, the lack of attention to comorbid psychiatric disorders may be one major explanation for the inconsistent research findings from previous research, as well as the lack of efficacy of many treatment and prevention programs for alcoholism. Integration of the role of comorbidity into existing models of the progression of alcohol use to dependence may advance knowledge regarding sources of heterogeneity in the development of alcoholism.

The parental marital relationship does not appear to have a direct impact on drug use, although it does appear to interact with other risk factors in enhancing the risk of drug use (Kaplan, 1995). However, some investigators have noted that family conflict is associated with the youngster's delinquency and drug use (Robins, 1980). Indeed, parental conflict may be a greater risk factor than disrupted family structure resulting in parental absence (Farrington, Gallagher, Morley, St. Ledger, & West, 1988). Adolescents with substance-abusing parents experience more stress (Brown, Vic, & Creamer, 1989) and more negative life events than those from non-substance-abusing families (Roosa, Beals, Sandler, & Pillow, 1990).

Parental substance abuse may also contribute to family dysfunction, which is then related to such negative outcomes as the initiation or escalation of substance abuse (Gabel & Shindledecker, 1991; McCarthy & Anglin, 1990). Dysfunction in the relationships between parents and adolescents is also associated with an elevated risk of adolescent substance abuse. Substance-abusing parents have been shown to provide less social or emotional support to their children (Holden, Brown, & Mott, 1988). Evidence from several studies reveals that strong parental-child bonding may inhibit drug use and delinquent behavior in adolescents (Hawkins, Catalano, & Miller, 1992), whereas poor relationships are associated with an increased risk of drug use in offspring (Brook, Lukoff, & Whiteman, 1980; Brook, et al., 1986b). Whereas poor communication and lack of parental support may directly lead to adolescent substance use, Brook and colleagues (Brook, Brook, Gordon, Whiteman, & Cohen, 1990; Brook, Whiteman, & Finch, 1993) show that drug use by an adolescent offspring may serve to further disturb parent-child interaction.

The effect of maternal drug use on parenting and the subsequent use of drugs in offspring was described by Kandel (1990), who found a strong relationship between maternal drug use and control problems with the children. Subsequent studies have shown that poor parental control is associated with drug use in offspring. Molina, et al. (1994) found that low levels of parental monitoring and socialization were both associated with substance use, irrespective of whether the parent was alcoholic or not. In contrast, increased levels of parental monitoring or control (Baumrind & Moselle, 1985; Duncan, et al., 1995) were associated with a decreased risk of substance use in offspring. Likewise, Brook, Whiteman, Gordon, and Cohen (1986a) and Brook, Whiteman, Nomura, Gordon, and Cohen (1988) found that both parental control and attachment served to inhibit drug use among adolescents. Appropriate parental monitoring is also effective in reducing delinquency (Patterson,

Chamberlain, & Reid, 1982). These studies all provide support for the current notion that the family is the single most influential childhood factor in buffering the child and in shaping later adaptation (Kumpfer, Molgaard, & Spoth, 1996).

The relationship between parental substance abuse and childhood behavioral problems indicative of abuse or maltreatment was studied by Gabel and Shindledecker (1990) in a sample of children hospitalized for suicidal ideation/behavior or aggressive/destructive behavior. Parental substance abuse was the major indicator of confirmed cases of child abuse. Even more commonly associated with parental substance abuse is neglect, which can have major physical and emotional consequences for exposed children.

YALE FAMILY/HIGH RISK STUDY

In the next section, the results of a high-risk study of substance use disorders are presented to illustrate the magnitude of impact of familial substance use. The major goals of the study were: (a) to investigate the magnitude and patterns of transmission of substance abuse in families; and (b) the role of parental drug and alcohol abuse on the development of emotional and behavioral problems, and substance use and abuse among offspring.

Study Description

The sample of the Yale Family Study includes a high-risk sample of children ages 7–17 of parents with substance use disorders or anxiety disorders, and controls from the general community. Families in the high-risk component of the study included a total of 88 families of 52 probands diagnosed with anxiolytic, sedative, or benzodiazepine abuse; marijuana abuse or dependence; or alcoholism (substance group); and 36 probands with a major anxiety disorder. In addition, the control families included 35 probands with no history of psychiatric disorder. A total of 137 biological offspring ages 7–17 were eligible for interview in this study, of whom 134 (98%) were interviewed directly. A modified version of the Kiddie-Schedule for Affective Disorders and Schizophrenia (K-SADS-E; Orvaschel, Puig-Antich, Chambers, Tabrizi, & Johnson, 1982) was used for diagnostic assessment of the children. All interviews were conducted by experienced interviewers blind to the diagnosis of the parent. The interview was administered independently with the child, and with the mother about the child by the same interviewer. Diagnostic criteria were evaluated using all available information (i.e., the diagnostic interview, family history reports on the child, teachers reports and medical records) by child psychiatrists blind to the diagnostic status of the parents and not involved in direct assessments of the sample. If the subject met criteria for any psychiatric disorder, the records were reviewed independently by a second diagnostician.

The Yale Family Study used the Parental Bonding Instrument (PBI; Parker, Tupling, & Brown, 1979), which is a self-report measure of two dimensions of parenting—care and protection—to assess perceived quality of the parent-child relationship. These dimensions have been investigated individually and jointly with respect to offspring psychopathology. Twenty-five attitudinal and behavioral items were completed on both parents by each offspring. The PBI was completed by children age 12 or older and by the parent who was directly interviewed about the child, who completed a PBI describing his or her parenting behavior towards that specific child. The PBI has high test-retest reliability (MacKinnon, Henderson, & Duncan-Jones, 1989; Plantes, Prusoff, Brennen, & Parker, 1988).

The Family Adaptability and Cohesion Evaluation Scale (FACES III; Olson, Portner, & Bell, 1985; Olson, Portner, & Lavee, 1985; Olson, Spenkle, & Russell, 1979) was used to assess family functioning. The FACES III is a 111-item self-report instrument which measures family cohesion and adaptability and includes a social desirability scale. The overall FACES has demonstrated acceptable internal consistency (.62–.77) and test-retest reliability (.80–.83), as well as content and construct validity. With respect to the self-report version of the FACES used in this study, it has recently been demonstrated that the scores should be interpreted linearly. The FACES III was administered to each interviewed family member older than age 11.

In addition to the FACES III, interviewed adults (older than age 18) also completed the McMaster Family Assessment Device (FAD; Epstein, Baldwin, & Bishop, 1983) to measure family functioning. The FAD is a 60-item self-report measure which contains seven subscales: (a) problem solving, (b) communication, (c) family roles, (d) affective responsiveness, (e) affective involvement, (f) behavior control, and (g) general functioning (overall measure of family health/pathology). In addition to the use of continuous scores, subscale cutoffs have been established (Miller, Kabacoff, Keitner, Epstein, & Bishop, 1986).

Major Findings

Substance Abuse in Offspring

The rates of alcohol and drug abuse among the adolescent offspring of these probands are presented in Table 2-2. Although the mean age of the sample is only 12, a striking association emerges between parental substance dependence and alcohol and drug abuse among the offspring. Whereas none of the offspring of parents without substance abuse or psychopathology exhibit substance abuse problems, 20.5% of the offspring of the substance abusing parents already meet criteria for alcohol or drug abuse themselves. Rates of alcohol abuse are two-fold greater than those of drug abuse, but no significant major sex differences emerged at this early stage of development. These findings suggest that the offspring of parents with substance use disorders are at increased risk for the development of substance abuse themselves. This is particularly striking when one considers the youthful age of this cohort and the

Table 2-2   Rates of drug and alcohol abuse and dependence in the Yale High-Risk
Study

Disorders in Children	Parent Proband					
	Substance			Normal		
Sex of Child	Male	Female	Total	Male	Female	Total
N of Children >12 Years	N = 19	N = 20	N = 39	N = 14	N = 14	N = 28
Substance Abuse/Dependence	21.1	20.0	20.5	0	0	0
Alcohol Abuse/Dependence	15.8	20.0	18.0	0	0	0
Drug Abuse/Dependence	5.3	15.0	10.3	0	0	0

inclusion of probands with either marijuana or anxiolytic abuse rather than
'hard' drugs such as cocaine or opioids.

Effects of Parental Concordance

The impact of parental concordance for substance use disorders and anxiety disorders is shown in Table 2-3. These results show both generalized effects
of parental psychopathology as well as specificity. With respect to anxiety
disorders, there is a direct increase in rates of anxiety disorders among offspring as a function of number of affected parents. Comorbid substance use disorders did not mediate this effect. In contrast, affective disorders, conduct
disorder and oppositional disorder were far more strongly associated with the
presence of two affected parents, irrespective of the specific disorder manifest
by the parents. These findings suggest that both depression and conduct disorder may be more strongly related to family dysfunction in general rather than
to specific effects of some underlying biologic/genetic factors.

Family Environment of Substance Abusers

Families share their environment as well as their genes, and both biology
and environment may increase their common risk for various psychiatric disorders. Physical (family structure and socioeconomic status) as well as social
characteristics (family functioning including dyadic relationships) constitute
the family environment. Parental psychopathology has been associated with
increased rates of marital discord and both divorce and separation. However,
the effects of parent(s)' psychiatric status appear global and impact negatively
on parenting and overall family functioning.

The associations observed between parental psychopathology and parent-
ing/family variables are important because of their potential impact on the
mental health of offspring. Low levels of care from parents have been associated with offspring psychopathology. Marital distress as well as unhealthy family functioning styles were also associated with both mood and behavior
disorders. Both extremes of the range of family cohesion and adaptability have
been associated with offspring psychopathology.

Table 2-3 Child diagnoses by parental mating type: Disorders in offspring by number of parents with substance use disorder and/or anxiety/affective disorder

	Both Parents		One Parent		Neither	
	Substance $N=18$	Substance+ Anxiety/ Affective[1] $N=54$	Anxiety/ Affective $N=23$	Substance $N=19$	Anxiety/ Affective $N=48$	Normal $N=26$	p value $(\chi^2, 5\ df)$
Child Disorders (%)							
Anxiety Disorders	0.0	14.8	39.1	5.3	16.7	3.9	**
Affective Disorders	5.6	14.8	21.7	15.8	4.2	0.0	n.s.
Conduct Disorder	16.7	16.7	8.7	0.0	0.0	0.0	**
Oppositional Disorder	16.7	11.1	21.7	0.0	8.3	3.9	n.s.

$^+p < .10$; $^*p < .05$; $^{**}p < .01$; $^{***}p < .00$.
[1] One parent with substance abuse; other parent with affective or anxiety disorder.

Table 2-4 Family/home environment of children by proband parent group

	Proband Parent		
	Substance $N = 77$	Normal $N = 54$	p
Family Characteristics			
Parents Divorced (%)	28.4	2.9	***
Low SES (%)	40.3	20.0	**
Parent Family Functioning			
Parental Care[a] (mean score)	21	26	**
Family Cohesion[b] (mean score)	3.4	4.2	**

$^*p < .05$; $^{**}p < .01$; $^{***}p < .001$.
[a] Parental Bonding Instrument. [b] Faces III.

Table 2-4 presents selected family structure and function domains for high- and low-risk families. Offspring of substance abusers were less likely to be living with both parents and more likely to be in a lower SES group. With respect to the care dimension of parenting style on the PBI, parents with substance disorders had significantly lower care scores. In addition, families containing a substance-abusing parent have lower family cohesion scores on the FACES III. Family functioning was further examined by parental mating type.

Analyses of the impact of parental concordance for substance use disorders revealed that families with two affected parents had higher proportions of unhealthy functioning regardless of the particular combination of parental diagnoses. Although the rate of unhealthy functioning was elevated among offspring of one parent with a substance use disorder, it did not significantly differ from the neither-affected mating type. The findings regarding family cohesion were similar; those families with two affected parents (one of whom has a substance abuse diagnosis) were significantly more disengaged than the comparison families (Dierker, et al., 1999).

Implications for Prevention and Treatment

The results of this review suggest that a family history of substance abuse is one of the most potent risk factors for the development of substance abuse among exposed offspring. Both specific and non-specific factors in the family contribute to the increased risk of substance abuse. Future research should seek an understanding of the mechanisms through which the family conveys an increased risk of substance abuse to offspring since a family history of substance abuse is the most potent predictor of vulnerability to its development. Study designs which incorporate the complexity of factors involved in familial transmission including genetic factors, transmitted biologic factors, and social and cultural factors are critical to gaining an understanding of these processes. The genetic epidemiologic approach is one of the most powerful to understanding the mechanisms through which families exert their influence on the transmission of substance abuse across generations to incorporate the components of the host vulnerability, factors associated with exposure to drugs or alcohol, and the contribution of the family, peer, neighborhood, and larger cultural environment conducive to its development.

Evidence presented herein strongly supports the critical importance of family-based programs for prevention of substance abuse. The findings suggest that targeted prevention should be geared towards offspring of substance abusers, even those who have not been identified in treatment settings. The majority of the substance abusers in the present study were identified from a random community sample, yet the magnitude of substance abuse in their offspring even at this early stage of adolescent development was quite striking.

These findings also have important implications for both primary and secondary prevention efforts. Primary prevention programs should identify those youth at increased risk for the development of substance abuse based not only on their own characteristics but also parental and family risk. More intensive effort may then be devoted to risk reduction among such youth and their families. The risk of substance abuse secondary to psychopathology may also be reduced through treatment of such primary disorders as conduct disorder, anxiety or depression (Kessler & Price, 1993). The finding of the superiority of lithium over placebo in reducing symptoms of both depression and alcoholism in a recent randomized clinical trial of adolescents with comorbid bipolar disorder and alcohol abuse or dependence is particularly promising (Geller, et al., 1998). In summary, a combination of individual and family treatment, in conjunction with broader efforts towards education and primary prevention at the community level, are likely to provide the optimal approach to reduce substance abuse.

ACKNOWLEDGMENTS

This research was supported in part by grants AA07080, DA05348 from Alcohol, Drug Abuse, and Mental Health Administration of the United States Public Health Service and by a Research Scientist Development Award K02-DA00293.

REFERENCES

Barnes, G. & Welte, J. (1986). Patterns and predictors of alcohol use among 1–12th grade students in New York State. *Journal of Studies in Alcohol, 47*, 53–62.

Baumrind, D. & Moselle, K. A. (1985). A developmental perspective on adolescent drug abuse. *Advances in Alcohol and Substance Abuse, 4*, 41–67.

Beidel, D. & Turner, S. (1997). At risk for anxiety: I. Psychopathology in the offspring of anxious parents. *Journal of the American Academy of Child and Adolescent Psychiatry, 36*, 918–924.

Biederman, J., Rosenbaum, J. F., Bolduc, E. A., Faraone, S. V., & Hirshfeld, D. R. (1991). A high risk study of young children of parents with panic disorders and agoraphobia with and without comorbid major depression. *Psychiatry Research, 37*, 333–348.

Bohman, M. (1978). Some genetic aspects of alcoholism and criminality: A population of adoptees. *Archives of General Psychiatry, 35*, 269–276.

Brook, J. S., Lukoff, I. F., & Whiteman, M. (1980). Initiation into adolescent marijuana use. *Journal of Genetic Psychology, 137*, 133–142.

Brook, J. S., Whiteman, M., Gordon, A. S., & Cohen, P. (1986a). Dynamics of childhood and adolescent personality traits and adolescent drug use. *Developmental Psychobiology, 22*, 403–414.

Brook, J. S., Whiteman, M., Gordon, A. S., & Cohen, P. (1986b). Some model mechanisms for explaining the impact of maternal and adolescent characteristics on adolescent stage of drug use. *Developmental Psychology, 22*, 460–467.

Brook, J., Whiteman, M., Nomura, C., Gordon, A., & Cohen, P. (1988). Personality, family, and ecological influences on adolescent drug use: A developmental analysis. *Journal of Chemical Dependency Treatment, 1*, 123–161.

Brook, J. S., Brook, D. W., Gordon, A. S., Whiteman, M., & Cohen, P. (1990). A psychosocial etiology of adolescent drug use: A family interactional approach. *Genetic, Social and General Psychology Monographs, 116*, 111–267.

Brook, J., Whiteman, M., & Finch, S. (1993). Role of mutual attachment in drug use: A longitudinal study. *Journal of the American Academy of Child and Adolescent Psychiatry, 32*, 982–989.

Brown, S. A., Vic, P. W., Creamer, V. A. (1989). Characteristics of relapse following adolescent substance abuse treatment. *Addictive Behaviors, 14*, 291–300.

Cadoret, R. J. (1992). Genetic and environmental factors in initiation of drug use and the transition to abuse. In M. Glantz & R. Pickens (Eds.), *Vulnerability to drug abuse* (pp. 99–113). Washington, DC: American Psychological Association.

Cadoret, R. J., Troughton, E., O' Gorman, T., & Heywood, E. (1986). An adoption study of genetic and environmental factors in drug abuse. *Archives of General Psychiatry, 43*, 1131–1136.

Cadoret, R. J., Yates, W. R., Troughton, E., Woodworth, G., & Stewart, M. A. (1995). Adoption study demonstrating two genetic pathways to drug abuse. *Archives of General Psychiatry, 52*, 42–52.

Cadoret, R. J., Yates, W. R., Troughton, E., Woodworth, G., & Stewart, M. A. (1996). An adoption study of drug abuse/dependency in females. *Comprehensive Psychiatry, 37*, 88–94.

Chassin, L., Rogosch, F., & Barrera, M. (1991). Substance use and symptomatology among adolescent children of alcoholics. *Journal of Abnormal Psychology, 100*, 449–463.

Clair, D. & Genest, M. (1987). Variables associated with the adjustment of offspring of alcoholic fathers. *Journal of Studies on Alcohol, 48*, 345–355.

Claridge, G., Ross, E., & Hume, W. I. (1978). *Sedative drug tolerance in twins.* Oxford, England: Pergamon Press.

Dawson, D. A. & Grant, B. F. (1993). Gender effects in diagnosing alcohol abuse and dependence. *Journal of Clinical Psychology, 49*, 298–307.

Dierker, L. C., Merikangas, K. R., & Szatmari, P. (1999). Influence of parental concordance for psychiatric disorders on psychopathology in offspring. *Journal of the American Academy of Child and Adolescent Psychiatry, 38*, 280–288.

Duncan, T. E., Duncan, S. C., Hops, H., & Stoolmiller, M. (1995). An analysis of the relationship between parent and adolescent marijuana use via generalized estimating equation methodology. *Multivariate Behavioral Research, 30*, 317–339.

Epstein, N. B., Baldwin, L. M., & Bishop, D. S. (1983). The McMaster family assessment device. *Journal of Marital and Family Therapy, 9*, 171–180.

Farrington, D. P., Gallagher, B., Morley, L., St. Ledger, R. J., & West, D. J. (1988). Are there any successful men from criminogenic backgrounds? *Psychiatry, 51*, 116–130.

Gabel, S. & Shindledecker, R. (1990). Parental substance abuse and suspected child abuse/maltreatment predict outcome in children's inpatient treatment. *Journal of the American Academy of Child and Adolescent Psychiatry, 29*, 919–924.

Gabel, S. & Shindledecker, R. (1991). Aggressive behavior in youth: Characteristics, outcome, and psychiatric diagnoses. *Journal of the Academy of Child and Adolescent Psychiatry, 30*, 982–988.

Gabel, S. & Shindledecker, R. (1992). Behavior problems in sons and daughters of substance abusing parents. *Child Psychiatry & Human Development, 23*, 99–115.

Geller, B., Cooper, T. B., Sun, K., Zimmerman, B., Frazier, J., Williams, M., & Heath, J. (1998). Double-blind and placebo-controlled study of lithium for adolescent bipolar disorders with secondary substance dependency. *Journal of the American Academy of Child and Adolescent Psychiatry, 37*, 171–178.

Gfroerer, J. (1987). Correlation between drug use by teenagers and drug use by older family members. *American Journal of Drug and Alcohol Abuse, 13*, 95–108.

Gordon, H. W. (1994). Human neuroscience at National Institute on Drug Abuse: Implications for genetics research. *American Journal of Medical Genetics, 54*, 300–303.

Grillon, C., Dierker, L., & Merikangas, K. R. (1998). Fear-potentiated startle in adolescent offspring of parents with anxiety disorders. *Biological Psychiatry, 44*, 990–997.

Grove, W., Eckert, E., Heston, L., Bouchard, T., Segal, N., & Lykken, D. (1990). Heritibility of substance abuse and antisocial behavior: A study of monozygotic twins reared apart. *Biological Psychiatry, 27*, 1293–1304.

Gurling, H., Grant, S., & Dangl, J. (1985). The genetic and cultural transmission of alcohol use, alcoholism, cigarette smoking and coffee drinking: A review and an example using a log linear cultural transmission model. *British Journal of Addiction, 80*, 269–279.

Hawkins, J. D., Catalano, R. F., & Miller, J. Y. (1992). Risk and protective factors for alcohol and other drug problems in adolescence and early adulthood: Implications for substance abuse prevention. *Psychological Bulletin, 112*, 64–105.

Heath, A. C., Bucholz, K. K., Madden, P. A., Dinwiddie, S. H., Slutske, W. S., Beirut, L. J., Statham, D. J., Dunne, M. P., Whitfield, J. B., & Martin, N. G. (1997). Genetic and environmental contributions to alcohol dependence risk in a national twin sample: Consistency of findings in women and men. *Psychological Medicine, 27*, 1381–1396.

Hill, S. H., Cloninger, C. R., & Ayre, F. R. (1977). Independent familial transmission of alcoholism and opiate abuse. *Alcoholism: Clinical and Experimental Research, 1*, 335–342.

Hill, S. Y., Steinhauer, S. R., & Zubin, J. (1992). Cardiac responsivity in individuals at high risk for alcoholism. *Journal of Studies on Alcohol, 53*, 378–388.

Holden, M. G., Brown, S. A., & Mott, M. A. (1988). Social support network of adolescents: Relation to family alcohol abuse. *American Journal of Drug and Alcohol Abuse, 14*, 487–498.

Jang, K. L., Livesley, W. J., & Vernon, P. A. (1995). Alcohol and drug problems: A multivariate behavioral genetic analysis of co-morbidity. *Addiction, 90*, 1213–1221.

Johnson, S., Leonard, K. E., & Jacob, T. (1989). Drinking, drinking styles and drug use in children of alcoholics, depressives, and controls. *Journal of Studies on Alcohol, 50*, 427–431.

Kandel, D. B. (1990). Parenting styles, drug use, and children's adjustment in families of young adults. *Journal of Marriage and the Family, 52*, 183–196.

Kandel, D. B. & Andrews, K. (1987). Processes of adolescent socialization by parents and peers. *International Journal of the Addictions, 22*, 319–42.

Kaplan, H. B. (Ed.). (1995). *Drugs, crime and other deviant adaptations: Longitudinal studies.* New York: Plenum.

Kendler, K. & Prescott, C. (1998). Cannabis use, abuse and dependence in a population-based sample of female twins. *American Journal of Psychiatry, 155*, 1016–1022.

Kendler, K., Neale, M., Kessler, R., Heath, A., & Eaves, L. (1992). A population-based twin study of major depression in women: The impact of varying definitions of illness. *Archives of General Psychiatry, 49*, 257–266.

Kendler, K., Neale, M., Kessler, R., Heath, A., & Eaves, L. (1993). Major depression and phobias: The genetic and environmental sources of comorbidity. *Psychological Medicine, 23*, 361–371.

Kendler, K. S., Eaves, L. J., Walters, E. E., Neale, M. C., Heath, A. C., & Kessler, R. C. (1996). The identification and validation of distinct depressive syndromes in a population-based sample of female twins. *Archives of General Psychiatry, 53*, 391–399.

Kessler, R. & Price, R. (1993). Primary prevention of secondary disorders: A proposal and agenda. *American Journal of Community Psychology, 21*, 607–633.

Kessler, R., McGonagle, K. A., Zhao, S., Nelson, C. B., Hughes, M., Eshleman, S., Wittchen, H. U., & Kendler, S. (1994). Lifetime and 12-month prevalence of DSM-III-R psychiatric disorders in the United States: Results from the National Comorbidity Survey. *Archives of General Psychiatry, 51*, 8–19.

King, M. C., Lee, G. M., Spinner, N. B., Thomson, G., & Wrensch, M. R. (1984). Genetic epidemiology. *Annual Review of Public Health, 5*, 1–52.

Kuller, L. H. (1979). The role of population genetics in the study of the epidemiology of cardiovascular risk factors. In D. C. Rao, R. Elston, L. H. Kuller, M. Feinleib, C. Carter, & R. Havlick (Eds.), *Genetic analysis of common disease: Application to predictive factors in coronary disease* (pp. 489–495). New York: Alan R. Liss.

Kumpfer, K., Molgaard, V., & Spoth, R. (1996). The Strengthening Families Program for the prevention of delinquency and drug use. In R. DeV. Peters & R. J. McMahon (Eds.), *Preventing childhood disorders, substance abuse, and delinquency* (pp. 241–267). Thousand Oaks, CA: Sage Publications.

Lewinsohn, P., Rohde, P., & Seeley, J. (1995). Adolescent psychopathology: III. The clinical consequences of comorbidity. *Journal of the American Academy of Child and Adolescent Psychiatry, 34*, 510–519.

Lipman, E. L., Offord, D. R., & Boyle, M. H. (1993). Follow-up of psychiatric and educational morbidity among adopted children. *Journal of the American Academy of Child and Adolescent Psychiatry, 32*, 1007–1012.

Luthar, S. S., Anton, S. F., Merikangas, K. R., & Rounsaville, B. J. (1992). Vulnerability to substance abuse and psychopathology among siblings of opioid abusers. *The Journal of Nervous and Mental Disorders, 180*, 153–161.

Lyons, M. J., Toomey, R., Meyer, J. M., Green, A. I., Eisen, S. A., Goldberg, J., True, W. R., & Tsuang, M. T. (1997). How do genes influence marijuana use? The role of subjective effects. *Addiction, 92*, 409–417.

MacKinnon, A., Henderson, A. S., & Duncan-Jones, P. (1989). The Parental Bonding Instrument (PBI): An epidemiological study in a general population sample. *Psychological Medicine, 19*, 1023–1034.

MacMahon, B. (1968). Gene environment interaction in human disease. *Journal of Psychiatric Research, 6*, 393–402.

Maier, W. & Merikangas, K. R. (1992). *Co-transmission and comorbidity of affective disorders, anxiety disorders and alcoholism in families*. Berlin: Springer-Verlag.

Maier, W., Buller, R., & Hallmayer, J. (1988). Comorbidity of panic disorder and major depression: Results from a family study. In I. Hand & H. U. Wittchen (Eds.), *Panic and phobias: Treatments and variables affecting course and outcome* (pp. 180–185). Berlin: Springer-Verlag.

Marley, R., Witkin, J., & Goldberg, S. (1991). Genetic factors influence changes in sensitivity to the convulsant properties of cocaine following chronic treatment. *Brain Research, 542*, 1–7.

Martin, C. S., Earleywine, M., Blackson, T. C., Vanyukov, M. M., Moss, H. B., & Tarter, R. E. (1994). Aggression, inattention, hyperactivity, and impulsivity in boys at high and low risk for substance abuse. *Journal of Abnormal Child Psychology, 22*, 177–203.

Mausner, J. S. & Kramer, S. (1984). *Epidemiology: An introductory text* (2nd ed.). Philadelphia: W.B. Saunders.

McCarthy, W. J. & Anglin, M. D. (1990). Narcotics addicts: Effect of family and parental risk factors on timing of emancipation, drug use onset, pre-addiction incarcerations, and educational achievement. *Journal of Drug Issues, 20*, 99–123.

McGue, M. (1994). Genes, environment, and the etiology of alcoholism. *Development of alcohol problems: Exploring the biopsychosocial matrix, 26* (Serial No. 94-3495), 1–40.

Meller, W., Rinehart, R., Cadoret, R., & Troughton, E. (1988). Specific familial transmission in substance abuse. *The International Journal of the Addictions, 23*, 1029–1039.

Merikangas, K. R. (1990). Comorbidity for anxiety and depression: Review of family and genetic studies. In J. D. Maser & C. R. Cloninger (Eds.), *Comorbidity of mood and anxiety disorders* (pp. 331–348). Washington, DC: American Psychiatric Press.

Merikangas, K. R. & Kupfer, D. J. (1995). *Mood disorders: Genetic aspects*. Baltimore, M.D.: Williams & Wilkens.

Merikangas, K. R., Leckman, J. F., Prusoff, B. A., Pauls, D. L., & Weissman, M. M. (1985). Familial transmission of depression and alcoholism. *Archives of General Psychiatry, 42*, 367–372.

Merikangas, K. R., Rounsaville, B. J., & Prusoff, B. A. (1992). *Familial factors in vulnerability to substance abuse*. Washington, DC: American Psychological Association.

Merikangas, K. R., Risch, N. J., & Weissman, M. M. (1994). Comorbidity and co-transmission of alcoholism, anxiety and depression. *Psychological Medicine, 24*, 69–80.

Merikangas, K. R., Dierker, L. C., & Szatmari, P. (1998a). Psychopathology among offspring of parents with substance abuse and/or anxiety: A high risk study. *Journal of the American Academy of Child and Adolescent Psychiatry, 39*, 711–720.

Merikangas, K. R., Stevens, D. E., Fenton, B., O'Malley, S., Woods, S. W., Stolar, M., & Risch, N. (1998b). Co-morbidity and familial aggregation of alcoholism and anxiety disorders. *Psychological Medicine, 28*, 773–788.

Merikangas, K. R., Stolar, M., Stevens, D. E., Goulet, J., Preisig, M., Fenton, B., O'Malley, S., & Rounsaville, B.J. (1998c). Familial transmission of substance use disorders. *Archives of General Psychiatry, 55*, 973–979.

Miller, I. W., Kabacoff, R. I., Keitner, G. I., Epstein, N. B., & Bishop, D. S. (1986). Family functioning in the families of psychiatric patients. *Comprehensive Psychiatry, 27*, 302–312.

Mirin, S. M., Weiss, R. D., & Michael, J. (1988). Psychopathology in substance abusers: Diagnosis and treatment. *American Journal of Drug and Alcohol Abuse, 14*, 139–157.

Mirin, S. M., Weiss, R. D., Griffin, M. L., & Michael, J. L. (1991). Psychopathology in drug abusers and their families. *Comprehensive Psychiatry, 32*, 36–51.

Molina, B. S. G., Chassin, L., & Curran, P. J. (1994). A comparison of mechanisms underlying substance use for early adolescent children of alcoholics and controls. *Journal of Studies on Alcohol, 55*, 269–275.

Morton, N. (1982). *Outline of genetic epidemiology*. Basel: Karger.

Moss, H. B., Majumder, P. P., & Vanyukov, M. (1994). Familial resemblance for psychoactive substance use disorders: Behavioral profile of high risk boys. *Addictive Behaviors, 19*, 199–208.

Moss, H. B., Mezzich, A., Yao, J. K., Gavaler, J., & Martin, C. S. (1995). Aggression among sons of substance-abusing fathers: Association with psychiatric disorder in the father and son, paternal personality, pubertal development, and socioeconomic status. *American Journal of Drug and Alcohol Abuse, 21*, 195–208.

Olson, D. H., Spenkle, D. H. J., & Russell, C. S. (1979). Complex model of marital and family systems. 1. Cohesion and adaptability dimensions, family types and clinical applications. *Family Process, 18*, 3–78.

Olson, D. H., Portner, J., & Bell, R. (1985a). Family Adaptability and Cohesion Evaluation Scales (FACES II). *Family Social Science*. Unpublished manual. St. Paul: University of Minnesota.

Olson, D. H., Portner, J., & Lavee, Y. (1985b). FACES III. *Family Social Science*. St. Paul: University of Minnesota.

Orvaschel, H., Puig-Antich, J., Chambers, W., Tabrizi, M. A., & Johnson, R. (1982). Retrospective assessment of prepubertal major depression with the Kiddie-SADS-E. *Journal of the American Academy of Child and Adolescent Psychiatry, 21*, 392–397.

Parker, G., Tupling, H., & Brown, L. B. (1979). A parental bonding instrument. *British Journal of Medical Psychology, 52*, 1–10.

Patterson, G. R. (1986). Performance models for antisocial boys. *American Psychologist, 41*, 432–444.

Patterson, G. R., Chamberlain, P., & Reid, J. B. (1982). A comparative evaluation of parent training programs. *Behavior Therapy, 13*, 638–650.

Pedersen, N. (1981). *Twin similarity for usage of common drugs*. New York: Alan R. Liss.

Peterson, J. L. & Zill, N. (1986). Marital disruption, parent-child relationships, and behavior problems in children. *Journal of Marriage and the Family, 48*, 295–307.

Pickens, R., Svikis, D., McGue, M., Lykken, D., Heston, L., & Clayton, P. (1991). Heterogeneity in the inheritance of alcoholism: A study of male and female twins. *Archives of General Psychology, 48,* 19–28.

Plantes, M. M., Prusoff, B. A., Brennen, J., & Parker, G. (1988). Parental representations of depressed outpatients from a U.S.A. sample. *Journal of Affective Disorders, 15,* 149–155.

Reich, W., Earls, F., Frankel, O., & Shayka, J. J. (1993). Psychopathology in children of alcoholics. *Journal of the American Academy of Child and Adolescent Psychiatry, 32,* 955–1002.

Rhodes, J. E. & Jason, L. A. (1990). A social stress model of substance abuse. *Journal of Consulting and Clinical Psychology, 58,* 395–401.

Robins, L. N. (1980). The natural history of drug abuse. *Acta Psychiatrica Scandinavica, Supplementum 284,* 7–20.

Robins, L. (1992). The future of psychiatric epidemiology. *International Journal of Methods in Psychiatric Research, 2,* 1–3.

Roosa, M. W., Beals, J., Sandler, I. N., & Pillow, D. R. (1990). The role of risk and protective factors in predicting symptomatology in adolescent self-identified children of alcoholic parents. *American Journal of Community Psychology, 18,* 725–741.

Rounsaville, B. J., Tierney, T., Crits-Christoph, K., Weissman, M. M., & Kleber, H. D. (1982). Predictors of treatment outcome in opiate addicts: Evidence for the multidimensionality of addicts' problems. *Comprehensive Psychiatry, 23,* 462–478.

Rounsaville, B. J., Kosten, T. R., Weissman, M. M., Prusoff, B., Pauls, D., Anton, S. F., Merikangas, K. (1991). Psychiatric disorders in the relatives of probands with opiate addiction. *Archives of General Psychiatry, 48,* 33–42.

Sher, K. J., Walitzer, K. S., Wood, P. K., & Brent, E. E. (1991). Characteristics of children of alcoholics: Putative risk factors, substance use and abuse, and psychopathology. *Journal of Abnormal Psychology, 100,* 427–448.

Smart, L. S., Chibucos, T. R., & Didier, L. A. (1990). Adolescent substance use and perceived family functioning. *Journal of Family Issues, 11,* 208–227.

Susser, M. (1985). Separating heredity and environment. *American Journal of Preventive Medicine, 1,* 5–23.

Sylvester, C. E., Hyde, T. S., & Reichler, R. J. (1987). Clinical psychopathology among children of adults with panic disorder. *Journal of the American Academy of Child and Adolescent Psychiatry, 26,* 668–675.

Sylvester, C., Hyde, T., & Reichler, R. (1988). Clinical psychopathology among children of adults with panic disorder. In D. Dunner, E. Gershon, & J. Barrett (Eds.), *Relatives at risk for mental disorder* (pp. 87–102). New York: Raven Press.

Tsuang, M. T., Lyons, M. J., Eisen, S. A., Goldberg, J., True, W., Lin, N., Meyer, J. M., Toomey, R., Faraone, S. V., & Eaves, L. (1996). Genetic influences on DSM-III-R drug abuse and dependence: A study of 3372 twin pairs. *American Journal of Medical Genetics, 67,* 473–477.

Tsuang, M. T., Lyons, M. J., Meyer, J. M., Doyle, T., Eisen, S. A., Goldberg, J., True, W., Lin, N., Toomey, R., & Eaves, L. (1998). Co-occurence of abuse of different drug in men: The role of drug-specific and shared vulnerabilities. *Archives of General Psychiatry, 55,* 967–972.

Turner, S. M., & Beidel, D. C. (1988). Some further comments on the measurement of social phobia. *Behaviour Research and Therapy, 26,* 411–413.

Turner, S. M., Beidel, D. C., & Costello, A. (1987). Psychopathology in the offspring of anxiety disorders patients. *Journal of Consulting and Clinical Psychology, 55,* 229–235.

Wahlberg, K. E., Wynne, L. C., Oja, H., Keskitalo, P., Pykalainen, L., Lahti, I., Moring, J., Naarala, M., Sorri, A., Seitamaa, M., Laksy, K., Kolassa, J., & Tienari, P. (1997). Gene-environment interaction in vulnerability to schizophrenia: Findings from the Finnish Adoptive Family Study of Schizophrenia. *American Journal of Psychiatry, 154,* 355–362.

Warner, L., Kessler, R., Hughes, M., Anthony, J., & Nelson, C. (1995a). Prevalence and correlates of drug use and dependence in the United States. *Archives of General Psychiatry, 52,* 219–229.

Warner, V., Mufson, L., & Weissman, M. (1995b). Offspring at high risk for depression and anxiety: Mechanisms of psychiatric disorder. *Journal of the American Academy of Child and Adolescent Psychiatry, 34,* 786–797.

West, M. O. & Prinz, R. J. (1987). Parental alcoholism and childhood psychopathology. *Psychological Bulletin, 102*, 204–218.

Wilens, T., Biederman, J., Kiely, K., Bredin, E., & Spencer, T. (1994). Pilot study of behavioral and emotional disturbances in the high-risk children of parents with opioid dependence. *Journal of the American Academy of Child and Adolescent Psychiatry, 34*, 779–785.

Zimmerman, M., Coryell, W., & Pfohl, B. (1986). Validity of familial subtypes of primary unipolar depression. *Archives of General Psychiatry, 43*, 1090–1096.

PART 2

Parental Dysfunctions

CHAPTER 3

A Longitudinal Study of Aggressive and Withdrawn Children into Adulthood

Patterns of Parenting and Risk to Offspring

Lisa A. Serbin, Dale M. Stack, Alex E. Schwartzman,
Jessica Cooperman, Vivianne Bentley,
Christina Saltaris, & Jane E. Ledingham

This chapter focuses on risk to offspring of parents from a prospective longitudinal study of individuals from inner-city, lower-socioeconomic status (SES) backgrounds (Serbin, et al., 1998). The parents in this sample have been followed since 1976, when they were elementary school children, through adolescence, early adulthood and, most recently, into parenthood (Schwartzman, Ledingham, & Serbin, 1985; Serbin, et al., 1998). Within this sample of socially and economically disadvantaged young adults, risk to offspring was examined as a function of parents' childhood histories and characteristics, measured when the parents were themselves children between the ages of 6 and 13. For purposes of the present chapter, the emphasis is on mothers and their children. Specifically, intergenerational risk and prediction of problems in offspring are examined in relation to the mothers' patterns of childhood aggression and social withdrawal.

In examining a community-based rather than a clinical sample, this chapter about children from families at higher risk for psychosocial problems (e.g., aggression, withdrawal, behavior difficulties) is anomalous in a volume on children of dysfunctional parents: It does not deal specifically with children of parents with a particular psychological problem or psychiatric disorder. Some of the parents in the study have diagnosable disorders (including anxiety-related problems, phobias, and depression), as well as elevated rates of substance abuse, and criminal convictions. Other parents have proven to be highly 'resilient,' considering the difficult circumstances they lived in as children and the behavioral and academic problems many of them exhibited when first entering the study.

In this chapter, we attempt to describe the complex, multiple challenges facing these individuals as they become parents. The focus of the chapter is on prediction of adverse birth circumstances and parenting problems in the first instance, and then on prediction of risk and negative outcomes for a new generation of children. Implications of these findings for prevention and intervention focusing on parents and their young children are also considered.

Children from lower-SES families growing up in the inner city represent an established 'high-risk' population (Lipman & Offord, 1997; McLoyd, 1998). Children developing under conditions of financial disadvantage are at greater risk for a variety of health and psychosocial problems, including physical health difficulties, cognitive, academic, emotional, and behavioral problems (e.g., Lipman & Offord, 1997; Lipman, Offord, Racine, & Boyle, 1994). For example, results from a large-scale Canadian study reveal that school-aged children who are poor are three times as likely to have one or more psychiatric disorders, attentional disorders, conduct disorders, or emotional disorders than are their non-poor counterparts (Lipman, et al., 1994). It is also clear that many of the offspring born to inner-city children when they reach adolescence and early adulthood are, in turn, disadvantaged (Harris & Marmer, 1996).

There is considerable ongoing research and debate about the nature of the lifespan and intergenerational risk processes involved within a disadvantaged sample (Caspi & Elder, 1988a,b). This debate has implications for understanding the etiology of the many problems with high prevalence in lower-SES, urban populations. The conceptualization of risk processes for disadvantaged children is also important in the design of prevention and intervention strategies.

A MODEL OF RISK

There are two distinct ways of conceptualizing risk to children coming from backgrounds of poverty: that of cumulative or 'additive' risk, versus the approach of examining specific developmental pathways for individuals faced with particular challenges. These perspectives are not mutually exclusive. Given the multiplicity, complexity, and high levels of comorbidity in the problems of inner-city populations, both additive and specific developmental models may be useful in identifying causes, predicting outcomes, and planning interventions.

It may be useful to start with an illustrative analogy from public health, which we will refer to as the 'Swamp Model' (after Angold, personal communication). Living near a swamp can involve exposure to multiple infectious agents (e.g., microbes causing malaria, cholera, and typhoid) within an environment (dampness, mud, insects, impure water, air pollution from rotting vegetation and swamp gas) conducive to acute infection and chronic illness. By analogy, impoverished inner-city environments carry with them a large variety of established risk factors, such as lower quality educational opportunities; low income and occupational status; poor quality housing; inadequate diet and malnutrition; poor health care; crowding; high crime rates and violence; limited vocational and recreational opportunities; and inadequate social support networks. In addition, living in poor, inner-city neighborhoods also increases the probability of exposure to a variety of infectious agents, lead, air pollution, and other established health hazards.

These multiple risks begin in the prenatal period, and accumulate across the lifespan. As a result, we are not surprised by a higher incidence and prevalence of many serious psychosocial and medical problems, including illiteracy, school dropout, adolescent childbearing, and physical and mental illness, ultimately resulting in shorter life expectancy (e.g., Cairns, Cairns, Xie, Leung, & Hearne, 1998; Furstenburg, Brooks-Gunn, & Morgan, 1987; Sameroff & Seifer, 1992; Scaramella, Conger, Simons, & Whitbeck, 1998). There is a clear additive (and multiplicative) risk operating in these populations. Depending on the number and severity of the risk factors present, individuals from these backgrounds can be expected to have one or more negative outcomes in various areas of psychosocial functioning and health. Also, these risk factors may be 'non-specific,' in that a variety of different negative outcomes may be influenced by common environmental risk factors in childhood.

Returning to the 'swamp' analogy, there are also specific disease processes operating within this population, just as there are in more advantaged groups. However, the 'swamp' population faces: (a) a greater risk of exposure to various causal agents; combined with (b) low resistance (due to malnutrition, for example); and (c) inadequate resources for coping with adversity and illness. Consequently, individuals from this population may be more likely to develop problems when challenged by specific stressors or causal agents, and also may be less likely to resolve health problems as they develop.

If, for example, a genetic risk for a mental illness or for a specific learning disability is present, a child from a disadvantaged environment might be more likely to develop the genetically-based illness. Similarly, if there is a perinatal problem or a closed-head injury in early childhood, a child from a disadvantaged background may be more likely to have severe and chronic learning problems than a child whose family has more resources and can provide the environment necessary for a favorable outcome (such as adequate nutrition, consistent and high quality health care, cognitive stimulation, and social-emotional support). In general, the lower nutritional status and greater likelihood of exposure to infection and injuries that are characteristic of this population are likely to affect whether the child will actually develop a disorder for which there may be a genetic or biological/temperamental risk or a specific environmental predisposition.

In a disadvantaged population, rates of medical and psychosocial problems are elevated, but specific etiological and outcome processes can still be identified against the intensifying background of environmental disadvantage. From an etiological and prevention research perspective, the elevated risk for mental illness found in a disadvantaged group provides an opportunity to identify developmental and etiological pathways for specific disorders. This is particularly true if specific subgroups of the population are followed and compared, based on the presence of particular risk factors (e.g., parental mental illness) or stable behavioral or temperamental characteristics of the individual. That is, against the background of social and economic disadvantage and elevated health risks, it may be possible to identify specific individual and environmental characteristics that predict specific social and health problems, or conversely, promote resiliency in the face of specific risks.

THE CONCORDIA STUDY

The Concordia Longitudinal Study of Children at Psycho-Social Risk was begun by Jane Ledingham and Alex Schwartzman in 1976. At that time, the project screened over 4,000 children enrolled in grades 1, 4, or 7 at French-language public schools serving lower income neighborhoods in urban Montreal. All of the children were in regular programs (i.e., they were not in special education classes) at the time of screening. Approximately equal numbers of girls and boys were selected for participation, based on a peer-nomination instrument that identified 1,770 children belonging to extreme groups based on aggression and/or withdrawal, or as normative for their school class, grade level, and gender (i.e., as members of a comparison group). About half the sample were divided among the three risk groups (aggressive, withdrawn, and aggressive-withdrawn) with similar numbers of male and female participants in each group, and about half were age- and gender-matched comparison children.

The rationale for the selection measure and criteria are described more fully in Serbin, et al. (1998). Results of this study and others confirm that childhood aggression and withdrawal are both stable dimensions, with implications for future functioning in many areas of development (Farrington, 1991; Moskowitz, Schwartzman, & Ledingham, 1985; Olweus, 1984). The use of gender-specific norms for aggression and withdrawal has also proven to be useful, as distinct developmental pathways for males and females identified as highly aggressive and/or withdrawn have been consistently observed (Schwartzman, Verlaan, Peters, & Serbin, 1995). Most relevant to this chapter, the use of within-sex norms for aggression and withdrawal allowed the identification of groups of highly aggressive and/or withdrawn girls from within a community-based sample, making the Concordia project one of the few large longitudinal studies in the world of aggression in women.

The three studies presented deal with subgroups of the Concordia sample who are now parents, their offspring, and their spouses. Our current focus is on the women in the study and their children, because the women generally had children earlier (i.e., at younger ages than the men), and their children were more likely to be available to participate, due to the relatively high prevalence of single parenthood and of maternal custody in the sample.

The three sections present a balance of research findings and illustrative clinical case descriptions. The focus is on several health and social/developmental themes. First, we focus on the general elevated risk for problematic birth circumstances and early health problems in the offspring of the Concordia sample, which is due to the presence of high rates of deviant social behavior, especially aggression, in the parent's childhood. Next, we predict parenting problems in a subsample who became parents in adolescence or early adulthood, based on mothers' histories of social behavior and their subsequent educational experiences in adolescence. Finally, we discuss parenting and early developmental outcomes in a larger sample of infants and preschool-aged children born when their parents were more mature (i.e., in their mid-20's to early 30's).

The specific pathways to parenthood and parenting predicted by childhood aggression and withdrawal, and the close integration of physical health with social/developmental progress in the children, are major themes illustrated in these results. Equally striking is the role of parental education, which emerged repeatedly as an important 'buffer' against negative outcomes for offspring in this high-risk sample.

ADVERSE CIRCUMSTANCES SURROUNDING THE BIRTH OF OFFSPRING

One important route through which children may be placed at risk is through the pre-, peri-, and postnatal care and environments that are provided to the developing child. These are considered to be important for healthy development (e.g., Casaer, de Vries, & Marlow, 1991; Prechtl, 1968). Numerous factors surrounding the birth of the child include potentially important variables, such as nutritional status prior to conception and during pregnancy, substance ingestion during pregnancy, prematurity, birth weight, medical status at birth, birth trauma, delivery complications, length of hospitalization, multiparity, chronic illness, injuries, and the family and home environment after birth. Moreover, these factors are associated with child outcomes. As one example, while they are developing in the womb, unborn children can be placed at risk through the prenatal care provided by parents (e.g., poor nutrition and unhealthy lifestyles) and through maternal ingestion of toxic substances. Thus, when a risk event occurs (pre-pregnancy, at conception, during prenatal development, during the perinatal period, or following birth), it is often interrelated with developmental outcome (Kopp & Kaler, 1989).

Adverse conditions during early development are clearly important considerations that can impact on child outcome. Pre-, peri-, and post-birth risk factors may be elevated in or complicated by poverty and teenage pregnancy.

For example, pre-pregnancy risks such as maternal chronic illness, history of drug use, and poor nutrition during childhood, may cyclically occur in generations of people who are economically disadvantaged (Kopp & Kaler, 1989). Chronic undernutrition during infancy and early childhood is known to have negative effects on cognitive development and school performance (Pollitt, et al., 1996), and the quality of neonatal nutrition has been linked to less rapid weight gain and poorer developmental outcome at 18 months in preterm babies (Lucas, Morley, Cole, & Gore, 1989). In studying undernutrition effects, the emphasis on cognitive development to the exclusion of biological and psychosocial effects, is no longer considered sufficient (Pollitt, et al., 1996). Moreover, Duncan, Brooks-Gunn, and Klebanov (1994) found that family income and poverty status were strongly related to the cognitive and behavioral development of children, and the duration of poverty was a key contributor. Education is another means through which these factors may operate. Maternal education has been found to be correlated with maternal behaviors and child outcome in numerous studies (e.g., Auerbach, Lerner, Barasch, & Palti, 1992; Serbin, et al., 1998), and it appears to serve both risk and protective functions. Thus, there may be pathways of risk, including income, education, medical or health status, emotional health, and home environment factors, through which child outcome is affected (e.g., Berlin, 1997).

The importance of the childrearing environment cannot be overlooked, as it is considered to be a powerful determinant of outcome (e.g., Werner & Smith, 1992). For example, Werner and Smith (1977, 1992), in their 30-year longitudinal study, state that 'prenatal and perinatal complications were consistently related to impairment of physical and psychological development in childhood and adolescence *only* when they were combined with chronic poverty, parental psychopathology, or persistently poor rearing conditions, unless there was serious damage to the central nervous system' (Werner & Smith, 1992, p. 191). This is not to argue that prenatal and perinatal factors are unimportant, as these were correlated with major physical handicaps of the central nervous system, mental retardation, serious learning difficulties, and chronic mental health problems in their sample. Rather, it elucidates a trend that the researchers themselves underscore, whereby the impact of reproductive stress decreased over time, and the developmental outcome of biological risk conditions seemed to interact with the quality of the rearing environment.

With data from the Concordia Risk Study, a community sample of individuals known to have a history of psychosocial and behavioral problems, we addressed five factors relating to reproductive patterns, birth circumstances, and early health, which have direct implications for the second generation of this sample, that is, their child offspring: (a) teen parenthood; (b) multiparity; (c) close birth spacing; (d) delivery complications; and (e) injuries and acute medical illnesses post-birth to 48 months. Our focus was on the presence of general elevated risk for problematic birth circumstances and early health problems in the offspring of the Concordia sample, as predicted by deviant social behavior, especially high rates of aggression and the pattern of combined aggression and social withdrawal, in the parent's childhood.

For the factors pertaining to gynecological, fertility and birth circumstances, we focused exclusively on the 909 female participants of the Concordia Study. Our objective was to examine differences in problematic fertility and delivery outcomes, as a function of mothers' childhood behavior classification. We used percentile cutoffs to identify children who exhibited extreme scores on the aggression and/or withdrawal scales, while at the same time enabling adequate sample sizes for statistical analysis. In the original 1976 sample, girls who scored above the 95th percentile on aggression and below the 75th percentile on withdrawal, relative to same-sex classmates, were selected for the aggressive group ($n=101$); the reverse criteria were used to select the withdrawn group ($n=112$). Z-scores equal to or above the 75th percentile on both aggression and withdrawal were criteria for membership in the aggressive-withdrawn group ($n=129$). Finally, age-matched children for whom z-scores on aggression and withdrawal scales fell in the average range (i.e., between the 25th and 75th percentile) were selected for the contrast group ($n=567$; see Schwartzman, et al., 1985, for a more extensive description of the methodology).

The data base for four of the five outcome variables—teen parenthood, multiparity, close spacing of births, and delivery complications—were obtained from medical records of the Régie de l'Assurance-Maladie du Québec (RAMQ). The fifth outcome—health, injuries, and accidents—is discussed below in the context of a different subsample of our longitudinal study. Of the 909 original female participants, medical records were obtained for 853 (95% retrieval rate). The medical records covered all contacts with the health care system occurring between 1981 and 1994. All women in the sample were at least 24 years of age by 1994, which allowed us to examine their adolescent and early adult medical histories. Each of the four maternal factors presents added developmental risk for offspring, as well as poorer prospects for mothers' future educational and occupational attainment (Baldwin & Cain, 1980; Conger, Elder, Lorenz, Simons, & Whitbeck, 1994; Furstenberg, Brooks-Gunn, & Chase-Landsdale, 1989; Hardy, et al., 1997; Layzer, St. Pierre, & Bernstein, 1996; Whitman, Borkowski, Schellenbach, & Nath, 1988).

The four outcomes are defined below and the results are described. Using the medical records up to age 24, women in each of the three risk groups (aggressive, withdrawn, and aggressive-withdrawn) were compared with women from the comparison group, employing the risk ratio (RR) statistic (Serbin, et al., 1998). The RR statistic enables the comparison of the prevalence of a specific outcome within a risk population and within a comparison group. A risk ratio of one is indicative of outcomes that are equivalent in the risk and comparison groups, while a risk ratio value greater than one is indicative of greater prevalence of the outcome in the risk group (Rothman, 1986; refer to Serbin, et al., 1998, for detailed information).

Risky sexual behavior and early sexual behavior can lead to *teenage pregnancy*. Early or off-time pregnancy has been shown to be associated with negative outcomes in childhood (Brooks-Gunn & Furstenberg, 1986; Scaramella, et al., 1998). Teen parenthood in our sample was defined as childbirth occurring before the age of 20 (i.e., ≤ 19 years of age). Rates of teen parenthood were significantly higher among women in the aggressive (17%) and aggressive with-drawn (15%) groups than in the comparison group (8%), ($RR = 2.17$, $p < .01$, and $RR = 1.86$, $p < .01$, for the aggressive and aggressive-withdrawn groups compared with the contrast group, respectively). The rate for the withdrawn group (9%) was not significantly different from the contrast group.

Multiparity, or having more than one offspring, has been related to nega-tive child outcomes, when combined with poverty, teenage mothers, or adverse rearing environments (e.g., Furstenberg, et al., 1987). Multiparity in the Con-cordia sample was defined as two or more childbirths before age 24. The multiparity rate was higher in the aggressive-withdrawn mothers (40%; $RR = 1.88$, $p < .05$) compared with the contrast group mothers (21%), and this elevated rate also tended to be the case for the aggressive group mothers (32%; $RR = 1.47$, $p < .10$).

Several longitudinal studies have identified the pattern of multiparity and *close spacing of children* (e.g., Furstenberg, et al., 1987; Werner & Smith, 1992). For purposes of our analyses, close spacing between sequential births was defined as less than 2 years between a first and a second birth. For those women who were multiparous by age 24 ($n = 72$), close birth spacing was observed in 81% of the aggressive-withdrawn women, relative to a rate of 56% for the multiparous women in the comparison group ($RR = 1.44$, $p < .05$).

Perinatal problems such as *delivery complications* have also been demon-strated to have effects on later outcome (Casaer, et al., 1991). However, why serious neonatal problems result from a cluster of risk factors in one pregnancy and not another is not always clear (Casaer, et al., 1991). Moreover, the inter-action between perinatal events and external influences during and past the neonatal period warrants clarification and elucidation (e.g., Casaer, et al., 1991). Associations between SES, home rearing environments, and later behav-ioral and intellectual development have been shown in some follow-up stud-ies (e.g., Beckwith & Parmalee, 1986). In addition, obstetric risk variables seem to be cumulative in their effects (Sepkoski, Coll, & Lester, 1982). In our sample, delivery problems during first childbirth were considered. These included fetal, placental, or amniotic problems, and delivery by caesarean section. In 33% of first births to aggressive-withdrawn mothers there were delivery complications, whereas delivery complications occurred in only 18% of first births to contrast group mothers ($RR = 1.80$, $p < .05$). Age of pregnancy was controlled by using the medical records only up to age 24.

In addition to the aforementioned four factors, the postnatal environment and care provided also contribute to the mental and physical status of the devel-oping child. For example, *illnesses, infections, accidents, and visits to hospital Emergency Rooms (ER)* are indices of postnatal care that relate to the child's health status. Wilms (1997) advocates including health outcomes and injuries in our models, arguing that there are 'super-highways' to childhood illness which include poverty, poor family functioning, depression, and smoking. Moreover, injuries are the leading cause of death and a significant cause of disability in childhood (Fingerhut & Kleinman, 1989; Rodriguez, 1990). With our sample, we were in a unique position to examine the relation between mothers' social behavior during childhood and subsequent injury in a second generation; such an examination of mothers' social behavior has not been studied in the context of injuries and hospital visits.

To assess some of these health status risks on the offspring of our sample, we examined the medical records (Medicare archives (RAMQ) as mentioned on page 49) of the sub-sample of firstborn children of adolescent mothers ($n = 94$) from our original sample. All of these women gave birth to their first child before their 21st birthday. We examined visits to the ER, non-emergency medical visits, diagnoses that were available for the ER visits (for 389 of the 613 records of ER treatment, i.e., 64%), emergency surgical consultations, and emergency hospitalizations for the children from birth to 4 years of age (Serbin, Peters, & Schwartzman, 1996).

In general, we found that across the sample, children of women in both the aggressive and aggressive-withdrawn groups showed higher rates of medical and ER visits and hospitalizations. The rate for children of the women in the aggressive group (average of 1.95 visits per year) was significantly higher than the rate for children in the comparison group (average of 1.17 visits per year). The rate for children in the aggressive-withdrawn group (average of 2.23 visits per year) was also higher than the rate for the children in the comparison group. However, a marginal interaction between gender and classification group suggested that for the aggressive-withdrawn group, both sons and daughters tended to have elevated rates of ER visits, whereas the elevated rate was limited to sons for the aggressive group.

Adding the diagnoses of acute illness and infections, asthma, and injury-related diagnoses accounted for 66% of the 258 records for which we had diagnostic information. Moreover, injury-related diagnoses (e.g., fractures, wounds, head injuries, burns, poisonings) made up about 22% of the 258 ER visits for which a diagnosis was submitted. Here again, elevated risks for offspring of mothers with childhood histories of aggression and aggression-withdrawal were seen. Comparison of the percentage of children from each of the risk groups with injury-related outcomes to the percentage of children from the comparison group using logistic regression indicated that the three risk groups and the comparison group differed for girls and boys (Chi Square $(1, N = 94) = 4.545$, $p < .04$). Conducting separate logistic regressions for each gender, sons from the aggressive group had a significantly higher risk for injury-related ER visits than did sons from the comparison group (Wald's $W = 5.43$, $p < .02$). Seventy percent of the aggressive group boys were seen in the ER, relative to 25% of the sons from the comparison group. In the case of girls, daughters of the aggressive-withdrawn group were at a marginally significant higher risk of an injury-related visit to the ER, compared with daughters of the contrast group (70% vs. 32%, $W = 3.778$, $p < .06$).

While only 15% of the 613 ER visits required the services of a surgeon, it is noteworthy that 67% of the children of the aggressive-withdrawn group who required these services received surgical consultations compared with 35% for the children of the comparison group. Finally, acute illness and infections accounted for 68% of the 258 ER visits for which diagnoses were available.

Here again, it was the children of the aggressive-withdrawn group who were at elevated risk compared with the comparison group (72% vs. 26%). It is also noteworthy that 9% of the diagnoses were for the treatment of asthma. Together, these results underscore the higher risk status of the aggressive and aggressive-withdrawn groups. Moreover, our findings suggest that it is possible to identify subgroups of children of adolescent mothers who are at risk for emergency treatment related to injuries and illnesses from the generally 'high-risk' group of children of adolescent mothers.

Taken together, our results indicate that there were more problematic outcomes for the groups with high levels of aggression relative to the comparison group. The largest number of problems occurred in the aggressive-withdrawn group, those women who as children had been high on both aggression and social withdrawal. Consistent with other findings from our project, social withdrawal appeared to add to the risk involved in childhood aggression, with regard to the adverse birth circumstances covered above, as well as postnatal ER visits and injuries that we documented. Offspring of mothers who were highly aggressive as children, and those that were high on both aggression and withdrawal, are at comparatively high risk for health and developmental problems. Moreover, the results underscore the importance of examining the circumstances surrounding the birth and the significance of adverse pre- and postnatal factors, especially when the environment is complicated by additional psychosocial problems. At the same time, it is important to note several limitations. First, the data were grouped using general categories of risk (the four groups); thus, no other individual characteristics of parents from the data set were used as predictors. Second, we were not able to ascertain pathways to risk and resilience. Third, we were not in a position with this data set to look beyond the early postnatal period and determine how adverse postnatal environments might affect subsequent processes. It is clear that each of these issues is important and would lead to increased understanding about the processes and mechanisms of risk from parent to offspring. In the next sections, we observe the outcomes or offspring born at disadvantage; that is, we examine the environmental processes and their outcomes.

The limitations notwithstanding, the resulting outcomes point to parenting as one pathway through which risks are elevated in children and highlight parenting as a potential mechanism through which risk might be transferred. For example, some of the outcomes may directly relate to the health practices of the family (e.g., postnatal care and environment, illnesses, injuries, accidents, asthma). In addition, the theme of additive risk is evident in the findings, where the same groups showed elevated rates on a number of risk factors, not merely one. These two themes of parenting and additive risk are underscored and are clearly evident when we turn to direct observations of our Concordia Risk Study mothers in interactions with their offspring. The unity of development is also salient; that is, there are interrelationships among risk factors and developmental domains. These, too, become more directly observable in the offspring's later development covered in the two following sections. Prenatal diet, neonatal nutrition, delivery complications, multiparity, frequent hospital visits, or development of asthma may not merely restrict themselves to the individual domain within which they occur; e.g., physical outcomes in the case of illnesses. Rather, these risk factors may impact on the child's cognitive, socio-emotional, and motor development, and combined with poor quality of home environment and poverty, exacerbate the situation.

MANIFESTATIONS OF RISK WITHIN THE CONTEXT OF MOTHER–CHILD INTERACTIONS: SCHOOL-AGE OFFSPRING

Results from the Concordia Risk Study presented to date indicate continued vulnerability to later-life problems not only for the women who were aggressive and/or withdrawn as children, but for their offspring as well. In the next phase of the project, we were interested in discovering whether this risk might manifest itself in observable behaviors displayed by both mothers and their school-aged children. Would women, identified not as a function of clinical diagnoses, but rather as a result of behavioral tendencies in childhood, manifest difficulties in their parenting behavior? Further, would an intergenerational transmission of risk occur, whereby maternal childhood risk factors are transferred to the next generation, beyond the realm of adverse birth circumstances and medical problems?

The intergenerational model of risk transmission, in its most basic form, suggests that patterns established in early life of the previous generation provide a context for the replication of such patterns by the succeeding generation (Caspi & Elder, 1988a,b). The process is hypothesized to occur as follows: Problem behavior is first manifested during the childhood of the parent. Moving from the family of origin to the family of procreation, behavioral tendencies of the at-risk individual persist into adulthood, creating circumstances that foster family dysfunction, such as parenting difficulties. In turn, problematic parenting serves as a possible link between problem behavior in parents and subsequent problem behavior in their offspring. Corresponding to this intergenerational model, our focus in this section is on the nature of interactions between mother and child.

The relationship between mother and child has been understood as one of the most important in the life of a child. It is within the context of early relationships that children develop skills and strategies that will serve them for the rest of their lives (Bowlby, 1980). When this relationship is adaptive, children are likely to emerge well-adjusted and free from major pathology. When this relationship is disrupted, however, be it through maternal psychosocial difficulty, maternal pathology, and/or family dysfunction, children are placed at risk for psychosocial disturbances (Beardslee, Bemporad, Keller, & Klerman, 1983; Caspi & Elder, 1988a,b; Dumas, LaFreniere, & Serketich, 1995; Hammen, et al., 1987; Patterson, 1982).

The principal aim of the current investigation was to answer the following questions: (a) Does intra-generational continuity—that is, behavioral continuity in aggression and social withdrawal over time within a single generation—reveal itself in the behavior of women during interactions with offspring? (b) Is there evidence for intergenerational risk transmission in the behavior of children within their interactions with their mothers? Based on the intergenerational model of psychosocial risk and previous research with the Concordia Risk Study, it was anticipated that mothers' childhood aggression and withdrawal would serve as risk factors in the prediction of certain behavioral responses within the interaction between mothers and their offspring (Caspi & Elder, 1988b; Lehoux, 1995; Patterson, 1982). With respect to mothers, elevated ratings of aggression and/or social withdrawal in childhood were anticipated to contribute to the prediction of mothers' engagement in more aversive and less supportive behavior within current interactions with their offspring. More specifically, with respect to the former, continuity in aggressive behavior was predicted, such that mothers who were rated as aggressive during childhood were anticipated to evidence more overt, aggressive behavior during the interaction sequence. Continuity in social withdrawal was also anticipated, such that mothers who were rated as withdrawn during childhood were predicted to evidence more ignoring and unresponsive behavior during the interaction sequence. In terms of supportive behavior, it was anticipated that mothers who were rated by their peers as aggressive and/or withdrawn during childhood would exhibit less supportive behavior when interacting with their offspring.

In the area of child behavior, elevated ratings on aggression and/or social withdrawal during mothers' childhood were anticipated to contribute to the prediction of aversive behavior in their offspring. Specifically, it was anticipated that continuity in aggressive behavior across generations would manifest itself with the transmission of overt aversive behaviors, including restlessness and displays of aggression, in children of women rated as aggressive during childhood. Maternal social withdrawal during childhood was expected to contribute to the prediction of a more unresponsive response style in the offspring of these women, reflecting intergenerational continuity.

In order to test these hypotheses, 84 women from the original sample, together with their eldest children, were recruited to participate. Due to the limitations associated with the small sample size, the four group classifications (i.e., aggressive, withdrawn, aggressive-withdrawn, and contrast) were not used. Instead, the entire sample was considered as a single unit with each mother having a peer nomination score from childhood along the dimensions of aggression and social withdrawal. Hence, aggression and withdrawal were treated as continuous variables.

With respect to demographic characteristics, participating mothers tended to be young, with the average age at first delivery being 20. At the time of testing, these women ranged in age from 24 to 33. Their first-born children, 37 boys and 47 girls, ranged in age from 5 to 13 years. In terms of marital status, 9 (11%) mothers were single, 22 (26%) were cohabiting, 39 (46%) were married, and the remaining 14 (17%) were either separated or divorced. Completed years of schooling ranged from 6 to 17 years, with the average reflecting high school completion. Thirty (35%) dropped out of school before completing high school. Of the 82 participants where information was available on welfare status, 26 (31%) were on welfare. The mean occupational prestige score for the sample was 3124.94, comparable to the level of a cashier.

The principal measure used in the completion of this study was the High-Risk Interaction Coding System (H-RICS; Cooperman & Steinbach, 1995), an observational coding system designed specifically to detect patterns of interaction characteristic of high-risk mother-child dyads. The H-RICS was developed from the original work of the researchers involved in this project, but also draws from extant coding systems, mainly, the Family Interaction Coding System (FICS; Patterson, Ray, Shaw, & Cobb, 1969). Interrater reliability was calculated and determined to be adequate (overall Kappa = .81).

In order to collect observational data, the mothers and their children were invited to a University laboratory to participate in a series of interaction tasks which were videotaped for subsequent behavioral coding. The four laboratory tasks used in this study were selected in order that a range of typical mother-child interaction scenarios might be observed. They included: a free-play task, a teaching task, a negotiation task, and finally, a conflict discussion task. The order of the tasks was designed to gradually move mother-child dyads from a relatively stress-free, optimal interaction situation through to a potentially anxiety-provoking, highly interactive, confrontational scenario in which a topic that provoked conflict between members of the dyad was selected for discussion. The sequence of the activities, save for the presence of the first task, was drawn from the work of Granger, Weisz, and Kauneckis (1994).

Six simultaneous-entry multiple regressions were conducted, in which the same predictors were included. The predictors consisted of three demographic characteristics of mothers, including those on which the hypotheses were based (peer-nominated aggression and social withdrawal from grades 1, 4, and 7), as well as maternal educational attainment. The association between low maternal education and subsequent risk for psychopathology in offspring is well-documented (Auerbach, Lerner, Barasch, & Palti, 1992; Furstenberg et al., 1987; Lehoux, 1995; Velez, Johnson, & Cohen, 1989). Further, research with the present sample has identified maternal educational achievement as a strong predictor of both family risk factors and behavior problems in children (Lehoux, 1995). Maternal education has also been found to play a mediating role in continued risk from childhood aggression and social withdrawal (Serbin et al., 1998).

The remaining two predictors, which reflected child characteristics, were gender and age. With respect to the former, previous risk and resilience research indicates that boys may be at an elevated risk for behavior problems in contrast to their female counterparts (Brooks-Gunn & Furstenberg, 1986; Lehoux, 1995; Rutter, 1985). The age of the child was also of interest due to the various developmental levels of children who participated in this study.

The first hypothesis centered on the notion that maternal psychosocial difficulties in childhood would predict maladaptive behaviors in current interactions with offspring. Specific behaviors considered included: reduced support, aggression, and unresponsiveness. With respect to *supportive maternal behavior*, no significant main effect for aggression was observed. However, a trend

($p < .10$) emerged for social withdrawal: The more elevated the mother's score on social withdrawal, the less supportive she was observed to be in her interactions with her offspring. In terms of the remaining predictors, significant main effects were uncovered for both mother's educational attainment and the age of the child. The more educated the mother, the more she was observed to be supportive with her offspring. As well, mothers of younger children were found to engage in more supportive behavior.

Results for the prediction of *maternal aggression* during interactions with offspring were somewhat surprising. Neither childhood aggression nor social withdrawal was predictive of maternal aggression during interactions with offspring. Education, however, was found to be an important variable, such that the less educated the mother, the more likely she was to engage in aggressive behavior within interactions with her child. Child characteristics were also found to be predictive of maternal aggression, such that mothers were more likely to be aggressive if interacting with a younger, male child.

With respect to the results of the regression predicting *maternal unresponsiveness*, social withdrawal emerged as a significant predictor while a trend was observed for aggression. These findings suggest that mothers who were more socially withdrawn and/or more aggressive during childhood were observed to be more unresponsive to or ignoring of their children during interactions. Once again, maternal education was found to be the strongest predictor, such that less educated mothers engaged in more unresponsive behavior than did their more highly educated counterparts. Child characteristics were not found to contribute significantly to the prediction of unresponsiveness.

The lack of support for the stability of aggression might be attributed to the way in which aggression was defined in this study. Over time, there occurs a metamorphosis in the expression of aggression in females, from a more direct expression in childhood to a more indirect form in adolescence manifested by social ostracism (Bjorkqvist & Niemela, 1992; Cairns, Cairns, Neckerman, Ferguson, & Gariepy, 1989). Perhaps the tendency of these women to engage in more unresponsive or ignoring behaviors with their offspring reflects a certain degree of ostracism, sending the subtle message to their children that they are not worthy of any attention, let alone positive attention. Considering this possible explanation, the present findings should not necessarily be taken as evidence for a lack of stability in aggression.

The second hypothesis, reflecting the theory of intergenerational risk transmission, proposed that mothers' psychosocial difficulties during childhood would predict the presentation of more maladaptive behavior patterns by offspring during mother-child interactions. Specific child behaviors evaluated included restlessness, aggression, and unresponsiveness. Mothers' aggression in childhood was predictive of *restlessness*, suggesting that the more aggressive mothers were as children, the more likely their children were to engage in restless behavior during an interaction requiring discussion and negotiation. Of the remaining predictors, only the age of the child made a significant, unique contribution to the prediction of child restlessness, with younger children being more restless than their older counterparts.

In the prediction of *aggression* in children, mothers' childhood social withdrawal was found to be a significant predictor, and a trend was observed for aggression. The more withdrawn a mother was as a child, the more aggressive her child was observed to be within the context of mother-child interactions. Similarly, the more aggressive a mother was as a child, the more aggressive her child was observed to be. Of the remaining secondary predictors, only the age of the child was found to contribute uniquely to the prediction of aggressive child behavior, suggesting that younger children tended to engage in more aggressive behavior in comparison with older children. The regression predicting *unresponsive* child behavior failed to show significance; however, univariate analyses revealed a significant relationship between mothers' aggression in childhood and their children's current unresponsive behavior, such that the more aggressive the mother was in childhood, the more likely her child was to engage in unresponsive behavior.

The purpose of these analyses was to explore the relationship between psychosocial problems within the childhood of mothers and the related maladaptive behavior patterns of both these mothers and their offspring. In essence, our aim was to determine, first, whether peer-identified psychosocial problems in childhood were stable characteristics and risk factors, manifesting themselves within mothers' interactions with their offspring. Second, we explored transmission of psychosocial problems, whereby maternal psychosocial difficulties during childhood were anticipated to predict aversive behaviors emitted by children during interactions with their mothers.

Overall, moderate support was obtained for the manifestation of problem behaviors in both mothers and their offspring. The amount of explained variance in both mother and child behavior attributed to the unique predictive abilities of maternal aggression and/or social withdrawal in childhood was small (range = 1–6% of the variance for each). However, the fact that these variables provided any predictive validity is important given the 20-year time lag between the collection of the aggression and social withdrawal variables in mothers when they were children and the current collection of mother and child data. Further analyses using path models with a larger female sample for the Concordia project (Serbin, et al., 1998) indicate that education is one pathway from aggression and social withdrawal in childhood to child outcome. These results suggest the need to take into consideration not only the direct effects of these behavioral tendencies in childhood, but their indirect effects as well.

Up to this point, the data presented have included a summary of group findings. On average, women who were evaluated by their peers in childhood as being aggressive and/or withdrawn were found to be at increased risk for less adaptive parenting behaviors. As well, these women are more likely to have children who are at elevated risk for pediatric illness, injury, and maladaptive behavior. In order to make group findings more tangible, the case of one of the participating dyads follows. The mother and son you are about to meet are among the most problematic pairs we observed. At the same time, their story provides a flavor for the observed behaviors highlighted within our data set.

CASE ILLUSTRATION

At the time when the Concordia Risk Study began, Suzanne was rated by her peers as demonstrating traits of both elevated aggression and social withdrawal. Twenty years later, Suzanne is now a 30-year-old mother of two closely spaced sons. Felix, the target child is five, while Jean is four. In terms of SES, Suzanne completed high school. Both she and her husband work at minimum wage jobs. As such, financial issues are of grave concern.

Suzanne characterizes herself as a woman with a close family yet, at the same time, she reports never feeling intimately connected to anyone and experiencing difficulties trusting others. Aside from this, Suzanne denies other psychosocial difficulties, but acknowledges her addiction to nicotine, indicating that she smokes three packages of cigarettes per day. With respect to her characterization of Felix, she describes him as a difficult child. Felix's scores on the Parent Report Form of the Child Behavior Checklist (CBCL; Achenbach, 1991) were in the clinical range for both his overall profile as well as the externalizing scale. Felix experiences attentional problems including difficulty concentrating and sitting still. Felix also has severe problems expressing himself. His language is barely comprehensible. Related to these difficulties, Suzanne notes that Felix is quite aggressive, with outbursts of temper, rapidly fluctuating moods, and a tendency to deliberately hurt himself, taunt other children, and destroy objects. Due to Felix's expressive language delays, we were unable to complete a cognitive assessment. His developmental score on a drawing task indicated that he is well behind his peers in terms of non-verbal abilities.

Observations of Suzanne and Felix during their interaction conform to research findings, as well as confirm Suzanne's concerns about Felix. Most salient was the aggressive behavior exhibited by both Suzanne and Felix as exemplified in the following episode. During the conflict discussion task, Suzanne was trying to explain to Felix why he should not punch his younger brother. Suzanne, speaking quickly at one point, inadvertently sprayed saliva into Felix's face. Felix was not able to process that this action was an accident and not a deliberate attack against himself. He became enraged and spat in his mother's face. In response, perpetuating the cycle of aggression, Suzanne slapped Felix in the face. Felix then alternated rapidly between hostility and sadness. He would yell at his mother in an accusatory fashion and then quickly break down into sobs and withdraw from the interaction, refusing to speak with his mother. In summary, both Suzanne and Felix exhibited elevated levels of aggression. In addition, Felix was also found to be extremely restless and at times, unresponsive.

The preceding scenario exemplifies the increased risk of maladaptive behavior observed in high-risk mothers and their offspring. It also underscores the importance of parenting as a socialization process and potential risk pathway and suggests the value of studying the dyad earlier. The implications of these findings include the fact that to address the behavior of mother or child in isolation is insufficient. Instead, coercive as well as adaptive processes within the dyads and their developing relationship should be evaluated and serve as targets for intervention.

MANIFESTATIONS OF RISK WITHIN THE CONTEXT OF MOTHER–CHILD INTERACTIONS: PRESCHOOL OFFSPRING

In the current phase of the Concordia Risk Study, we are continuing to study parenting and other processes through which intergenerational transfer of risk may occur by exploring the social and family environments within which children of this high-risk sample develop. Findings to date suggest that by the time children arrive at grade school, they are already showing problems in the form of emotional and behavioral maladjustment (Serbin, et al., 1998). The focus of this ongoing project is on the preschool years, an important period for a child's social and emotional development, and during which important developmental transformations take place (Cicchetti, Cummings, Greenberg, & Marvin, 1990). Our aim is to identify patterns of risk that may be most detrimental for young children. This knowledge can, in turn, be used to develop appropriate interventions for implementation prior to these children entering school, a time when preventive strategies may be most effective.

This ongoing study differs from the other intergenerational studies conducted thus far within the Concordia Risk Study. The parents are in their mid 20's and early 30's; therefore, they are more mature than those in previous investigations. Thus, we might not necessarily expect these parents to face the same challenges of teenage mothers that have been identified. To what extent, and how the parents' age and maturity can act as a buffer for families with risk-backgrounds, is unknown. The age span of the children, 12 to 72 months, is younger than we had previously studied and provides an opportunity to examine the interactions of mothers and their young children using naturalistic observations of mother-child play.

The participants for the present study were recruited as a subsample from the pool of 1,770 subjects making up the Concordia Risk Study and were selected on the basis of their having one offspring in the target age range of 12 to 72 months. In total, the sample consisted of 114 risk mothers, and 61 risk fathers with their children. The parents' ages ranged from 25 to 34 years. In terms of marital status, 40% were married, 43% were co-habitating, 10% were single, and 6% were divorced/separated. In terms of education, mothers had between 5 and 17 years ($M = 11.58$, 28% did not complete high school), and fathers had between 8 and 16 years ($M = 11.57$, 26% were high-school dropouts, i.e., <11 years of schooling). Typical employment for these parents corresponded to jobs such as salesperson, filing clerk, cashier, and hairdresser. In sum, compared with the sample of mothers described in the previous section, these parents were older, more of them were married or co-habiting, and on average they had slightly more education. By including male participants for the project, we will be able to examine how transfer of risk for fathers compares to that of mothers in the future. However, because of the fewer number of fathers, to date the focus of our investigations has been on the risk mothers.

All participants were contacted by telephone in order to arrange an appointment for two home visits. The research team typically consisted of two members: an M.A. level psychologist, and a research assistant. At the start of the first home visit, an intellectual assessment of the child was conducted in order to evaluate the current status of the child's cognitive and language abilities and, in the case of the younger children, motor development was also assessed. The Bayley Scales of Infant Development (Second Edition, Bayley, 1993) were administered to children aged 12 to 42 months. The Stanford Binet Intelligence Scale (Fourth Edition; Thorndike, Hagen, & Sattler, 1986) was administered to children aged 42 to 72 months. While the child was being evaluated, face-to-face interviews were conducted with the mother. The purpose of the interviews was to gather information concerning the target child's prenatal environment, delivery, birth complications, and current health status, as well as gather information concerning family stresses. Questionnaires, completed by participants in between the two home visits, provided further information concerning parents' current psychosocial functioning. During the home visits, mother-child interactions were videotaped in a variety of situations, which permitted us to directly observe the patterns of behavior of mothers and their children.

Data collection for this current phase of the Concordia Risk Study has recently been completed. Although all the coding and a complete analysis of the data have not, as yet, been undertaken, we do have some preliminary results from analyses conducted on a sub-sample of mothers and their children, the youngest in the study, aged 12 to 42 months (Bentley, Stack, & Serbin, 1998). In these preliminary analyses, we explored unresponsive parenting or ignoring behaviors, previously observed with school-aged offspring, to see whether these would be also apparent in mothers' interactions with their toddlers and preschool children.

In our search for important parenting and family variables that may place these children at risk, a primary focus is the mother-child relationship. As previously mentioned, this first relationship is one of the most salient relationships in a child's life. During the first 3 years of life, important attachment processes and emotional organization take place (Emde, 1989; Fogel, 1993; Sameroff & Seifer, 1992). A parent's ability to be emotionally available, responsive, and attentive during these early years will ultimately impact the developmental outcome of their child (Biringen & Robinson, 1991; Egeland & Erickson, 1987). The primary objectives of this present inquiry were to consider whether mothers' childhood aggression and social withdrawal might interfere with their abilities to effectively parent their young children.

For the purposes of this study, we assessed the quality of the mother-child relationship during a 15-minute free-play session using the Emotional Availability Scales (Biringen, Robinson, & Emde, 1988). These scales consist of five relational measures of emotional availability capturing both maternal and child behaviors (i.e., maternal sensitivity, scaffolding, and hostility; and child responsiveness and involvement).

At the outset, it was hypothesized that maternal childhood risk status would disrupt levels of emotional availability towards the next generation. However, within the context of the present study, it was found that many mothers who had elevated levels of childhood aggression or withdrawal alone were able to demonstrate adequate levels of emotional availability in interacting with their children. Mothers who were identified in their childhoods as being both aggressive and socially withdrawn were more likely to demonstrate hostile behaviors when interacting with their children. Other investigations have also found similar patterns of interactions within risk samples (Crittenden, 1981; Dix, 1991; Egeland & Erickson, 1987). It is interesting, however, that, within this sample, primarily covert forms of hostility were seen such as sarcasm, boredom, and irritability. Although perhaps manifesting themselves in a slightly different form, these behaviors are consistent with those found in previous investigations within the Concordia Risk Study in which aggressive and withdrawn mothers were more likely to be unresponsive and ignoring, which also transmit messages of social rejection to their children. Previous findings have indicated that children with combined levels of aggression and withdrawal may be particularly at risk for maladaptive psychosocial functioning in adulthood (Moskowitz & Schwartzman, 1989). These documented problems in social functioning may now be revealed in mothers' interactions with their own children which suggest both continuity for the aggressive and withdrawn behaviors and a potential pathway for the intergenerational transfer of risk.

Surprisingly, within this present study, maternal education was not found to be significantly associated with either the maternal or child emotional availability measures. Seventy-two percent of the mothers within this sub-sample were fairly well educated, with between 11 (high-school completion in Quebec) to 15 years of education. The mothers were also older when they had their first child compared to previous investigations within the Concordia Risk Study. Taken together, these factors may have resulted in education having a reduced influence on the quality of interactions in a mature sample of mothers, most (72%) of whom had completed high school.

Given that analyses of these data are only preliminary in nature, however, it is premature to draw conclusions regarding the quality of the parent-child relationship and the intergenerational transfer of risk in this sample. Nevertheless, the observations to date indicate the presence of many parenting problems among these parents and developmental difficulties in their offspring. As mentioned previously, we assessed the children's intellectual functioning, along with their behavioral and socio-emotional development, parental characteristics, and family relationships. Using this information, an evaluation of the level of risk to the child's cognitive and psychosocial development was made, and each case was classified into one of three categories. If the child was functioning at an age-appropriate level and no significant risk factor was threatening his/her development, the case was considered to be a *low-risk* case. *Moderate-risk* cases were those where some level of developmental risk was noted. In these cases, concern was raised by the child's cognitive and socio-emotional adjustment, or problems with the family environment, such as stress or marital conflict, which might impede or impact on the child's development. Finally, the case was judged to be a *high-risk* case when the child was found to be experiencing significant delays in his/her intellectual and/or social-emotional functioning compared to same age peers.

Using this classification system, we were able to demonstrate general elevated risk in our sample. Across the entire sample of 175 children, 64% were considered to be at moderate to high risk for developmental problems. Importantly, although the rates of referral were high in children from the comparison group (47% of these children, whose parents came from disadvantaged backgrounds but did not have histories of aggression and/or social withdrawal, were showing moderate to severe cognitive delays and/or behavioral problems), the offspring of individuals with histories of problematic behavioral tendencies were still more likely to experience problems. Overall, almost 70% of the children from the aggressive, withdrawn, and aggressive/withdrawn groups were judged to be at moderate to high risk for developmental problems. In most of these cases, the concern was directly related to delays in the children's intellectual functioning and/or behavioral adjustment.

Our clinical assessments illustrated the presence of various negative outcomes in the children of our sample, including health problems, language difficulties, cognitive delays, and behavioral problems (measured by direct observation, or parental report), as well as family problems that may interfere with the provision of cognitive stimulation and socio-emotional support and development. Such findings highlight the necessity to study these different areas of psychosocial functioning and health simultaneously, to obtain a global understanding of the developmental problems affecting high-risk children. Indeed, the risk profiles of many of the children in our sample were serious and complex. The following case provides an illustration of the multiple risk factors that can affect children's development and the close links between different negative outcomes they experience.

CASE ILLUSTRATION

Carole is one of the mothers we visited as part of this phase of the project. She comes from a severely disadvantaged background, and in 4th grade was identified by peer nominations as highly aggressive and withdrawn. Both her parents had minimal education, and worked in menial jobs. She was sexually abused by her father during childhood, and has suffered from several episodes of depression since the age of 16. Although she did poorly in school, she managed to complete her high school education. She is now a 29-year-old mother of two, with a 5-year-old daughter and a 2 1/2-year-old son, Sylvain, the 'target' child in this study. Carole separated from the children's father, who was drug dependent and physically abusive towards her, when Sylvain was 2 years of age. At that time, she experienced a 'nervous breakdown,' and was taken to the emergency room of a psychiatric hospital. She then spent 2 weeks in a halfway house. She currently lives alone with her two children, and is dependent on welfare as her only source of income.

Sylvain's medical history is marked by many problems. While pregnant, Carole suffered from anemia and gestational diabetes. She also had to take medication to stop contractions that began at the 7th month of the pregnancy. Sylvain was born prematurely, with the umbilical cord around his neck. He was diagnosed with asthma when he was 4 months old. He also suffers from chronic otitis and diarrhea. Since the age of 1, he has been taking medication for hyperactivity-related problems. Carole expresses feelings of inadequacy in dealing with her son's difficult behavior. Sylvain often has temper tantrums, acts aggressively, and has a tendency to deliberately hurt himself. These behavioral tendencies were evident during our clinical assessment, as he was very uncooperative and required firm limit-setting. On the Bayley Scales of Infant Development (Second edition; Bayley, 1993), Sylvain showed a significant delay on the Mental Development Index, primarily attributable to language delays. As well, he evidenced a mild delay on the Motor scales. Due to these extensive problems, Sylvain was classified as a *high-risk* case, and was referred for a comprehensive psychological assessment. An evaluation for speech therapy was also recommended, in addition to a parenting program to help his mother manage her child's behavioral problems.

An extreme illustration of the multiple risks to the offspring in our sample, Sylvain's case also highlights another important finding from this phase of the project. That is, boys appear more at risk for severe developmental problems than girls; there were more sons (26.3%) than daughters (17.9%) who received a *high-risk* classification, indicating immediate need for clinical services. This potential gender difference in referral rates for behavioral problems and/or cognitive delays is consistent with previous studies (Brooks-Gunn & Furstenberg, 1986; Rutter, 1985).

In the near future, we plan to systematically explore these multiple risk factors as well as the various negative outcomes facing the young children in our sample, in order to examine specific pathways of risk. This approach will also enable us to study the processes underlying resilience. Thirty-six percent of the children in our sample appear to be functioning at an age-appropriate level across developmental domains, despite the presence of various risk factors in their profiles. We are interested in identifying specific characteristics of the family situation, the parents, and/or the child that promote adjustment in the face of psychosocial disadvantage. Previous studies have emphasized the role of parental education as a protective factor (Auerbach, et al., 1992; Furstenberg, et al., 1987; Serbin, et al., 1998). We intend to examine other variables, such as parental characteristics, family relationships, and the availability of social support, since a number of our clinical assessments, as well as previous research (Cowen, Wyman, Work, & Parker, 1990; McLoyd, 1990), indicate that these variables may represent important buffers against negative outcomes.

GENERAL DISCUSSION

The present studies suggest some of the processes involved in prediction of intergenerational risk and in the transfer of risk to offspring within a disadvantaged population of women. Aggression appears to be a general risk factor within this sample. For many years, aggression in girls was a relatively neglected topic in the research literature. This pattern has begun to change as it becomes clear that aggression and other atypical behavior in girls may predict patterns of negative adolescent and adult outcomes that are distinct from the overt delinquency and other problems typical of aggressive boys. Although it is not yet clear from the Concordia Risk Study results, aggression in males may also predict intergenerational patterns of risk (Fagot, Pears, Capaldi, Crosby, & Leve, 1998). We will have the opportunity to explore these predictions in the future with our sample of fathers.

In contrast to aggression, withdrawal may have more subtle interactive or additive effects within subgroups who are at highest risk. The existence of different forms of social withdrawal has been postulated (Mash & Barkley, 1998; Rubin, Hymel, & Mills, 1989), and may also account for the somewhat variable results produced by this factor in different subgroups of the Concordia sample. The highly withdrawn girls who are also aggressive and/or who have poor academic skills are apparently at highest risk from within the larger group of withdrawn girls.

Highlighted in the three different studies presented are a number of predictors of intergenerational risk, including problematic obstetric and fertility patterns, school dropout, teen parenthood, and difficulty functioning as a responsive parent. Together with previously reported findings on offspring health and injuries, the results suggest that some of the young women followed have difficulty sustaining (or may not realize the importance of) regular medical care and adequate nutrition, either for themselves, or for their children. Moreover, the unity of development is underscored; that is, there are interrelationships between risk factors and developmental domains. In addition to problems addressing their children's physical needs, some of these young mothers may exhibit difficulty in appropriately monitoring, stimulating and responding to the psychological needs of their children, with serious potential consequences for their cognitive and social-emotional development. The generally high rates of behavioral, emotional and medical problems reported for their offspring, as well as the children's observed aggression and unresponsiveness in interacting with their mothers, suggest that these conditions exact a toll that is visible by the time children reach elementary school.

One factor predicted outcomes consistently within the highest-risk sub-sample described here, the mothers with school-aged offspring: mothers' education. 'Education' in this model probably represents a cluster of socio-economic factors extending beyond the completion of schooling, such as mothers' economic and occupational status, quality of environment, social support, and physical and psychological health. All of these factors probably affect parenting and children's well being, in addition to various aspects of formal education that may influence parenting ability directly.

In the present set of studies, educational attainment predicted teen parenthood, observed parental behavior, mother's reports of depression, anxiety, and other symptoms, and reports of behavioral-emotional problems in offspring. In turn, mother's educational attainment was predicted by both childhood aggression and by elementary school achievement test results (see also Serbin, et al.,

1998). The association between the dimensions of aggression and withdrawal and poor achievement scores highlights the complexity of the challenges facing these children. One implication of these findings is that children who have behavioral problems may also have poor academic skills or cognitive and attentional problems that require assessment and intervention.

It is beyond the scope of this chapter to identify the intervening factors or processes that were not measured or included in this set of studies (e.g., role of fathers, additional family factors). What is clear from the present results is that childhood aggression and withdrawal play a role in predicting intergenerational outcomes. Whether similar results would be found in a different context (e.g., in a less disadvantaged population) or a different geographic, cultural or ethnic milieu, remains an important issue for further research. It may be that childhood social behavior is a less important predictor in populations at lower risk (e.g., middle income samples) for negative outcomes, and it appears that mothers' years of education may be a less important predictor of child well-being in women who postpone their childbearing into their mid to late 20's.

The risk patterns examined here will continue to evolve as the participants develop through adulthood. The present results indicate that during the child-rearing years, parenting must be considered a domain for the expression and transfer of behavioral problems that may be visible years earlier. Unresponsiveness to offspring and lack of emotional support were the patterns seen in both observational studies. Parental unresponsiveness may be linked to the development of coercive styles of interaction between parents and children (Fagot, et al., 1998), as seen in the aggressive behavior of the Concordia sample offspring towards the more withdrawn mothers.

Further issues to pursue with the Concordia data set include the relation between boys' childhood behavior and future parenting. Based on the findings of the Oregon Social Learning Centre project (Fagot, et al., 1998), we anticipate that the children of men with childhood histories of aggression will also be a problematic group. The effects of spousal characteristics obviously also need to be included in models of prediction for offspring. For the present, however, it seems clear that girls' childhood behavior, in particular aggression and withdrawal, present risk factors for both generations. The social, economic, and personal costs of these intergenerational patterns are substantial, and warrant consideration by makers of educational, health, and social policy.

ACKNOWLEDGMENTS

This research was partially supported by grants from the Seagram Fund for Innovative Research (Concordia University), the Strategic Fund for Children's Mental Health (Health Canada), and the National Institute of Mental Health. Portions of this paper were presented at the biennial meeting of the Society for Research in Child Development, April 1997, Washington, D.C. and the International Conference on Infant Studies, April 1998. The Concordia

Longitudinal Risk Research Program was originated in 1976 under the direction of Jane Ledingham and Alex Schwartzman. We thank Claude Senneville, Xiaoming Tang, Irfan Yaqub, and Dany Lacroix for their assistance in data collection and analysis. Furthermore, we thank Julie Brousseau, Pascale Lehoux, Manon St. Germain, Sandra Thibault, and Natalie Vaudry for their aid in data collection for one subsample, and Marie-Claude Ouimet for help with data organization. We are particularly grateful to the Regie d' Assurance-Maladie du Quebec for their assistance in the analysis of medical records. Finally, we are most indebted to the participants in the study. Correspondence concerning this chapter should be addressed to Lisa A. Serbin, Centre for Research in Human Development and Department of Psychology, Concordia University, 7141 Sherbrooke Street West, Montreal, Quebec, Canada, H4B 1R6. Electronic mail may be sent via Internet to LSERBIN@VAX2.CONCORDIA.CA.

REFERENCES

Achenbach, T. M. (1991). *Manual for the Child Behavior Checklist/4-18 and 1991 Profile.* Burlington, VT: University of Vermont, Department of Psychiatry.

Auerbach, J., Lerner, Y., Barasch, M., & Palti, H. (1992). Maternal and environmental characteristics as predictors of child behavior problems and cognitive competence. *American Journal of Orthopsychiatry, 62*, 409–420.

Baldwin, W. & Cain, V. S. (1980). The children of teenage parents. *Family Planning Perspectives, 12*, 34–43.

Bayley, N. (1993). *The Bayley Scales of Infant Development* (2nd ed.). New York: The Psychological Corporation.

Beardslee, W., Bemporad, J., Keller, M., & Klerman, G. (1983). Children of parents with major affective disorder: A review. *American Journal of Psychiatry, 140*, 825–832.

Beckwith, L. & Parmelee, A. H. (1986). EEG patterns of preterm infants, home environment and later IQ. *Child Development, 57*, 777–789.

Bentley, V. M., Stack, D. M., & Serbin, L. A. (1998, April). *Maternal childhood risk status as a predictor of emotional availability in mother-child interactions.* Poster presented at the meeting of the International Conference on Infant Studies, Atlanta, GA.

Berlin, L. (1997, November). *Poverty, early development and early intervention.* Symposium on Poverty and Academic Achievement, conducted at University of Montreal, Montreal, Québec.

Biringen, Z. & Robinson, J. (1991). Emotional availability in mother-child interactions: A reconceptualization for research. *American Journal of Orthopsychiatry, 61*, 258–271.

Biringen, Z., Robinson, J. L., & Emde, R. N. (1988). *The Emotional Availability Scales.* Unpublished manuscript. University of Colorado Health Sciences Center, Denver.

Bjorkqvist, K. & Niemela, P. (1992). New trends in the study of female aggression. In K. Bjorkqvist & P. Niemela (Eds.), *Of mice and women: Aspects of female aggression* (pp. 1–16). San Diego, CA: Academic Press.

Bowlby, J. (1980). *Attachment and loss. Vol. 1: Loss, sadness and depression.* New York: Basic Books.

Brooks-Gunn, J. & Furstenberg, F. F. (1986). The children of adolescent mothers: Physical, academic, and psychological outcomes. *Developmental Review, 6*, 224–251.

Cairns, R. B., Cairns, B. D., Neckerman, H. J., Ferguson, L. L., & Gariepy, J. L. (1989). Growth and aggression: 1. Childhood to early adolescence. *Developmental Psychology, 25*, 320–330.

Cairns, R. B., Cairns, B. D., Xie, H., Leung, M. C., & Hearne, S. (1998). Paths across generations: Academic competence and aggressive behaviors in young mothers and their children. *Developmental Psychology, 34*, 1162–1174.

Casaer, P., de Vries, L., & Marlow, N. (1991). Prenatal and perinatal risk factors for psychological development. In M. Rutter & P. Casaer (Eds.), *Biological risk factors for psychosocial disorders* (pp. 139–174). New York: Cambridge University Press.

Caspi, A. & Elder, G. H. (1988a). Childhood precursors of the life course: Early personality and life disorganization. In E. M. Hetherington, R. M. Lerner, & M. Perlmutter (Eds.), *Child development in lifespan perspective* (pp. 115–142). Hillsdale, NJ: Lawrence Erlbaum Associates.

Caspi, A. & Elder, G. H. (1988b). Emergent family patterns: The intergenerational construction of problem behavior and relationships. In R. Hinde & J. Stevenson-Hinde (Eds.), *Relationships within families: Mutual influences* (pp. 218–240). Oxford: Oxford University Press.

Cicchetti, D., Cummings, E. M., Greenberg, M. T., & Marvin, R. A. (1990). An organizational perspective on attachment beyond infancy: Implications for theory, measurement and research. In M. T. Greenberg, D. Cicchetti, & E. Mark Cummings (Eds.), *Attachment in the preschool years: Theory, research, and intervention* (pp. 3–50). Chicago: University of Chicago Press.

Conger, R. D., Elder, J. H. Jr, Lorenz, F. O., Simons, R. L., & Whitbeck, L. B. (1994). *Families in troubled times: Adapting to change in rural America*. New York: Aldine de Gruyter.

Cooperman, J. M. & Steinbach, L. (1995). *The High-Risk Interaction Coding System: Coding manual*. Unpublished manuscript, Concordia University, Centre for Research in Human Development, Montreal, Quebec.

Cowen, E. L., Wyman, P. A., Work, W. C., & Parker, G. R. (1990). The Rochester Child Resilience Project: Overview and summary of first year findings. *Development and Psychopathology, 2*, 193–212.

Crittenden, P. M. (1981). Abusing, neglecting, problematic and adequate dyads: Differentiating by patterns of interaction. *Merrill-Palmer Quarterly, 27*, 201–218.

Dix, T. (1991). The affective organization of parenting: Adaptive and maladaptive processes. *Psychological Bulletin, 110*, 3–25.

Dumas, J. E., LaFreniere, P., & Serketich, W. (1995). 'Balance of Power': A transactional analysis of control in mother-child dyads involving socially competent, aggressive, and anxious children. *Journal of Abnormal Psychology, 104*, 104–112.

Duncan, G. J., Brooks-Gunn, J., & Klebanov, P. K. (1994). Economic deprivation and early childhood development. *Child Development, 65*, 296–318.

Egeland, B. & Erickson, M. F. (1987). Psychologically unavailable caregiving. In M. R. Brassard, R. Germain, & S. M. Hart (Eds.), *Psychological maltreatment of children and youth* (pp. 110–120). New York: Pergamon Press.

Emde, R. N. (1989). The infant's relationship experience: Developmental and affective aspects. In A. J. Sameroff & R. N. Emde (Eds.), *Relationship disturbances in early childhood* (pp. 33–51). New York: Harper Collins.

Fagot, B. I., Pears, K. C., Capaldi, D. M., Crosby, L. & Leve, C. S. (1998). Becoming an adolescent father: Precursors and parenting. *Developmental Psychology, 34*, 1209–1219.

Farrington, D. P. (1991). Childhood aggression and adult violence: Early precursors and later life outcomes. In D. J. Pepler & K. H. Rubin (Eds.), *The development and treatment of childhood aggression* (pp. 5–29). Hillsdale, NJ: Lawrence Erlbaum Associates.

Fingerhut, L. & Kleinman, J. (1989). Trends and current status in childhood mortality, United States, 1900–1985. *Vital Heath Statistics, 26*, 1–44.

Fogel, A. (1993). *Developing through relationships: The origins of communication, self, and culture*. New York: Harvester Wheatsheaf.

Furstenberg, F. F., Brooks-Gunn, J., & Morgan, S. P. (1987). *Adolescent mothers in later life*. New York: Cambridge University Press.

Furstenberg, F. F., Jr., Brooks-Gunn, J., & Chase-Landsdale, L. (1989). Teenage pregnancy and childbearing. *American Psychologist, 44*, 313–320.

Granger, D. A., Weisz, J. R., & Kauneckis, D. (1994). Neuroendocrine reactive, internalizing behavior problems and control-related cognitions in clinic-referred children and adolescents. *Journal of Abnormal Psychology, 103*, 267–276.

Hammen, C., Gordon, D., Burge, D., Adrian, C., Jaenicke, C., & Hiroto, D. (1987). Maternal affective disorders, illness, and stress: Risk for children's psychopathology. *American Journal of Psychiatry, 144*, 736–741.

Hardy, J. B., Shapiro, S., Mellits, E. D., Skinner, E. A., Astone, N. M., Ensminger, M. E., Laveist, T., Baumgardner, R. A., & Starfield, B. H. (1997). Self-sufficiency at ages 27 to 33 years: Factors present between birth and 18 years that predict educational attainment among children born to inner-city families. *Pediatrics, 99*, 80–87.

Harris, K. M. & Marmer, J. K. (1996). Poverty, parental involvement, and adolescent well-being. *Journal of Family Issues, 17*, 614–640.

Kopp, C. B. & Kaler, S. R. (1989). Risk in infancy: Origins and implications. *American Psychologist, 44*, 224–230.

Layzer, J., St. Pierre, R., & Bernstein, L. (1996, March). *Early life trajectories of teenage mothers vs. older mothers.* Paper presented at the meeting of the Society for Research on Adolescence, Boston, MA.

Lehoux, P. M. (1995). *The intergenerational transmission of psychosocial problems: Family process and behavioral outcome in offspring of high-risk mothers.* Unpublished master's thesis, Concordia University, Montreal, Quebec.

Lipman, E. L. & Offord, D. R. (1997). Psychosocial morbidity among poor children in Ontario. In G. J. Duncan & J. Brooks-Gunn (Eds.), *Consequences of growing up poor* (pp. 239–287). New York: Russell Sage Foundation.

Lipman, E. L., Offord, D. R., Racine, Y. A., & Boyle, M. H. (1994). Psychiatric disorders in adopted children: A profile from the Ontario Child Health Study. *Canadian Journal of Psychiatry, 37*, 627–633.

Lucas, A., Morley, R., Cole, T. J., & Gore, T. J. (1989). Early diet in preterm babies and developmental status in infancy. *Archives of Disease in Childhood, 64*, 1570–1578.

Mash, E. J. & Barkley, R. A. (Eds.). (1998). *Treatment of childhood disorders* (2nd ed.). New York: Guilford Press.

McLoyd, V. C. (1990). The impact of economic hardship on black families and children: Psychological distress, parenting, and socio-emotional development. *Child Development, 61*, 311–346.

McLoyd, V. C. (1998). Socioeconomic disadvantage and child development. *American Psychologist, 53*, 185–204.

Moskowitz, D. S. & Schwartzman, A. E. (1989). Painting group portraits: Studying life outcomes for aggressive and withdrawn children. *Journal of Personality Psychology, 57*, 723–746.

Moskowitz, D. S., Schwartzman, A. E., & Ledingham, J. (1985). Stability and change in aggression and withdrawal in middle childhood and adolescence. *Journal of Abnormal Psychology, 94*, 30–41.

Olweus, D. (1984). Stability in aggressive and withdrawn, inhibited behavior patterns. In R. M. Kaplan, V. J. Konecni, & R. W. Novaco (Eds.), *Aggression in children and youth* (pp. 104–137). Netherlands: Martinus Nijhoff Publishers.

Patterson, G. R. (1982). *A social learning approach to family intervention: Volume 3. Coercive family processes.* Eugene, OR: Castalia.

Patterson, G. R., Ray, R. S., Shaw, D. A., & Cobb, J. A. (1969). *Manual for coding family interactions.* New York: Microfiche Publications.

Pollitt, E., Golub, M., Gorman, K. Grantham-McGregor, S. Levitsky, D., Schürch, B., Strupp, B., & Wachs, T. (1996). A reconceptualization of the effects of undernutrition on children's biological, psychosocial, and behavioral development. *Social Policy Report: Society for Research in Child Development, 10*(5), 1–30.

Prechtl, H. (1968). Neurological findings in newborn infants after pre- and perinatal complications. In J. Jonix, H. Visser, & J. Troelstra (Eds.), *Aspects of prematurity and dysmaturity* (pp. 303–312). Leiden, Netherlands: Stenfert Kroese.

Rodriguez, J. G. (1990). Childhood injuries in the United States: A priority issue. *American Journal of Diseases of Children, 144*, 625–626.

Rothman, K. J. (1986). *Modern epidemiology.* Toronto: Little, Brown.

Rubin, K. H., Hymel, S., & Mills, R. S. L. (1989). Sociability and social withdrawal in childhood: Stability and outcomes. *Journal of Personality, 57*, 237–255.

Rutter, M. (1985). Resilience in the face of adversity. *British Journal of Psychiatry, 147*, 598–611.

Sameroff, A. J. & Seifer, R. (1992). Early contributors to developmental risk. In J. Rolf, A. S. Masten, D. Cicchetti, K. H. Nuechterlein, & S. Weintraub (Eds.), *Risk and protective factors in the development of psychopathology* (pp. 52–66). New York: Cambridge University Press.

Scaramella, L. V., Conger, R. D., Simons, R. L., & Whitbeck, L. B. (1998). Predicting risk for pregnancy by late adolescence: A social contextual perspective. *Developmental Psychology, 34*, 1233–1245.

Schwartzman, A. E., Ledingham, J. E., & Serbin, L. A. (1985). Identification of children at risk for adult schizophrenia: A longitudinal study. *International Review of Applied Psychology, 34*, 363–380.

Schwartzman, A., Verlaan, P., Peters, P., & Serbin, L. (1995). Sex roles as coercion. In J. McCord (Ed.), *Coercion and punishment in long-term perspective* (pp. 362–375). New York: Cambridge University Press.

Sepkoski, C., Coll, C. G., & Lester, B.M. (1982). The cumulative effects of obstetric risk variables on newborn behavior. In L. P. Lipsitt & T. M. Field (Eds.), *Perinatal risk and newborn behavior* (pp. 33–39) Norwood, NJ: Ablex Publishing.

Serbin, L. A., Peters, P. L., & Schwartzman, A. E. (1996). Longitudinal study of early childhood injuries and acute illnesses in the offspring of adolescent mothers who were aggressive, withdrawn, or aggressive-withdrawn in childhood. *Journal of Abnormal Psychology, 105*, 500–507.

Serbin, L. A., Cooperman, J. M., Peters, P. L., Lehoux, P. M., Stack, D. M., & Schwartzman, A. E. (1998). Intergenerational transfer of psychosocial risk in women with childhood histories of aggression, withdrawal or aggression and withdrawal. *Developmental Psychology, 34*, 1246–1262.

Thorndike, R. L., Hagen, E. P., & Sattler, J. M. (1986). *The Stanford-Binet Intelligence Scale: Fourth Edition*. Chicago: Riverside Publishing Company.

Velez, C. N., Johnson, J., & Cohen, P. (1989). A longitudinal analysis of selected risk factors for childhood psychopathology. *Journal of the American Academy of Child and Adolescent Psychiatry, 28*, 861–864.

Werner, E. E. & Smith, R.S. (1977). *Kauai's children come of age*. Honolulu: University of Hawaii Press.

Werner, E. E. & Smith, R. S. (1992). *Overcoming the odds: High risk children from birth to adulthood*. London: Cornell University Press.

Whitman, T. L., Borkowski, J. G., Schellenbach, C. J., & Nath, P. S. (1988). Predicting and understanding developmental delay of children of adolescent mothers: A multidimensional approach. *American Journal of Mental Deficiency, 92*, 40–56.

Wilms, D. (1997, November). *The Quebec advantage: The superior literacy and mathematical skills of Quebec youth*. Symposium on Poverty and Academic Achievement, conducted at University of Montreal, Montreal, Québec.

CHAPTER 4

Preventing Depression in Children Through Resiliency Promotion

The Preventive Intervention Project

WILLIAM R. BEARDSLEE, EVE M. VERSAGE,
POLLY VAN DE VELDE, SUSAN SWATLING, & LIZBETH HOKE

The Preventive Intervention Project is a longitudinal study that works with families to prevent difficulties in children from homes where parental affective illness is present. The primary aim of our project is the prevention of childhood disorder through the promotion of resilient traits and the modification of risk factors associated with parental affective illness (e.g., poor marital communication, dysfunctional parenting practices, a lack of focus on the children, and confusion and misunderstanding in families). In this chapter, the theoretical constructs and the content of the individual sessions of the clinician-facilitated intervention are described.

OVERVIEW

The first phase of the project was initiated in 1989. Currently 100 families from the greater Boston area have enrolled in the study and are being assessed at 8-month intervals. Families in which one or both parents had been diagnosed with an affective illness with non-ill children between the ages of 8–15 were recruited. The mean age of the children enrolled in the study at the time of initial assessment was 11.6 ± 1.9 yrs. In 77% of the families, the identified affectively ill parent was the mother and in 23% of the families both parents suffered from an affective disorder.

(Each family was randomly assigned and participated in either a two-part lecture series or a short-term clinician-facilitated intervention.) In choosing a format for the interventions, the ease and consistency with which they could be delivered were considered. The interventions were designed to be administered by a wide range of health care professionals and were manual-based to insure the reliability of their delivery. Over time, through the enhancement of family understanding, the promotion of resilient traits, improved problem solving, and a greater focus on the children, overall improvement in child and family functioning is expected.

(The two interventions (clinician-facilitated and lecture format) are similar in content but differ in the degree in which cognitive materials are linked to the unique illness experience of the family.) In the lecture condition, the parents attend a two-part lecture series without their children. There is no direct attempt to link the psycho-educational material presented to the families' experience of the illness, except in response to specific questions raised by parents during the discussion portion of the lectures(During the lectures, the parents are encouraged to talk with their children about their illness and what they learned during the meetings.)(In the clinician-facilitated condition, the intervener actively works with the family to link their unique experience of the illness to the presented cognitive materials. The children participate in a family meeting in which the parents are given an opportunity to discuss their illness with them.)

Improved communication about the illness between spouses, with children, and as a family have been observed in participants of both intervention conditions (Beardslee, Salt, et al., 1997). (Both interventions were reported to reduce levels of parental guilt regarding the illness, and to increase understanding of parental illness by the child) (Beardslee, Wright, et al., 1997). Overall, significantly greater levels of change regarding illness-related behaviors, attitudes and overall change were found for participants in the clinician-facilitated condition than for participants from the lecture condition (Beardslee, Salt, et al., 1997). Additionally, significantly more parents from the clinician-facilitated condition were rated as having higher levels of self-understanding and improved focus on their children than participants from the lecture condition (Beardslee, Salt, et al., 1997). Children whose parents reported a positive response to intervention correspondingly reported better outcomes in terms of depressive symptoms and current global functioning (Beardslee, Wright, et al., l997). Both interventions have proved to be safe and feasible, and to offer considerable sustained benefits to families (Beardslee, Wright, Rothberg, Salt, & Versage, 1996; Beardslee, Salt, et al., 1997). The clinician-facilitated intervention has consistently provided much greater benefits. In this chapter, the main ingredients of the intervention sessions are presented in the hope that they will be useful to a wide range of clinicians.

RISKS ASSOCIATED WITH PARENTAL AFFECTIVE ILLNESS

Parental affective illness has been associated with increased rates of psychiatric disorders in children (Beardslee, et al., 1988; Grigoroiu-Serbanescu, et al., 1991; Hammen, Burge, Burney, & Adrian, 1990; Orvaschel, Walsh-Allis, & Ye, 1988; Radke-Yarrow, Nottelmann, Martinez, Fox, & Belmont, 1992; Weissman, Fendrich, Warner, & Wickramaratne, 1992). Rates of observed disorder have varied greatly, with estimates as low as 8% to as high as 74% reported in the children of unipolar depressed parents (Lavoie & Hodgins, 1994) and from 23% to 92% in the children of bipolar parents (Radke-Yarrow, et al., 1992). Meta-analytic findings indicate that approximately 61% of the offspring of parents with Major Depressive Disorder (MDD) will develop psychiatric disorder during childhood or adolescence and are four times more likely to develop an affective disorder than children with non-ill parents (Lavoie & Hodgins, 1994). Life table estimates suggest that by the age of 20 a child with an affectively ill parent has a 40% chance of experiencing an episode of depression, and by the age of 25 this rate increases to 60% (Beardslee, Keller, Lavori, Staley, & Sacks, 1993).

Parental affective illness has been associated with poor marital relationships (Fendrich, Warner, & Weissman, 1990) and family cohesion/parenting problems (Billings & Moos, 1983; Rutter & Quinton, 1984). High rates of marital conflict, separation and divorce have been found in couples with a depressed spouse (Coyne, et al., 1987; Hautzinger, Linden, & Hoffman, 1982). Children in families with parental affective disorder who are exposed to marital conflict are significantly more likely to experience some form of psychopathology during their lifetime (including MDD) than are children in families with affective illness but no marital conflict (Fendrich, et al., 1990).

In families with a depressed adult, family functioning and parenting disturbances are common in both the acute phase of the disorder and thereafter (Keitner & Miller, 1990), and have been connected to emotional and health problems in children (Billings & Moos, 1983, 1985). Specifically, interaction studies of young children and their depressed parents have demonstrated disturbances in parenting, including decreased attention, less intensity of interaction, and an inability to focus on the child (Beardslee & Wheelock, 1994; Downey & Coyne, 1990). Depressed mothers are less effective than non-depressed mothers at disciplining and setting limits with their children (Kochanska, Kuczynski, Yarrow, & Welsh, 1987). With older children, maladaptive interpersonal patterns between mothers and children have also been described (Gordon, et al., 1989), as have higher levels of criticism and verbal abuse (Cox, Puckering, Pound, & Mills, 1987; Gordon, et al., 1989). Research using Vaughn and Leff's (1976) measure of expressed emotion has demonstrated a strong association between high levels of criticism and poor outcome in spouses (Hooley, Orley, & Teasdale, 1986) and children (Schwartz, Dorer, Beardslee, Lavori, & Keller, 1990) of depressed individuals.

Recent research has indicated that a single risk factor may lead to a variety of different negative outcomes, emphasizing that risk factors are unlikely to be specific to one disorder. Perhaps more importantly, the sum of several risk factors are better predictors of poor outcome than any one risk factor (Rutter, 1986; Simons & Miller, 1987). In a sample of adolescents followed over 4 years, Rutter (1986) examined six adversity factors for childhood depression and found that the sum of risk factors was far more important than any single risk factor in predicting future depression. Similar results have been reported by Sameroff, Seifer, Zax, and Barocas (1987) with young children, and by Offord (1989) for general behavioral difficulties.

Beardslee and colleagues (Beardslee, Keller, et al., 1996) applied this approach to predicting onsets of affective disorder in a non-referred sample of adolescents drawn from a prepaid health plan, many of whose parents were affectively ill. They developed an adversity index to predict the onset of disorder in these adolescents who were followed over 4 years. They found that the presence of factors from different domains best predicted poor outcome, including duration of parental affective disorder, number of parental non-affective diagnoses, and total number of prior child diagnoses (Beardslee, Keller, et al., 1996). These findings indicate the need to view parental affective disorder as a marker for a constellation of risk factors that, taken together, predict poor outcome, and indicate that affective disorder must be understood in its component parts, rather than as a single entity.

Although these findings indicate that children growing up in homes where affective illness is present are at an increased risk for a variety of emotional difficulties, not all children at risk become ill. This observation is part of a larger awareness that many youngsters who are expected to do poorly as a function of growing up in highly disadvantaged circumstances actually do well (Garmezy, 1985; Rutter, 1987). As part of a larger study, Beardslee and Podorefsky (1988) examined the resilient traits of 18 young adults whose parents had affective disorders and had displayed high adaptive functioning at the time of initial assessment. These children were then interviewed 2 1/2 years later. They were asked specifically what they believed had enabled them to deal with the illness, what aspects were most difficult for them, and what advice they would give to others. At the second interview, 15 of the 18 children continued to function well. These resilient youngsters were involved in school and extracurricular activities, and had strong interpersonal relationships. In addition, they described self-understanding as essential to their ability to deal with their parents' illnesses (Beardslee & Podorefsky, 1988).(They were aware of their parents' affective disorder and knew they were not the cause of their parent's illness. This was reported as being crucial to their ability to deal with the situation.)These qualities were consistent with other studies of self-understanding (Beardslee, 1989).

Summary

Across studies employing varied samples, assessment methods, and theoretical perspectives, research has indicated that children of affectively ill parents are more likely to experience difficulties in behavior and/or mood than children in homes with no parental affective disorder (Beardslee & Wheelock, 1994; Downey & Coyne, 1990). Longitudinal studies have shown that the disadvantages associated with growing up in a home with an affectively ill parent persist over time (Beardslee, Keller, et al., 1993; Billings & Moos, 1983, 1985; Forehand & McCombs, 1988; Hammen, et al., 1990; Sameroff, et al., 1987; Zahn-Waxler, et al., 1988). Moreover, difficulties in children of parents with affective disorder also have been documented in studies of community samples as well as in clinically referred samples, emphasizing the need to attend to all children who grow up in homes with affective disorder, not just those in which parents present for clinical treatment (Beardslee, Keller, et al., 1993). These findings emphasize the seriousness of parental affective illness and the need for prevention and early intervention.

THEORETICAL FRAMEWORK OF THE CLINICIAN-FACILITATED INTERVENTION

As previously mentioned, the primary goal of this project is the prevention of illness in at-risk children through the promotion of resilient traits. Hearing resilient youth talk about the value and significant role 'self understanding' played in their lives (Beardslee & Podorefsky, 1988) promoted the hypothesis that through improved communication and creating a shared family understanding of parental affective illness, the effects of the illness might be lessened. The intervention is designed to be a safe place in which parents are able to express their fears and concerns regarding their children and their illness. Providing parents with factual information regarding the risks associated with parental illness, the etiology of the disorder and the characteristics of resilient children, parents are empowered to take protective action on their child's behalf (Beardslee, et al., 1998).

Our approach was to address the processes through which difficulties arose in families; in particular, interferences with communication, misunderstanding and parenting. Three tenets guided the development of this intervention: (a) the intervention needed to be family centered; (b) factual information would be linked to family experiences; and (c) the intervention would be child focused. In addition, we believe that the sustained success of the intervention was related to the establishment of a strong therapeutic alliance between the clinician and the family.

Family Centered

All family members are asked to participate in both the intervention and assessment process. The involvement of the family is expected to assist in the development of a shared understanding of the illness. The intervention provides family members with an opportunity to voice their perceptions and experiences of the illness to other family members. For many of the families this is the first opportunity that they have had to discuss their experience of the illness as a unit. The development of self-understanding is encouraged not only in the child but in all family members. As the family begins to talk openly about the illness it is expected that any feelings of guilt, blame or shame that have been associated with the disorder will be removed or lessened.

Factual Information Linked to Life Experience

The clinical focus of the intervention is to help family members understand, and discuss with one another, the effects of parental depression on individuals and on the family. It is our assumption that affective illness in the family becomes part of the family identity. Construction of the individual and family histories elicits the life experiences of the family that are related to the parent's illness and facilitates the open discussion of what may not have been talked about previously.

The inclusion of the psychoeducational component in sessions with the couple, the children and the family accomplishes several aims. Teaching about affective illness serves as a stimulus or focus around which life experiences are presented and organized. There is an attempt to link the life experience with the educational material, for the purpose of providing hope, destigmatization and understanding. When increased awareness occurs, in many families a reduction in blaming and the dissipation of some degree of shame attached to having a family member with a mental illness results. Generally attaching information about the illness to one's own experience of depression or bipolar illness makes it personally relevant and thus more readily integrated and understood. It has been our experience that as the teaching process proceeds, each family finds many ways to personalize the factual information. This makes the information more meaningful and it normalizes individual experiences.

Perhaps more than anything else, the intervention deals with families' hopes and dreams for the future and how these hopes and dreams have been affected by the presence of a severe mental illness. For many of our families, their view of the future has been negatively tainted by the illness. A fundamental goal of the intervention is to encourage hope for the future based on knowledge of realistic action that can be initiated in the present.

Child Focused

Despite the severe and often incapacitating effects affective illness can have, parents are often able to rally in response to their children's needs and put their best efforts into helping their children cope with the effects of the illness. Since parenting itself is often a strength that is preserved in spite of the illness, using these skills may enhance a parent's own sense of competency as well as increase their hopefulness about the future.

It is essential that the parents recognize the impact of the illness on the child. Although it may be difficult for parents to acknowledge that their illness has been stressful for their child, it is quite possible that their fears about the harm done to their children are exaggerated. Therefore, a realistic appraisal of a child's strengths and problem areas is often very reassuring for parents. The parents are assisted in planning strategies that will protect their child and enhance the child's coping skills. The clinician works with the parents to help them verbalize their fears and concerns regarding their children. The clinician also encourages the parents to develop supportive networks for the child and to talk openly with the child about the parent's illness.

Therapeutic Alliance

Parents are frequently motivated to participate in the intervention because they are offered concrete information about affective illness as well as direct ways to strengthen their children's coping skills. In the research project, the presentation of educational material about the illness was perceived by the parents as immediately useful and less intrusive than other types of contact with mental health providers.

The therapeutic alliance is fostered initially by the clinician's acknowledgment of, and respect for, the parents' wish to help their children as well as the clinician's ability to identify and reinforce the family's strengths and resources. The clinician's offer of straightforward strategies also helps to foster a positive alliance. Couples for whom the intervention has seemed most helpful have been those who can anticipate possible difficulties for their children based on their children's present experiences. These parents may not necessarily see their children as troubled, but they do see the children's present need for help in understanding what's happening in their family. The parents' ability to focus on their children, separately and as a couple, seems to have far more influence on the success of the intervention than the level of impairment in the affectively ill parent. Ongoing work for the parents includes eliciting and helping their children articulate their experiences of the parents' illness and reinforcing the fact that they are neither to blame nor responsible for the illness.

Rather than emphasizing individual difficulties, this intervention makes use of the family's style of problem solving. This approach is specified in the principles of brief couples therapy described by Budman and Gurman (1988, p. 122). As Budman and Gurman emphasize, the clinician should function not as an expert lecturing to the family, but as a facilitator who is joining with the family to mobilize existing strengths to help their children. The development of the alliance depends on the conduct of the clinician, on the hope and responsiveness of the family, and on the fit between the family and the clinician. The alliance depends in part on a shared belief between the clinician and the family that the intervention will be of benefit.

The clinician works in a flexible manner, both in scheduling appointments (meeting with parents and families in an office setting or in their home) and in providing a variety of services. The flexibility of the clinician to meet the changing needs of the family is a vital component of the intervention and in our view is the most basic tenet of prevention.

CONTENT OF THE CLINICIAN-FACILITATED INTERVENTION SESSIONS

The clinician-facilitated intervention is an intensive, short-term intervention with a psycho-educational format. The intervention consists of 6–8 sessions that include meetings with the parents, individual meetings with the children and a family meeting. Although the manual contains information outlining the content of six sessions, additional sessions may be added at the therapist's discretion. Although the research protocol requires that there be at least one child in the family between the ages of 8–15, the intervention has been used with families whose children ranged in age from 4–25. The intervention has been effectively used with both single- and dual-parent families. The sessions are held either in the family's own home or in the clinician's office. During the first two sessions, the clinician meets just with the couple. The third meeting consists of individual meetings with the children. During the fourth meeting the clinician meets with the couple to plan a family meeting which takes place during the fifth session. In the final session, the clinician meets with the couple to review what happened during the family meeting and to make a strategic plan for the future.

The content of the intervention sessions is summarized in a manual.* An examination of the fidelity of our measure found that the intervention was delivered consistently across families by different clinicians (Beardslee, Versage, Wright, & Salt, 1999).

First Session—Constructing a Family History of the Illness

The clinician-facilitated intervention is based on the premise that parental affective illness is a family experience. Before change can take place in a family, the parents need to recognize the various ways the illness influences family life. One step in this process is eliciting a family history of the affective disorder. The intervener helps the family articulate events that they identify as having particular emotional valence. The clinician provides continuity between sessions, as he or she recalls the unfolding of the history from session to session and encourages the family members to review their own and each other's recollections of the illness. Thus, a process in which the family is learning together is facilitated.

During the first and second sessions of the intervention, the clinician constructs a history of the illness with the family. The clinician views the parents'

*Copies of the intervention manual can be obtained from the first author.

roles as experts, both with respect to their experience of their own illness and with regard to their children. The experiences of the family are elucidated and integrated in new ways, enabling them to address misunderstandings and confusions.

The process is started by inquiring about the ill parent's most recent episode of illness. Six main areas of interest are covered: (a) the stressors or precipitating events that may have exacerbated the episode; (b) symptoms or behavior changes that occurred during and prior to the onset of the episode; (c) treatment received; (d) course and duration of the episode; (e) evidence of recovery and; (f) the ill parent's perspective on how the illness may have affected the family. The clinician also inquires about the ill parent's first episode of affective illness, and then asks for a brief history of subsequent episodes.

Second Session—Perspective of the Non-ill Parent and the Psychoeducational Component

In the second session with the parents, the emphasis shifts to the non-ill spouse's experience. For many of these parents, this is the first time they have had a chance to verbalize their experience of their spouse's affective illness. For some couples, the process of understanding their spouse's perspective can begin to unearth misperceptions and fears that have previously remained unexplored. Because depression most often negatively affects both mood and self-concept, depressed people are vulnerable to distortions of thinking which include a high degree of self-blame. Similarly, spouses often express guilt that they may have contributed to or were unable to alleviate their partner's depression. When these concerns can be clarified, some couples begin to experience improved communication and decreased feelings of anxiety and guilt as similarities and differences in each other's perception of the illness experience unfold. The clinician encourages the parents to elaborate on their responses to particular events or beliefs associated with the illness, especially when it becomes apparent that their views are divergent. The capacity to both express and tolerate another's perspective is a central tenet of the intervention's effectiveness and is modeled throughout the session. A significant feature of the intervention is the presentation of cognitive information. This involves teaching about aspects of parental depression and bipolar illness and about the risks to, and resiliency of, children exposed to parental affective disorder. During the second meeting with the parent(s), the clinician reviews the etiology of depression or bipolar disorder, its biological/physiological base, its psychosocial manifestations, and the risks to children growing up in families with serious affective illness. Specific characteristics of resilient children are described.

Etiology

A review of etiologic factors, both genetic and psychosocial, is provided. Depression and bipolar disorder are presented as illnesses that have multiple etiologies, with physical manifestations and a specified constellation of signs and symptoms. The importance of psychosocial stressors, such as loss of a job or family transitions, as precipitants of affective symptomatology is discussed. The responsiveness of the illness to appropriate treatments is emphasized.

Signs and Symptoms

A review of the signs and symptoms of affective illness (both bipolar and depression) is helpful for both the spouse and the ill parent even in families that are knowledgeable about depression. The symptoms that are most confusing are irritability and loss of energy. Irritability places a great strain on others in the family, as they often feel attacked or rejected by the ill parent, and in turn, find it difficult to offer support. When the clinician points out that irritability, like sadness, is indicative of a disturbance in mood, and that it is independent of behaviors of other family members, tension and blame are generally reduced.

A closely related area to be covered in the psycho-educational component of the intervention is a discussion of how the symptoms of depression or mania often disrupt the everyday life of the family. Many families report that the illness limits their social life and affects the organization and planning of their family routines and special events. This is often a source of strain and resentment for both the partner and children of the ill parent. Clarifying how the symptoms of depression and mania can affect family life is often associated with a greater understanding and tolerance of the disruptions.

Resiliency

In many families, discussion of resilient characteristics provides an opportunity for parents to express pride in their children's accomplishments. Information about resiliency can be disseminated to children at all developmental stages. Even young children can understand that individual pursuits are important for oneself and that the parent wants the child to engage in them.

Three main areas of resilient characteristics in children are discussed: (a) self understanding; (b) involvement in activities outside the home; and (c) having a confiding relationship with an adult. Providing examples of the qualities of resilient children usually results in the parents identifying their child's resilient qualities or deciding to encourage them. Involvement in outside activities is the most concrete example of resiliency. If the child is not already participating in activities the parents often respond by deciding to encourage these behaviors. In cases where the child is already involved in activities outside of the home, parents are given an opportunity to recognize positive ways in which they have fostered their child's competence.

As previously noted, self-understanding has been identified as an essential element in the maintenance of resiliency in response to parental depression (Beardslee & Podorefsky, 1988). The child with a capacity for self-understanding is able to recognize and acknowledge the effects of the parent's illness on himself and his family. In light of this awareness, the child is able to maintain a sense of himself or herself as separate from concerns for the parent. In turn, this allows the child to continue the investment of energy in his or her own interests, activities, and relationships despite any disruptions in family functioning. This separate sense of self makes it possible for the child to acknowledge concern for his or her parent without assuming the burden of responsibility for the illness.

Third Session—Individual Meetings With the Child(ren)

It is during the third meeting that the clinician is first introduced to the children. The clinician meets individually with each child that will be participating in the family meeting. The meeting with the child has several objectives: (a) to acknowledge the importance of the child's perspective and to develop a rapport with the child; (b) to assess the child's current functioning with particular attention to his or her understanding and response to the affectively ill parent's previous episode(s) of illness; and (c) to help the child articulate questions or concerns which might be presented at the family meeting. The sequence of the child's interview is designed to stimulate the process of perspective taking.

At the start of the session, the clinician elicits from the child what he or she has been told about the interview and what the child expects that it will be like. The clinician presents a clear explanation of the reason for the interview. Throughout the meeting, the clinician gathers information regarding the child's functioning in a format similar to a standard diagnostic interview. In developing a judgment about the child's functioning, the clinician bases his understanding on both his clinical impressions of the child's presentation and on the parents' observations and concerns for their child. Many parents decide to participate in the study because of their concerns about how their children are functioning. Parents usually are seeking reassurances that their child's psychological development is normal and that no serious difficulty has gone undetected. Thus, this meeting and evaluation of the child allows the clinician to reassure the parents when appropriate or help the parents seek clinical/professional assistance when necessary.

During the meeting, the clinician asks the child about his or her family life and understanding of the parent's affective illness. If the child acknowledges an awareness of the parent's symptoms and is comfortable in talking about his or her experience, the clinician pursues this line of conversation. The clinician engages the children in a manner that allows them to connect their perceptions to the experience of their parents. During the session, the clinician talks to the child about the upcoming family meeting. The clinician asks the child to consider what he or she would like to discuss or what questions the child might have for the parents during the meeting. Many children are reluctant to disclose concerns themselves, but are comfortable in having the clinician relate their questions to their parents during the family meeting.

Fourth Session—Planning for the Family Meeting

During the fourth meeting, the clinician meets with just the parent(s). This meeting has three main objectives: (a) to provide the parents with a general review of their child's functioning; (b) to link the parents' perception of depression or mania with that of the child's experience of the parental affective illness; and (c) to facilitate the parents' participation in the joint task of planning the family meeting.

As parents approach this planning process, the clinician reviews the psychoeducational information presented in earlier sessions. The parents are encouraged to incorporate this material as well as the belief that they can act on their children's behalf in specifically defined ways in their efforts toward planning the family meeting. Even in marriages fraught with conflict, parents are often able to cooperate in planning a family session when they recognize that they can proactively work together to benefit their children.

In presenting an evaluation of the child's functioning, the clinician is careful to frame his or her perceptions as an overview and not as a comprehensive psychological assessment. The child's strengths and areas of successful adjustment are highlighted. Indications of emotional distress or less optimal functioning are also discussed. When the evaluation raises concerns about the child's emotional state, the clinician may suggest that the parents seek a referral for therapy or other resources to support their child's adjustment. The clinician is available to assist the parents in pursuing this option on their child's behalf.

To help parents in developing a focus for the family meeting, the clinician shares specific concerns or questions that the children wished to discuss. The parents are also asked to identify their concerns regarding their own or the family's experience of the illness. Preparing for the family meeting might involve, for example, the parents' decision to review the course of the illness, to reassure children that they are not to blame for the parent's symptoms, and to discuss their concerns for the future. Some parents elect to discuss specific events in the course of the illness; e.g., a parent's hospitalization or suicide attempt. Others choose a more general approach, focusing on a description of the symptoms associated with the illness and treatment options. Although there may be some resistance, the expectation that they will conduct a family meeting helps the parents further acknowledge their own experience of the illness. For some parents, the act of coming together as a family is a major step toward perceiving the depression as an illness that can be identified and treated. It is a fundamental premise of the intervention that parents' abilities to alter their perspectives about the experience of depression in ways that alleviate guilt and blaming will consequently allow for greater tolerance of individual expression within the family. In the intervention's format, the planning session with the parents represents an important step toward this goal.

Fifth Session—Family Meeting

The primary objective of the family meeting is to facilitate the creation of a shared understanding of the parental illness, which incorporates the affective experience of all family members. Secondly, the family meeting serves to empower parents to conceptualize and present the depression to their children as an illness that may have affected the family in various ways and can now be discussed and understood. As a precursor to developing this understanding, the clinician helps family members to relate this general information about depression to the family's specific experience. When parents are able to describe their symptoms and to attribute reactions which have been upsetting or confusing to the effects of depression, children often are able to express more openly their own responses to their parents' behaviors or moods.

The family meeting represents an opportunity for individuals to begin to develop a shared experience around the events associated with the parental affective illness. For some families, the meeting involves minimal discussion with considerable input from the clinician, while in other instances, families may focus on a specific topic for the entire session. It is important to remember that the form of the meeting, however limited it might seem, is less important than the family members' ability to share aspects of their individual experience of the illness in an atmosphere which encourages acceptance of differences and disagreements.

Sixth Session—Intervention Review and Plans for the Future

During this session, the clinician encourages the parents to talk between themselves about their reactions to the family meeting. Reviewing the family meeting helps the parents to understand and integrate any new information that was learned and gives them the opportunity to anticipate future challenges related to the illness. During the session, the clinician inquires about each child's reaction to the family meeting, and if needed helps the parents strategize ways that they can address any concerns or questions that might have come up. The clinician reviews with the parents whether their concerns were addressed, whether some goals were not accomplished, and ways that they can work toward accomplishing these goals after the intervention is completed. The process of developing a shared meaning of affective illness is ongoing and the parents are encouraged to continue to talk between themselves and with their children about their experience of the illness. The clinician helps the parents make a plan for dealing with future illness-related difficulties. The families' strengths and accomplishments during their participation in the intervention are acknowledged.

CONCLUSION

This chapter represents a brief guideline of the material contained in the intervention manual. It is our hope that this intervention will be used by a variety of health professionals who come in contact with affectively ill parents. This intervention is part of a large-scale empirical study. It has been shown to be safe (Beardslee, Salt, et al., 1993) and has resulted in long-lasting changes in both behaviors and attitudes regarding parental affective illness (Beardslee, Wright, et al., 1996).

Although our primary goal is to prevent depression in at-risk children, we realize that it is unlikely that affective illness can be prevented in all children due to the genetic component of this disorder. Parental education about the symptoms of childhood depression is a vital part of this intervention. As children experiencing difficulty are identified, it is then expected that these informed parents will seek treatment for their children. Early intervention is expected to both lessen the duration and severity of the child's difficulty, as well as limit developmental disruptions that might result.

We encourage families to continue to talk about the illness after the intervention sessions have ended, and to use the skills and strategies that were developed during their sessions with the clinician. It is important to remember that the intervention represents the beginning of an ongoing process of understanding, and that the main effects occur over time as families apply the approaches learned in their discussions of how to handle the disease.

ACKNOWLEDGMENTS

Special thanks to Donna Podorefsky and Lynn Focht for their contribution to the manual from which this chapter is based. This project was funded by a grant from the William T. Grant Foundation.

REFERENCES

Beardslee, W. R. (1989). The role of self-understanding in resilient individuals: The developement of a perspective. *American Journal of Orthopsychiatry, 59*, 266–278.

Beardslee, W. R. & Podorefsky, D. (1988). Resilient adolescents whose parents have serious affective and other psychiatric disorders: The importance of self-understanding and relationships. *American Journal of Psychiatry, 145*, 63–69.

Beardslee, W. R. & Wheelock, I. (1994). Children of parents with affective disorders: Empirical findings and clinical implications. In W. M. Reynolds & H. F. Johnston (Eds.), *Handbook of depression in children and adolescents* (pp. 463–479). New York: Plenum Press.

Beardslee, W. R., Keller, M. B., Lavori, P. W., Klerman, G. K., Dorer, D. J., & Samuelson, H. (1988). Psychiatric disorder in adolescent offspring of parents with affective disorders in a nonreferred sample. *Journal of Affective Disorders, 15*, 313–322.

Beardslee, W. R., Keller, M. B., Lavori, P. W., Staley, J. E., & Sacks, N. (1993). The impact of parental affective disorder on depression in offspring: A longitudinal follow-up in a nonreferred sample. *Journal of the American Academy of Child and Adolescent Psychiatry, 32*, 723–730.

Beardslee, W. R., Salt, P., Porterfield, K., Rothberg, P. C., Van de Velde, P., Swatling, S., Hoke, E., Moilanen, D. L., & Wheelock, I. (1993). Comparison of preventive interventions for families with parental affective disorder. *Journal of the American Academy of Child and Adolescent Psychiatry, 32*, 254–263.

Beardslee, W. R., Keller, M. B., Seifer, R., Lavori, P. W., Staley, J., Podorefsky, D., & Shera, D. (1996). Prediction of adolescent affective disorder: Effects of prior parental affective disorders and child psychopathology. *Journal of the American Academy of Child and Adolescent Psychiatry, 35,* 279–288.

Beardslee, W., Wright, E., Rothberg, P., Salt, P., & Versage, E. (1996). Response of families to two preventive intervention strategies: Long-term differences in behavior and attitude change. *Journal of the American Academy of Child and Adolescent Psychiatry, 35,* 774–782.

Beardslee, W. R., Salt, P., Versage, E., Gladstone, T.R.G., Wright, E., & Rothberg, P.C. (1997). Sustained change in parents receiving preventive interventions for families with depression. *American Journal of Psychiatry, 154,* 510–515.

Beardslee, W. R., Swatling, S., Hoke, L., Rothberg, P. C., Van de Velde, P., Focht, L., & Podorefsky, D. (1998). From cognitive information to shared meaning: Healing principles in preventive intervention. *Psychiatry: Interpersonal and Biological Processes, 61,* 112–129.

Beardslee, W. R., Wright, E., Salt, P., Drezner, K., Gladstone, T. R. G., Versage, E. M., & Rothberg, P. C. (1997). Examination of children's responses to two preventive intervention strategies over time. *Journal of the American Academy of Child and Adolescent Psychiatry, 36,* 196–204.

Beardslee, W. R., Versage, E. M., Wright, E., & Salt, P. (1999). The development and evaluation of two preventive intervention strategies for children of depressed parents. In D. Cicchetti & S. L. Toth (Eds.), *Developmental approaches to prevention and intervention* (pp. 111–115). Rochester, NY: University of Rochester Press.

Billings, A. G. & Moos, R. H. (1983). Comparisons of children of depressed and non-depressed parents: A social-environmental perspective. *Journal of Abnormal Child Psychology, 11,* 463–486.

Billings, A. G. & Moos, R. H. (1985). Children of parents with unipolar depression: A controlled 1-year follow-up. *Journal of Abnormal Child Psychology, 14,* 149–166.

Budman, S. H. & Gurman, A. S. (1988). *Theory and practice of brief therapy.* New York: Guilford Press.

Cox, A. C., Puckering, C., Pound, A., & Mills, M. (1987). The impact of maternal depression in young children. *Journal of Child Psychology and Psychiatry, 28,* 917–928.

Coyne, J. C., Kessler, R. C., Tal, M., Turnbull, J., Wortman, C. B., & Greden, J. F. (1987). Living with a depressed person. *Journal of Consulting and Clinical Psychology, 55,* 347–352.

Downey, G. & Coyne, J. C. (1990). Children of depressed parents: An integrative review. *Psychological Bulletin, 108,* 50–76.

Fendrich, M., Warner, V., & Weissman, M. M. (1990). Family risk factors, parental depression, and psychopathology in offspring. *Developmental Psychology, 26,* 40–50.

Forehand, R. & McCombs, A. (1988). Unraveling the antecedent-consequence conditions in maternal depression and adolescent functioning. *Behaviour Research and Therapy, 26,* 399–405.

Garmezy, N. (1985). Stress-resistant children: The search for protective factors. In J.E. Stevenson (Ed.), *Recent research in developmental psychology. Journal of Child Psychology and Psychiatry Book Supplement No. 4* (pp. 213–233). Oxford: Pergamon Press.

Gordon, D., Burge, D., Hammen, C., Adrian, C., Jaenicke, C., & Hiroto, D. (1989). Observations of interactions of depressed women with their children. *American Journal of Psychiatry, 146,* 50–55.

Grigoroiu-Serbanescu, M., Christodorescu, D., Magureanu, S., Jipescu, I., Totoescu, A., Marinescu, E., Ardelean, V., & Popa, S. (1991). Adolescent offspring of endogenous unipolar depressive parents and of normal parents. *Journal of Affective Disorders,* 185–198.

Hammen, C., Burge, D., Burney, E., & Adrian, C. (1990). Longitudinal study of diagnoses in children of women with unipolar and bipolar affective disorder. *Archives of General Psychiatry, 47,* 1112–1117.

Hautzinger, M., Linden, M., & Hoffman, N. (1982). Distressed couples with and without a depressed partner: An analysis of their verbal interaction. *Journal of Behavior Therapy and Experimental Psychiatry, 13,* 307–314.

Hooley, J. M., Orley, J., & Teasdale, J. D. (1986). Levels of expressed emotion and relapse in depressed patients. *British Journal of Psychiatry, 148,* 642–647.

Keitner, G. I. & Miller, I. W. (1990). Family functioning and major depression: An overview. *American Journal of Psychiatry, 147,* 1128–1137.

Kochanska, G., Kuczynski, L., Yarrow, M. R., & Welsh, J. D. (1987). Resolutions of control episodes between well and affectively ill mothers and their young children. *Journal of Abnormal Child Psychology, 15*, 441–456.

Lavoie, F. & Hodgins, S. (1994). Mental disorders among children with one parent with a lifetime diagnosis of major depression. In S. Hodgins, C. Lane, M. Lapalme, C. LaRoche, F. Lavoie, L. Kratzer, R. Palmour, & N. Rubin (Eds.), *A critical review of the literature on children at risk for major affective disorders* (pp. 37–82). Ottawa, ON: The Strategic Fund for Children's Mental Health.

Offord, D. R. (1989). Conduct Disorder: Risk factors and prevention. In D. Shaffer, I. Philips, & N. B. Enzer (Eds.), *Prevention of mental disorders, alcohol and other drugs in children and adolescents* (DHHS Publication No. ADM 89–1626, pp. 273-307). Rockville, MD: Office for Substance Abuse Prevention.

Orvaschel, H., Walsh-Allis, G., & Ye, W. (1988). Psychopathology in children of parents with recurrent depression. *Journal of Abnormal Child Psychology, 16*, 17–28.

Radke-Yarrow, M., Nottelmann, E., Martinez, P., Fox, M. B., & Belmont, B. (1992). Young children of affectively ill parents: A longitudinal study of psychosocial development. *Journal of the American Academy of Child and Adolescent Psychiatry, 31*, 68–77.

Rutter, M. (1986). The developmental psychopathology of depression: Issues and perspectives. In M. Rutter, C. E. Izard, & P. B. Read (Eds.), *Depression in young people: Developmental and clinical perspectives* (pp. 3–30). New York: Guilford Press.

Rutter, M. (1987). Psychosocial resilience and protective mechanisms. *American Journal of Orthopsychiatry, 57*, 316–331.

Rutter, M. & Quinton, D. (1984). Parental psychiatric disorder: Effects on children. *Psychological Medicine, 14*, 853–880.

Sameroff, A. J., Seifer, R., Zax, M., & Barocas, R. (1987). Early indicators of developmental risk: Rochester Longitudinal Study. *Schizophrenia Bulletin, 13*, 383–394.

Schwartz, C. E., Dorer, D. J., Beardslee, W. R., Lavori, P. W., & Keller, M. B. (1990). Maternal expressed emotion and parental affective disorder: Risk for childhood depressive disorder, substance abuse, or Conduct Disorder. *Journal of Psychiatric Research, 24*, 231–250.

Simons, R. L. & Miller, M. G., (1987). Adolescent depression: Assessing the impact of negative cognitions and socioenviromental problems. *Social Work, 32*, 326–330.

Vaughn, C. E. & Leff, J. P. (1976). The measurement of expressed emotion in the families of psychiatric patients. *British Journal of Social and Clinical Psychology, 15*, 157–165.

Weissman, M. M., Fendrich, M., Warner, V., & Wickramaratne, P. (1992). Incidence of psychiatric disorder in offspring at high and low risk for depression. *Journal of the American Academy of Child and Adolescent Psychiatry, 31*, 640–648.

Zahn-Waxler, C., Mayfield, A., Radke-Yarrow, M., McKnew, D. H., Cytryn, L., & Davenport, Y. B. (1988). A follow-up investigation of offspring of parents with bipolar disorder. *American Journal of Psychiatry, 145*, 506–509.

CHAPTER 5

Learning and Intimacy in the Families of Anxious Children

MARK R. DADDS

Humans have an inherent capacity to react to threat stimuli with fear and anxiety. For the majority of children and adolescents, fears and anxieties are common, functional, and transitory. For this reason, both parents and other caregivers often correctly view childhood anxiety as a passing complaint. Unfortunately, epidemiological studies using self-report measures indicate that anxiety problems are the most common form of child and adolescent psychological problems. More tentative evidence indicates that these problems may, in their severest forms, be disabling and chronic and may have some continuity with adult anxiety problems (Keller, et al., 1992; Pfeiffer, Lipkins, Plutchik, & Mizruchi, 1988; cf. Last, Perrin, Hersen, & Kazdin, 1996).

Where chronicity of childhood anxiety is the case, it is associated with general social problems such as negative self-image, dependency on adults in social situations, comparatively poor problem-solving skills, unpopularity, and low rates of interaction with peers (Kashani & Orvaschel, 1990; Messer & Beidel, 1994; Panella & Henggeler, 1986; Rubin & Clark, 1983; Strauss, Frame, & Forehand, 1987). In clinical samples, anxious children are less successful in peer relationships than their non-referred counterparts (Strauss, Lahey, Frick, Frame, & Hynd, 1988). Regardless of the causal direction of the relationship between anxiety and its psychosocial correlates, it makes sense that anxiety continually strengthens the psychosocial factors and vice versa, thus contributing to the chronicity of anxiety in children and adolescents who have not received treatment.

As we will see, the social context in which anxiety problems develop cannot be ignored, and converging evidence suggests that high levels of control, restriction, attention to social threat, and endorsement of avoidant coping strategies are characteristic of families of anxious children. The aim of this chapter is to review literature on the role of the family in the development of anxiety problems in children. It should be noted that comorbidity among childhood anxiety disorders is common, and there is precious little evidence of differences in etiology or treatment outcomes between the major categories of anxiety problems in young people (i.e., social fears, separation problems, generalized anxiety). Thus, this paper will focus on anxiety as a general construct, rather than specifying particular categories of symptomatology.

FAMILY TRANSMISSION

It is not possible to include a comprehensive review of the literature on the familial transmission of anxiety in this paper. However, as a context to the following review, some comments are warranted. Anxiety problems tend to run in families, with support coming from both studies of parents of children with anxiety/depression disorders and children of parents with anxiety/depression disorders. However, there is little evidence that transmission is specific to individual disorder categories and a number of other clinical conditions may be associated with increased risk for anxiety and depression. For example, a comparison of non-clinic families and families with a member diagnosed with Antisocial Personality Disorder found that children from these latter families had higher rates of ADHD, major depression, anxiety disorders, and substance use disorder (Faraone, et al., 1995). In a comparison of children with Major Depressive Disorder (MDD) and psychiatric controls, it was found that the families of children with MDD also had symptomatology of MDD, any mood disorder, Antisocial Personality Disorder, and anxiety disorders (Weller, et al., 1994). Thus, it appears that little will be gained by considering family transmission in terms of broad psychiatric categories. Future research in this area is needed to clarify interactive processes between possible genetic transmission of vulnerabilities (e.g., behavioral inhibition, see Kagan, Resnick, & Snidman, 1988) and family environment in the development of affective and anxiety disorders in children, rather than simply focusing on the presence or absence of disorder. As well as examining risks for the development of child and adolescent anxiety, familial protective factors need to be explored.

SOME ISSUES IN DIRECTLY MEASURING ANXIETY IN CHILDREN AND FAMILIES

Anxiety is a very difficult phenomenon to measure in ecologically meaningful ways. To operationalize a person's ability to approach a snake in a laboratory is reasonably simple. However, to operationalize more complex forms of anxiety, such as generalized anxiety and panic, and then measure them in real-world situations is a challenge. The common but generalized forms of anxiety remain elusive to observational strategies, and the discriminative validity of existing self-report measures is poor. Progress has occurred in diagnostic systems but the validity of these remains controversial.

Thus, most current research into childhood anxiety uses self-report and rating scale measures and the use of observational measures has become quite rare. This is regrettable. The development of observational strategies for measuring child anxiety mostly took place in the 1960s and 1970s. Since that initial burst of activity, little has occurred in terms of the development and refinement of these methodologies. Most existing observational strategies focus solely on the child. Creative attempts to operationalize the social context of the child's anxiety and examine its functional relationship to the development of anxiety are sorely needed. I believe there is enormous unrealized potential in the use of direct observations of anxiety in young children.

Dadds, Rapee, and Heard (1994) suggested two major areas for development. First, there is the need to understand the development of the child's anxiety in terms of its social context. Thus, observation systems that score both the child's anxiety as well as contextual stimuli need to be developed. Second, observations need to be designed and used in a way that allows for conceptual integration with other aspects of anxiety such as cognitive processing style, family interaction, and physiological reactivity. For example, much progress is currently being made in understanding the way anxious people process information about threat in their environment (e.g., Butler & Mathews, 1983; Vasey & MacLeod, 2001). That is, anxious people show an exaggerated tendency to perceive, attend to, and respond to threat in their environments. We may ask whether this processing style is learned through interaction with significant others, namely anxious parents. A methodology that integrates information processing and direct observation of the child in interaction with others may yield important insights into this process. The recent work by Krohne and colleagues (Krohne, 1992; Krohne & Hock, 1991), Vasey and MacLeod (2001), and our group (Barrett, Rapee, Dadds, & Ryan, 1996; Dadds, Barrett, Rapee, & Ryan, 1996) reviewed below, are examples of fruitful attempts in this direction. Similarly, the recent work examining the complex interplay of temperament, attachment styles, and parent-child interactions are innovative for their use of direct observational methodologies (e.g., Calkins & Fox, 1992; Nachmias, Gunnar, Mangelsdorf, Parritz, & Buss, 1996).

STUDIES OF FAMILY PROCESS

In research up until the 1970's reviewed by Hetherington and Martin (1972), mothers of anxious children were consistently described as domineering, overprotective, and overinvolved with the child. However, as Hetherington and Martin also noted, this image of the overprotective mother and the highly structured family system were based on 'rather indirect sources of data' (p. 61). Empirical studies have been more limited in the support they provided for family factors, but include elevated levels of anxiety in the parents of anxious children (Bernstein & Borchardt, 1991), and marital conflict as a correlate of anxiety in nonclinic children (Dadds & Powell, 1991). However, evidence that anxiety problems in children are associated with broader aspects of family dysfunction is conspicuously absent from the literature. Green, Loeber, and Lahey (1992) found no evidence for the presence of deviant family hierarchies, as predicted by family systems theory (Haley, 1976; Minuchin, 1974), in the families of overanxious boys. A study by Stark, Humphrey, Crook, and Lewis (1990) showed that anxious children saw their families as less supportive, less sociable, and more conflictual and enmeshed than nonclinic children. However, the results were even more striking for depressed and mixed depressed/anxious children, and so these factors are unlikely to be specific correlates of childhood anxiety.

More impressive data have come from direct observational studies of social learning processes. Krohne and Hock (1993) argued that a child's competencies are related to the parents' tendency to help the child develop problemsolving and coping skills, and inversely, to overly control the child (restriction). The idea of parental overcontrol has often been related to anxiety problems in children (see Rapee, 1997, for a review). Solyom, Silberfeld, and Solyom (1976) reported that mothers of agoraphobic patients scored significantly higher on measures of maternal control than mothers of normals. Krohne and Hock (1991) found that the mothers of high-anxious girls were judged by independent observers to be more restrictive than mothers of low-anxious girls during a common problem-solving task. Similarly, Dumas, LaFreniere, and Serketich (1995) observed parent-child interactions between aggressive, anxious, and non-distressed dyads. The anxious dyads were characterized by relatively high parental control and aversiveness.

In our research clinic, the emphasis has been on using an integrative theoretical and methodological approach. Using observational strategies of family processes, we have focused on the ways in which parents influence the child's problem solving in courageous versus avoidant directions. We emphasize the importance of parental control and restriction (Dumas, et al., 1995; Krohne & Hock, 1991), most readily measured via parent-child contingencies (Patterson, 1982), in reinforcing a bias toward high levels of threat interpretation (Butler & Mathews, 1983; Clark & Ehlers, 1993), thus increasing the child's susceptibility to avoidance and aversive conditioning experiences (Dadds, Bovbjerg, Redd, & Cutmore, 1997; Davey, 1992). This process is thought not to occur for all children in the family, but rather becomes focused on the child or children who show early signs of an anxious/inhibited temperament.

Barrett, Rapee, Dadds, and Ryan (1996) asked samples of 8 to 14 year old anxious, aggressive, and nonclinic children to interpret various ambiguous social and physical scenarios and plan what they would do in response to the scenario (e.g., 1: You want to join in with some children playing ball at school. As you approach you notice they are all laughing; 2: You are on your way to school and you notice that your tummy feels a little sick.). Parents were also asked to interpret the scenarios as they thought their child would. Interpretations were coded into Threat and NonThreat categories, and plans were coded into Avoid, Proactive, Aggressive response categories. Results demonstrated that both anxious and aggressive children and their parents make relatively high numbers of threat interpretations in response to ambiguous situations. However, in response to those interpretations, anxious children and their families predominantly chose avoidant solutions, whereas the aggressive

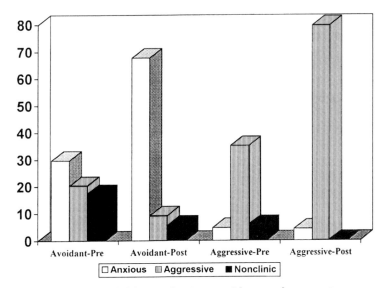

Figure 5-1 Percentage of children selecting avoidant and aggressive responses pre- and post-family discussion for anxious, aggressive, and non-clinic children in the Barrett, Rapee, Dadds, and Ryan (1996) study.

children and parents chose aggressive solutions when faced with ambiguous hypothetical social problems.

In the second part of the experimental procedure, the families of anxious, aggressive, and nonclinic children were brought together for 10 minutes to discuss how the child should deal with these ambiguous situations. They were told that while all could express their opinions during the discussion, the final plan was to be decided by the child. Figure 5-1 shows the percentage of avoidant and aggressive solutions chosen by the child before and after the family discussions. For anxious children only, the likelihood that the child would devise an avoidant solution increased dramatically after the family discussion. For aggressive children, the likelihood of aggressive solutions showed a similar increase, whereas the nonclinic children stayed with a preference for prosocial solutions throughout. It appears as if the family process can facilitate expression of the child's vulnerabilities.

In an attempt to identify the specific family processes responsible for the facilitation of avoidance in anxious children, Dadds, Barrett, Rapee, and Ryan (1996) analyzed the contingent stream of family behaviors that had been videotaped in these family discussions. Parent and child behaviors were coded using the Family Anxiety Coding System (Dadds, et al., 1994), and the conditional probabilities that certain parent behaviors would reliably follow child anxious and courageous behaviors were calculated. Parents of anxious children were more likely to reciprocate the child's proposals of avoidant solutions and were less likely to encourage prosocial solutions to ambiguous social situations, than parents of nonclinic and aggressive children. In a final test of the influence of these parent-child sequences, it was found that the more likely the parents were to reciprocate avoidance and fail to reinforce prosocial behavior, the more likely the child was to choose a final avoidant solution.

Cobham, Dadds, and Spence (1999) elaborated on these studies by substituting a real threat task for the ambiguous scenarios used by Barrett, Rapee, et al. (1996). Using similar samples of anxious, aggressive, and nonclinic children, the methodology invited the children to give a short talk about themselves in front of a small audience and a videotaping camera. Parent-child discussions were held before and after the talks and ratings of the child's confidence and anxiety were made by the child and parents at various points in the procedure. Contrary to Barrett, Rapee, et al. (1996), the parent-child discussions did not increase the child's anxiety or avoidance of the task. Rather, the discussions tended to lessen anxiety and avoidance. Our surprise at these results was heightened by analysis of the actual content of the parent-child discussions. Similar to Barrett, et al., the parents of anxious children were consistently observed to use an openly domineering and controlling style with their children, directing the child what to talk about and giving very little room for the children to direct their own behavior. We hypothesize that the differences are due to differences in the timing of the tasks. In the Barrett, Rapee, et al. (1996) study, the threat and family discussion tasks were part of the intake assessment and parents were not informed of the decision about the eligibility for the (free) treatment until after the experimental procedure. Thus parents were motivated to emphasize their child's anxiety for the researchers to see, and in the discussion they tended to push the child to admit to his or her anxiety. In the Cobham, et al. (1999) study, the experimental procedure was inadvertently presented after parents were accepted into the program; thus, parents were more likely to see the task as part of the treatment and were more likely to push the child to participate and be confident. However, in both cases we clearly observed a highly controlling style in the parents of anxious children. To give readers a sense of this control, a typical conversation we observed between a mother, father, and an anxious 10-year-old boy about the scenario in which the boy is approaching other children and notices they are laughing, is shown in Table 5-1. The parents' behavior is very controlling and results in the boy changing his initial prosocial plan into one of avoidance.

Chorpita, Albano, and Barlow (1996) observed similar parental influences to Dadds, et al. (1996) in four children aged 9 to 13 with a clinical diagnosis of anxiety disorder. Although their low numbers prohibit generalization, in this study low- and high-anxious children exhibited high threat interpretation, but only high-anxious children also included avoidance as the method of dealing with the perceived threat. This supports contentions that avoidance is a learned phenomenon. Reinforcement for avoidance may come not only from the removal of the distressing stimuli (negative reinforcement), but also through parental positive reinforcement of avoidant solutions. One possible explanation is that this cognitive bias could arise as a result of maternal overprotectiveness, which conveys not only a threat bias, but also the need to avoid, rather than take action against, perceived threat (Hirshfeld, Biederman, Brody, Faraone, & Rosenbaum, 1997a,b). Examination of anxious child–mother dyads

Table 5-1 An example of mother-father-anxious child discussions in response to the ambiguous social problem-solving task

Boy:	I'd just ask them; just go up and say "Can I please join in?"
Mother:	Do you reckon maybe they'd let you?
Boy:	Maybe.
Mother:	What sort of games do they usually play?
Boy:	Tiggy or handball.
Father:	Do you think they would let you if it was handball?
Boy:	No.
Father:	Why?
Boy:	I'm not that good at it.
Father:	You any good at tiggy?
Boy:	No.
Mother:	Why is this?
Boy:	Because I can't run fast enough.
Mother:	So do you think they would let you play or you don't think they would let you play?
Boy:	No.
Mother:	Would you be brave enough to go and ask them in the first place?
Boy:	I wouldn't bother.
Mother:	No.
Father:	Why wouldn't you bother?
Boy:	Because I know what the answer would be. Its always "no".
Mother:	You don't think they would be laughing at you before you even turned up, thinking "he's going to ask".
Boy:	Oh. Yes.
Mother:	They might do that?
Boy:	Yes.
Mother:	So what do you think you would do? Just avoid these situations or would you really like to play?
Boy:	Handball I'd like to play.
Mother:	But you've just got to learn more ball skills.
Boy:	Yes.
Mother:	It's hard isn't it?
Boy:	Yes.
Mother:	(Comforts boy)

(Dumas, et al., 1995) also showed mothers of anxious children as demonstrating high levels of aversive control, using such strategies as criticism, intrusiveness, and punishment. Studies including paternal influences are rare, yet Chorpita, et al. found that paternal verbalizations were more influential in children's post-family discussion threat interpretations and avoidant plans. This is certainly an area that deserves further investigation.

Chorpita, Brown, and Barlow (1998) pursued the idea of cognitive biases further through path analysis in an attempt to understand the relationship between children's attributional style, locus of control, and the degree of control within the family environment. Although there were problems with some of the child cognitive measures, two of their structural models offer preliminary support for a model in which the influence of parental control on children's negative affect is mediated by variations in children's locus of control.

In agreement with the reviews by Rapee (1997) and Dadds and Roth (2001), Chorpita and Barlow (1998) suggest a growing body of support for the role of control in a child's early development. Specifically, when a child's sense of control is compromised either through uncontrollable and unpredictable environmental influences, or through parental overcontrol, the child may be at greater risk of problems of helplessness (anxiety) or hopelessness (depression).

Early experience of the world as uncontrollable may later foster the sense of helplessness and anxious responding, regardless of the actual controllability of events. Recent research and theorizing (Chorpita & Barlow, 1998) indicates that early experiences of uncontrollability increase the activation of the Behavioral Inhibition System (BIS; Gray, 1982), as well as increasing the probability of exposure to perceived novel stimuli. The work by Fox and Calkins (1993) and Nachmias, et al. (1996) show that behavioral inhibition in infants is associated with clinging to parents and this can result in a parental style that pushes the child toward novelty, which in turn, activates their inhibition system. Clearly, this line of research is highly consistent with ideas of uncontrollability discussed by Chorpita and Barlow (1998) with reference to Gray's BIS, and demonstrates that learning about novelty and control, and their implications for self-confidence versus anxiety, begin early in life within the parent-child system.

These studies highlight the gains that can be made by studying anxiety in its social context using direct observational procedures and integrative theoretical models. Clearly, the task-discussion method is particularly useful for examining the relationships between individual factors such as child cognitions and behavior, and family factors such as threat emphasis and contingent responses to those individual variables.

Recent studies have also utilized the construct of expressed emotion (EE). Used extensively in research with adult psychiatric patients and their families, EE is a measure of criticism and/or emotional overinvolvement in relatives, usually parents. EE in relatives is a risk factor for poor prognosis in the developmental course of a number of psychiatric disorders, and more specifically, high maternal emotional overinvolvement has shown some association with anxiety disorders. Hirshfeld, et al. (1997a) examined maternal EE and child behavioral inhibition in children of parents with a range of emotional disorders (the 'at risk' sample). Comparison children were either high or low on behavioral inhibition, but without other familial mental health problems. Mothers' descriptions of the parent-child relationship were coded for EE, specifically criticism and emotional overinvolvement (EOI). In the at-risk sample, maternal criticism was associated with higher incidence of child behavioral inhibition, and maternal EOI was associated with higher incidence of separation anxiety problems independently of the children's other behavior and mood disorders. In an epidemiological sample, Stubbe, Zahner, and Goldstein (1993) observed a similar association between high EOI and child anxiety disorders. Thus, preliminary investigations of maternal EE point towards an association between maternal criticism and behavioral inhibition, irrespective of comorbid psychiatric diagnoses. High maternal EOI appears to be connected with separation anxiety in at-risk children.

In a continuation of the above study (Hirshfeld, et al., 1997b), maternal criticism was positively associated with a lifetime history of maternal anxiety disorder, with or without comorbidity. The occurrence of both maternal anxiety disorder and child behavioral inhibition predicted the rate of maternal criticism; however, maternal criticism was not related to the incidence of behavioral inhibition in their children in families where mothers were nonanxious. This suggests a reciprocal interaction between maternal anxiety and child inhibition. Child inhibition would be challenging for parents, as they could be expected to be easily frustrated and upset by their difficult child, as well as finding it difficult to calm themselves or their child once aroused. Anxious parents may therefore be more likely to respond irritably to their child, as well as overestimating the degree of threat to themselves or their child, and underestimating their own coping resources.

One aspect of interactional research that has received little attention from social learning theorists is that the contextual relationships we are studying are the most basic of our intimate and long-term relationships. Historically, learning theories have been relatively silent on issues of attachment and intimacy but the studies reviewed below show clearly that it is worth asking more about the nature of close relationships and context they provide for the learning of fear versus courage. Over the last few decades, a number of strategies for operationalizing attachment processes have been developed, including observational measures of parent-infant bonds (Ainsworth, 1989), and self-report and structured interview measures of current adult relationships and past relationships to parents (Main, 1996). A number of manifestations of insecure attachment have been described and empirically verified, including dismissive (or avoidant; e.g., avoiding or failing to seek out intimate contact) and preoccupied (or anxious/ambivalent styles; e.g., showing distress at separation, clinging, failure to show independent exploration). Using various methods of categorizing attachment, numerous studies have been published showing that different attachment processes characterize psychologically healthy versus distressed adults and children. Clinic-referred samples of children and adults show relatively low rates of secure attachment (i.e., intimate relationships marked by predictable, stable, and generous levels of care and support) compared to nonclinic samples (Main, 1996).

In general, however, it has been difficult to find specific relationships between particular forms of psychopathology and specific types of insecure attachment (see van IJzendoorn & Bakermans-Kranenburg, 1996, and van IJzendoorn, Schuengel, & Bakermans-Kranenburg, 1999, for meta-analytic reviews). Recent improvements in the design of studies may overcome this lack of specificity. For example, Rosenstein and Horowitz (1996) found that clinically referred adolescents with a 'preoccupied' or 'anxious ambivalent' attachment style were much more likely to have anxiety and depression problems than those with a 'dismissive' style, who tended to show conduct problems. Clearly these results are intuitively appealing and careful research is worth pursuing in this area. If valid, they indicate that relationships marked by high involvement but low security may be associated with internalizing profiles.

It should be noted, however, that the attachment area still tends to be characterized by reliance on global typology categories and absence of specific descriptions of behavioral processes mediating attachment and psychopathology. This is highlighted by the DeKlyen (1996) study, which showed that maternal attachment added no predictive power to the child's behavioral problems once direct observational measures of parent-child interactions were considered. Further, few treatment developments from an attachment perspective have been subjected to controlled outcome and process studies.

Gender effects also need to be considered and more effort is needed to include fathers in this area. For example, Cowan, Cohn, Pape-Cowan, and Pearson (1996) found that mothers' and fathers' attachment styles were differentially related to internalizing versus externalizing problems in their children. They assessed attachment history, family interaction and children's externalizing/internalizing behaviors over a 2-year period. With respect to the internalizing behaviors of anxiety disorder, Cowan, et al. found that the mothers' attachment history and family interaction accounted for 60% of the variance in children's internalizing behavior, with positive marital relationships functioning as a buffer between a mother's history of insecure attachment and subsequent ineffective parenting style. The fathers' profile was associated with children's externalizing behaviors. In effect, by examining parental attachment styles researchers are afforded a view of three generations of interaction in examining children's adaptive and dysfunctional patterns.

Warren, Huston, Egeland, and Sroufe (1997) examined whether infants who were anxiously/resistantly attached in infancy develop more anxiety disorders during childhood and adolescence than do infants who were securely attached. To test different theories of anxiety disorders, newborn temperament and maternal anxiety were included in multiple regression analyses. Infants participated in Ainsworth's Strange Situation Procedure at 1 year of age. The Schedule for Affective Disorders and Schizophrenia for School-Age Children was administered to the 172 children when they reached 17.5 years of age. Maternal anxiety and infant temperament were assessed near the time of birth. The hypothesized relation between anxious/resistant attachment and later anxiety disorders was confirmed. Anxious/resistant attachment continued to significantly predict child/adolescent anxiety disorders, even when entered last, after maternal anxiety and temperament, in multiple regression analyses.

In a longitudinal study, Fox and Calkins (1993) assessed children's behavioral and physiological responses to novelty and restraint, attachment styles, and maternal ratings of child temperament, from birth to 24 months. As is common in this area, the infants could be reliably grouped according to two distinct patterns of observed behavior and physiological reactivity. Even in the first days of life, some infants were frustrated by the imposition of limits to their behavior (e.g., arm restraint) and remained undistressed by novelty (peek-a-boo with a stranger, novel visual stimuli). Other infants reacted by accepting the imposition of limits but were clearly distressed by novelty. Similar to Kagan, et al.'s (1988) measures, the autonomic responses of fearful infants reflected an inability to respond adaptively to changes and novelty in the environment.

Fox and Calkins suggest that this group of infants are showing temperamental features that logically appear to be early signs of behavioral inhibition.

No relationship was found between the early measures of infant reactivity and behavioral inhibition measured at 24 months, suggesting that early temperament alone is not sufficiently able to account for the development of behavioral inhibition. However, a stable, consistent pattern emerged from the maternal reports of infant behavior across the 24-month period in association with later signs of behavioral inhibition. Maternal ratings of low positive affect and activity subscales at 5 months, and social fear at 14 months and 24 months, correlated positively with inhibition in toddlerhood. Thus, mothers were able to report on characteristics of their infants that were predictive of later inhibition, even though the independent measures of early behavioral reactivity did not.

Further, there were clear relationships between the early reactivity measures and the styles of attachment that the mother–child dyads formed. The freedom/novelty seeking infants tend to elicit negative responses from their parents, and actually avoid the controlling parent in an attempt to maintain their freedom. They were termed 'insecure-avoidant' according to attachment classifications. In contrast to this group, the infants who were easily distressed by novelty (insecure resistant), placed high demands upon parents for proximity and soothing, which parents were likely to meet with variable consistency.

Manassis, et al. (1994) found high rates of insecure attachment in a sample of inhibited children. Fox and Calkins (1993) found that attachment style interacted with the early behavioral measures in predicting behavioral inhibition. In particular, those infants who were behaviorally and physiologically distressed by novelty *and* had high insecure-anxious attachments tended to move into higher levels of behavioral inhibition. Both of the above groups elicited negative responses from parents, either bids for control which the child avoided, or frustration at the child's excessive proximity and soothing demands, which ironically increased the child's stress and demanding behavior. This interaction between insecure-anxious attachment styles and behavioral processes in which the child's demanding leads to a coercive cycle of parental frustration and rejection, and thus, increasing child demands, emerges from several diverse theoretical and empirical approaches to understanding families and anxiety. Further discussion of these processes will be presented at the end of this chapter.

Nachmias, et al. (1996) studied 18-month-old toddlers in another attempt to integrate attachment theory and physiological correlates of behavioral inhibition. In this study children were presented with three novel events: an exuberant live clown, a robot clown, and some lively puppets. Behavioral inhibition was rated as 'ease of approach.' Physiological stress reactions were operationalized as the activation of neuroendocrine responses in the hypothalamic-pituitary-adrenocortical (HPA) system, which is measured through cortisol secretions in the child's saliva. To reduce confounding the influence of inhibition with attachment, the measurement of attachment via the Strange Situation (see Ainsworth, 1989) occurred at least 1 week apart from the inhibition session. The results indicated that variance in children's physiological signs of anxiety/stress problems was accounted for by the interaction of the child's temperament and the quality of the parent-child relationship. Specifically, only children who were *both* insecurely attached and behaviorally inhibited were unsuccessful at reducing the activation of their neuroendocrine response to stress. No other group (i.e., securely attached, inhibited children; secure/insecure-noninhibited children) showed similar elevations in cortisol levels after exposure to the novel, arousing events. When inhibition extremes were used in a subsequent analysis, this inhibition by attachment interaction was reduced to a trend and no longer achieved significance. This could have been due to the reduced statistical power that is commonly associated with using split rather than whole/continuous samples.

A previous study (Calkins & Fox, 1992) that tested both attachment and inhibition in the same experimental session showed a different pattern of results in support of links between high inhibition and resistant attachment, and low inhibition and avoidant attachment. Nachmias and her colleagues (1996) have argued that Calkins and Fox's testing of inhibition immediately prior to testing attachment may have increased resistant behavior in children, who under different circumstances would not have been observed to have a resistant (insecure) attachment style. Secondly, fussing and crying are often considered behavioral indicators of behavioral inhibition (Calkins & Fox, 1992; Kagan, et al., 1988). In the Nachmias, et al. study, fussing and crying were measured as separate aspects of children's behavior, reflecting irritability, and not included in the definition of inhibition. Nachmias, et al. cite studies (Belsky & Rovine, 1987; Goldsmith & Alansky, 1987) which point to irritability as a distinguishing feature of resistant attachment style. The disentanglement of observations of fussing and crying with constructs of resistant attachment, inhibition, and irritability provides avenues for further research.

Children's and parents' behaviors were also extensively coded and then factor analyzed by Nachmias, et al. (1996) into comfort-seeking (including fussing), coping-competence, and distraction for children, and encourage-approach, comfort-giving, or demand-approach factors, for mothers. Overall, there was no significant interaction between attachment and inhibition. However, inhibited toddlers received more maternal comforting and encouragement to approach than less inhibited toddlers. Inhibited toddlers also sought more comfort from the mother, suggesting a reciprocal cycle as discussed in Patterson (1982). As would be expected, securely attached toddlers demonstrated significantly more coping competence than insecurely attached toddlers.

When average pre- and post-cortisol levels were examined, inhibition accounted for a large portion of the variance in both pre- and post-measures. Children who were able to cope competently with the novel situations showed significantly lower elevations of cortisol. Additionally, when mothers of insecurely attached children intruded upon their child's coping efforts by overly encouraging their children to interact or approach an arousing stimulus, high posttest cortisol levels resulted. This maternal style is hypothesized to have interfered with the toddler's tendency to cautiously regulate their own proximity and contact with the stimulus, which could have increased the child's perception of imminent threat. Thus behavioral inhibition, hypothesized to be the child's preferred coping mechanism in the face of arousing stimuli, was not allowed to operate due to maternal intrusiveness. In these cases cortisol levels were atypically elevated, a sign of stress. Additionally, and less clear, was the association observed between comfort giving and higher cortisol levels. It is possible that mothers' increased efforts to calm their children may actually extend beyond the immediate needs of the child for comforting, and indirectly convey messages of increased threat, simultaneously undermining the child's own coping strategies.

In summary, the above studies show important interactions between infant temperament, parent-child interactions, and attachment styles in the prediction of anxious outcomes for young children. These studies also highlight the difficulties of parenting a child with high levels of inhibition and fear of novelty. Pushing such children too forcefully toward challenge, or alternatively, being overly protective, both appear to enhance fearful responding, prevent anxious children from developing a sense of their own ability to cope, and reduce opportunities for them to experience and become familiar with novel challenges.

These models of how problematic parent-child interactions can escalate into behavior problems and psychopathology are highly consistent and complementary with the coercive operant model of parenting (Patterson, 1982; see also Greene & Doyle, 1999) that has been so successfully applied to conduct problems in children. The insecure (or 'behaviorally-inhibited' or 'anxious' child) who seeks closeness which is beyond the comfort level of the parent will in the short-term be rewarded with proximity, talk, contact and so on. However, when the parent's tolerance levels are exceeded, the parent will be pushed, now and then, into a rejecting stance. The rejection, although it may be very temporary and mild, will reinforce the child's construction that high levels of coercive or fearful, dependent behavior are needed to regain and then maintain closeness. As such cycles repeat, the more the relationship can be characterized as insecure and the more operant factors ensure their continued existence and strength. Such cycles have been eloquently described by Patterson (1982) with respect to aggression in families but clinical observations and the above studies indicate that may also contribute to the development of anxiety problem early in life.

A model that elucidates this integration of learning theory and attachment processes was the seminal but now largely ignored work of the Harlows (Harlow & Harlow, 1962). They described patterns of insecure attachment and 'approach-avoidance' conflicts using infant monkey–mechanical mother monkey dyads in which both food and comfort, as well aversive stimuli, were delivered via the mechanical mother. The delivery of aversive stimuli originating from the mother monkey led to increases in clinging rather than avoidance behavior, as well as anxiety and distress, in the infant monkeys.

Both a strength and limitation of the Harlow's research was that the mother's behavior was controlled by the experimenter and could not be shaped by the infant. In the real world, the increased clinging behavior by the infant monkey would have powerful effects on the mother. In some cases, the mother would react with displeasure to the clinging and thus would increase rejecting behaviors. This would lead to increases in the likelihood of further aversive clinging behavior from the infant, thus setting up an escalating cycle into anxiety and insecurity. The parent might also try to comfort the clinging infant; if this was done consistently, the clinging might be reduced as the infant gained confidence. However, parents are only human (well, not the parents in the Harlow study). Most likely is that the parent would fluctuate between comforting and rejection according to variations in a host of factors including the infant's behavior, her mood, the quality of her own adult relationships, and so on. Thus, intermittent patterns of reinforcement would be established which would strengthen the infant's demonstrations of anxiety and insecurity.

TOWARD THEORY DEVELOPMENT

The literature briefly reviewed here indicates that both social learning and attachment theory have established explanatory power and empirical support in explaining the role of the family in the development of anxiety disorders. However, both these models are incomplete without concurrent consideration of the child's temperament. That is, social learning and attachment processes can facilitate, and no doubt diminish, anxiety problems in children who have inhibited, shy temperaments, and conversely, such children appear to facilitate the expression of social learning and attachment processes that further promote anxiety.

There may be a number of potential benefits to be made by comparing, contrasting, and possibly integrating aspects of these models (Dadds & Barrett, 1996; Dadds & Roth, 2001). In its purest forms, social learning theory takes all stimuli as potentially equal and has little to say about the biological and development relevance of various stimulus settings and intimate relationships. By contrast, attachment theory correctly recognizes that particular settings may be very potent for learning fear versus courage, such as the parents' and child's first experiences of separation and reunion. Conversely, attachment theory places little emphasis on the microprocesses that establish and maintain behaviors, or the methodologies by which these microprocesses can be examined under controlled conditions. Social learning theory has a rich and successful history in these domains.

The two models make predictions that are seemingly contradictory, as least in terms of our current understanding, with respect to the development and expression of fear. For example, social learning theory would predict that contingent parental soothing should reinforce fear displays, and punishment of fear responses should suppress them. By contrast, attachment theory predicts that parental soothing will facilitate the child's skills in self-soothing, leading to a decrease in future fear displays, whereas punishment of fear responses will lead to an insecure attachment and an increase in fear behavior. Both of these have received indirect empirical support (e.g., Dadds, et al., 1996; King,

Hamilton, & Ollendick, 1988, for social learning theory and Harlow & Harlow, 1962, for attachment theory). In Harlow and Harlow's work, the cessation of aversive stimuli and the provision of comforting contingent upon clinging should increase clinging according to social learning theory, but should reduce clinging according to attachment theory.

SUMMARY

Anxiety tends to run in families. Emerging evidence shows that specific parent-child social learning processes, operating within the context of the quality and consistency of intimate relationships, are important in the development of anxiety problems. These processes interact with the child's (and parent's) temperament in predicting the development of anxiety problems, and families with both an inhibited child and anxious parents, are particularly prone to becoming entrapped in social learning processes that foster escalating anxiety problems. It was also argued that aspects of attachment theory may complement such social learning/temperament models, and recent empirical evidence supports a transactional view in which child temperament, parent-child interactions, and more global attachment processes interact to influence risk for, versus protection against, anxiety problems.

ACKNOWLEDGEMENTS

The author would like to thank colleagues Paula Barrett, Janet Roth, and Ron Rapee for contributions to the research described in this chapter.

REFERENCES

Ainsworth, M. D. S. (1989). Attachments beyond infancy. *American Psychologist, 44,* 709–716.

Barrett, P. M., Rapee, R. M., Dadds, M. R., & Ryan, S. (1996). Family enhancement of cognitive styles in anxious and aggressive children: The FEAR effect. *Journal of Abnormal Child Psychology, 24,* 187–203.

Belsky, J. & Rovine, M. (1987). Temperament and attachment security in the Strange Situation: An empirical rapprochement. *Child Development, 58,* 787–795.

Bernstein, G. A. & Borchardt, C. M. (1991). Anxiety disorders of childhood and adolescence. *Journal of the American Academy of Child and Adolescent Psychiatry, 30,* 519–532.

Butler, G. & Mathews, A. (1983). Cognitive processes in anxiety. *Advances in Behaviour Research and Therapy, 5,* 51–62.

Calkins, S. & Fox, N. (1992). The relations among infant temperament, security of attachment, and behavioral inhibition at twenty-four months. *Child Development, 63,* 1456–1472.

Chorpita, B. F. & Barlow, D. H. (1998). The development of anxiety: The role of control in the early environment. *Psychological Bulletin, 124,* 3–21.

Chorpita, B. F., Albano, A. M., & Barlow, D. H. (1996). Cognitive processing in children: Relation to anxiety and family influences. *Journal of Clinical Child Psychology, 25,* 170–176.

Chorpita, B. F., Brown, T. A., & Barlow, D. H. (1998). Perceived control as a mediator of family environment in etiological models of childhood anxiety. *Behavior Therapy, 29,* 457–476.

Clark, D. & Ehlers, A. (1993). An overview of cognitive theory and treatment of panic disorder. *Applied and Preventive Psychology, 2*, 131–139.

Cobham, V. E., Dadds, M. R., & Spence, S. H. (1999). Anxious children and their families: What do they expect? *Journal of Clinical Child Psychology, 28*, 220–231.

Cowan, P. A., Cohn, D. A., Pape-Cowan, C. P., & Pearson, J. L. (1996). Parents' attachment histories and children's externalizing and internalizing behaviors. *Journal of Consulting and Clinical Psychology, 64*, 53–63.

Dadds, M. R. & Barrett, P. M. (1996). Family process in childhood anxiety and depression. *Behaviour Change, 13*, 231–239.

Dadds, M. R. & Powell, M. B. (1991). The relationship of interparental conflict and marital adjustment to aggression, anxiety and immaturity in aggressive and nonclinic children. *Journal of Abnormal Child Psychology, 19*, 553–567.

Dadds, M. R. & Roth, J. (2001). Family factors. In M. W. Vasey & M. R. Dadds (Eds.), *The developmental psychopathology of anxiety* (pp. 278–303). New York: Oxford University Press.

Dadds, M. R., Rapee, R. M., & Heard, P. M. (1994). Behavioral observation. In T. Ollendick, N. King, & W. Yule (Eds.), *Handbook of childhood anxiety and phobic disorders* (pp. 349–364). New York: Plenum Press.

Dadds, M. R., Barrett, P. M., Rapee, R. M., & Ryan, S. (1996). Family process and child anxiety and aggression: An observational analysis. *Journal of Abnormal Child Psychology, 24*, 715–734.

Dadds, M. R., Bovbjerg, D., Redd, W. H., & Cutmore, T. H. (1997). Imagery and human classical conditioning. *Psychological Bulletin, 122*, 89–103.

Davey, G. C. L. (1992). Classical conditioning and the acquisition of human fears and phobias: A review and synthesis of the literature. *Advances in Behaviour Research and Therapy, 14*, 29–66.

DeKlyen, M. (1996). Disruptive behavior disorder and intergenerational attachment patterns. *Journal of Consulting and Clinical Psychology, 64*, 357–365.

Dumas, J. E., LaFreniere, P. J., & Serketich, W. J. (1995). 'Balance of power': A transactional analysis of control in mother–child dyads involving socially competent, aggressive, and anxious children. *Journal of Abnormal Psychology, 104*, 104–113.

Faraone, S., Chen, W., Warburton, R., Biederman, J., Milberger, S., & Tsuang, M. (1995). Genetic heterogeneity in Attention Deficit Hyperactivity Disorder: Gender, psychiatric comorbidity and maternal ADHD. *Journal of Abnormal Psychology, 104*, 334–345.

Fox, N. A. & Calkins, S. D. (1993). Pathways to aggression and social withdrawal: Interactions among temperament, attachment, and regulation. In K. H. Rubin & J. B. Asendorph (Eds.), *Social withdrawal, inhibition, and shyness in childhood* (pp. 81–100). Hillsdale, NJ: Lawrence Erlbaum Associates.

Goldsmith, H. H. & Alansky, J. A. (1987). Maternal and infant temperamental predictors of attachment: A meta-analytic review. *Journal of Consulting and Clinical Psychology, 55*, 805–816.

Gray, J. A. (1982). *The neuropsychology of anxiety*. Oxford: Clarendon.

Green, S. M., Loeber, R., & Lahey, B. B. (1992). Child psychopathology and deviant family hierarchies. *Journal of Child and Family Studies, 1*, 341–350.

Greene, R. W. & Doyle, A. E. (1999). Toward a transactional conceptualization of Oppositional Defiant Disorder: Implications for assessment and treatment. *Clinical Child and Family Psychology Review, 2*, 129–148.

Harlow, H. F. & Harlow, M. (1962). Social deprivation in monkeys. *Scientific American, 207*, 136–146.

Haley, J. (1976). *Problem-solving therapy*. San Francisco: Jossey-Bass.

Hetherington, E. M. & Martin, B. (1972). Family interaction. In H. C. Quay & J. S. Werry (Eds.), *Psychopathological disorders of childhood* (pp. 30–82). New York: Wiley.

Hirshfeld, D. R., Biederman, J., Brody, L., Faraone, S. V., & Rosenbaum, J. F. (1997a). Associations between expressed emotion and child behavioral inhibition and psychopathology: A pilot study. *Journal of the American Academy of Child and Adolescent Psychiatry, 36*, 205–213.

Hirshfeld, D. R., Biederman, J., Brody, L., Faraone, S. V. & Rosenbaum, J. F. (1997b). Expressed emotion toward children with behavioral inhibition: Associations with maternal anxiety disorder. *Journal of the American Academy of Child and Adolescent Psychiatry, 36*, 910–917.

Kagan, J., Reznick, J. S., & Snidman, N. (1988). Biological bases of childhood shyness. *Science, 240,* 167–171.

Kashani, J. H. & Orvaschel, H. (1990). A community study of anxiety in children and adolescents. *American Journal of Psychiatry, 147,* 313–318.

Keller, M. B., Lavori, P., Wunder, J., Beardslee, W. R., Schwarts, C. E., & Roth, J. (1992). Chronic course of anxiety disorders in children and adolescents. *Journal of the American Academy of Child and Adolescent Psychiatry, 31,* 595–599.

King, N. J., Hamilton, D. J., & Ollendick, T. H. (1988). *Children's phobias: A behavioral perspective.* Chichester: Wiley.

Krohne, H. W. (1992). Developmental conditions of anxiety and coping: A two-process model of child rearing effects. In K.A. Hagtvet (Ed.), *Advances in test anxiety research* (Vol. 7, pp. 143–155). The Netherlands: Swets & Zeitlinger.

Krohne, H. W. & Hock, M. (1991). Relationships between restrictive mother–child interactions and anxiety of the child. *Anxiety Research, 4,* 109–124.

Krohne, H. W. & Hock, M. (1993). Coping dispositions, actual anxiety, and the incidental learning of success- and failure-related stimuli. *Personality and Individual Differences, 15,* 33–41.

Last, C.G., Perrin, S., Hersen, M., & Kazdin, A.E. (1996). A prospective study of childhood anxiety disorders. *Journal of the American Academy of Child and Adolescent Psychiatry, 35,* 1502–1510.

Main, M. (1996). Overview of the field of attachment. *Journal of Consulting and Clinical Psychology, 64,* 237–243.

Manassis, K., Bradley, S., Goldberg, S., & Hood, J. (1994). Attachment in mothers with anxiety disorders and their children. *Journal of the American Academy of Child and Adolescent Psychiatry. 33,* 1106–1113.

Messer, S. C., & Beidel, D. C. (1994). Psychosocial correlates of childhood anxiety disorders. *Journal of the American Academy of Child and Adolescent Psychiatry, 33,* 975–983.

Minuchin, S. (1974). *Families and family therapy.* Cambridge, MA: Harvard University Press.

Nachmias, M, Gunnar, M., Mangelsdorf, S., Parritz, R. H., & Buss, K. (1996). Behavioral inhibition and stress reactivity: The moderating role of attachment security. *Child Development, 67,* 508–522.

Panella, D. & Henggeler, S. W. (1986). Peer interactions of conduct-disordered, anxious-withdrawn, and well-adjusted black adolescents. *Journal of Abnormal Child Psychology, 14,* 1–11.

Patterson, G. R. (1982). *Coercive family process.* Eugene, OR: Castalia Press.

Pfeiffer, C. R., Lipkins, R., Plutchik, R., & Mizruchi, M. (1988). Normal children at risk for suicidal behavior: A two-year follow-up study. *Journal of the American Academy of Child and Adolescent Psychiatry, 27,* 34–41.

Rapee, R. M. (1997). Potential role of childrearing practices in the development of anxiety and depression. *Clinical Psychology Review, 17,* 47–67.

Rosenstein, D. S. & Horowitz, H. A. (1996). Adolescent attachment and psychopathology. *Journal of Consulting and Clinical Psychology, 64,* 244–253.

Rubin, K. H. & Clark, M. L. (1983). Preschool teachers' ratings of behavioral problems: Observational, sociometric, and social-cognitive correlates. *Journal of Abnormal Child Psychology, 11,* 273–286.

Solyom, L., Silberfeld, M., & Solyom, C. (1976). Maternal overprotection in the etiology of agoraphobia. *Canadian Psychiatric Association Journal, 21,* 109–113.

Stark, K. D., Humphrey, L. L., Crook, K., & Lewis, K. (1990). Perceived family environments of depressed and anxious children. *Journal of Abnormal Child Psychology, 18,* 527–548.

Strauss, C. C., Frame, C. L., & Forehand, R. (1987). Psychosocial impairment associated with anxiety in children. *Journal of Clinical Child Psychology, 16,* 235–239.

Strauss, C. C., Lahey, B. B., Frick, P., Frame, C. L., & Hynd, G. W. (1988). Peer social status of children with anxiety disorders. *Journal of Consulting and Clinical Psychology, 56,* 137–141.

Stubbe, D. E., Zahner, G. E. P., & Goldstein, M. J. (1993). Diagnostic specificity of a brief measure of expressed emotion: A community study of children. *Journal of Child Psychology and Psychiatry, 34,* 139–154.

van IJzendoorn, M. H. & Bakermans-Kranenburg, M. J. (1996). Attachment representations in mothers, fathers, adolescents and children: A meta-analytic search for normative data. *Journal of Consulting and Clinical Psychology, 64*, 8–21.

van IJzendoorn, M. H., Schuengel, C., & Bakermans-Kranenburg, M. J. (1999). Disorganized attachment in early childhood: Meta-analysis of precursors, concomitants, and sequelae. *Development and Psychopathology, 11*, 225–249.

Vasey, M. W. & MacLeod, C. (2001). Information-processing factors in childhood anxiety: A review and developmental perspective. In M.W. Vasey & M.R. Dadds (Eds.), *The developmental psychopathology of anxiety* (pp. 253–276). New York: Oxford University Press.

Warren, S. L., Huston, L., Egeland, B., & Sroufe, L. A. (1997). Child and adolescent anxiety disorders and early attachment. *Journal of the American Academy of Child and Adolescent Psychiatry, 36*, 637–644.

Weller, R., Kapadia, R., Weller, W., Fristad, R., Lazaroff, L., & Preskorn, S. (1994). Psychopathology in families of children with Major Depressive Disorder. *Journal of Affective Disorder, 31*, 247–252.

CHAPTER 6

Understanding the Association between Parent and Child Antisocial Behavior

PAUL J. FRICK & BRYAN R. LONEY

Understanding the causes of antisocial and criminal behavior has long been a major focus of social science research. There are many reasons for this focus. First, the most severe patterns of antisocial behavior often emerge early in life and show fairly substantial continuity across the lifespan (Frick & Loney, 1999). Second, antisocial individuals operate at quite a high cost to society, both in terms of monetary costs, such as the costs of incarceration, and in terms of social costs, such as reduced quality of life for victims of antisocial acts and other persons living in crime-prone areas (Zigler, Taussig, & Black, 1992). Third, partly because of the disruptions they cause to others around them and partly due to the pervasive problems in adjustment these individuals often have, they make up a substantial number of referrals to mental health clinics, especially those clinics serving children (Frick, 1998a).

Given the importance of this research, it is not surprising it has spanned a number of social science disciplines with each discipline using somewhat different definitions for these behaviors. For example, sociologists and criminologists often use legal definitions of antisocial behavior, focusing on any behavior that breaks codified societal norms (McCord, 1991). Often these acts are classified into more discrete types of illegal acts, such as violent crimes (e.g., rape, assault, homicide), property crimes (e.g., vandalism, theft of property), drug offenses (e.g., possession or selling of illegal drugs), and status offenses (e.g., truancy). In contrast, psychologists and psychiatrists often use definitions of 'antisocial disorders' or 'conduct disorders' that focus on chronic patterns of severe aggressive and antisocial behavior that lead to impairments in a person's psychosocial functioning (Frick, 1998a). In adults, such chronic patterns of behavior are typically classified based on the criteria from the Diagnostic and Statistical Manual of Mental Disorders—4th Edition (DSM-IV; American Psychiatric Association, 1994) for Antisocial Personality Disorder (APD). In children, these severe and impairing types of behaviors are often classified based on the DSM-IV criteria for Oppositional Defiant Disorder (ODD) or Conduct Disorder (CD).

EARLY STUDIES OF AN INTERGENERATIONAL LINK TO CRIMINALITY AND AGGRESSION

Within this rather substantial and important body of research, a finding that has long intrigued social scientists is the familial link to antisocial and criminal behavior. Early studies conducted in the United States (Glueck & Glueck, 1968; McCord, 1979; Robins, West, & Herjanic, 1975; Wilson, 1975) and elsewhere (Farrington, 1978; Osborn & West, 1979) investigating the family backgrounds of juveniles who were arrested or convicted of delinquent acts consistently found an association between juvenile delinquency and parental arrests. These studies also documented that this link seemed to be independent of such potential confounds as the family's socioeconomic status (Farrington, 1978; Glueck & Glueck, 1968; McCord, 1979) and parent and child intelligence (Farrington, 1978; Glueck & Glueck, 1968; Osborn & West, 1979). Although these studies did not find that the types of crimes committed by parents and their children were highly correlated, the risk of delinquency in children increased as the rate of arrests in their parents increased (Osborn & West, 1979; Wilson, 1975).

These early studies focused on legal definitions (e.g., arrest rates, referrals to juvenile court) of antisocial behavior in both the parent and child. In contrast, Huesmann, Eron, Lefkowitz, and Walder (1984) obtained multiple measures of aggression (e.g., self-report, peer-rated aggression) in a large community sample of children ($n = 399$) who were originally assessed at 8 years of age and followed over a 22-year study period. At the follow-up assessments, these authors measured aggression in the offspring of their sample and found significant correlations ($r = .31$ to .40) between parent and child aggression scores. Like studies of criminality, the parent-child correlations on measures of aggression remained significant after partialling out the influence of social class and intelligence. The findings of Huesmann, et al. (1984) were particularly important because they provided evidence that the intergenerational link to antisocial behavior is not confined to studies using legal definitions of criminal behavior.

THE INTERGENERATIONAL LINK TO ANTISOCIAL DISORDERS

More recent research has used psychiatric definitions of antisocial disorders to study the link between parent and child antisocial behavior. This research has documented a consistent link between the presence of an antisocial disorder in parents and the presence of a conduct disorder in their children (Biederman, Munir, & Knee, 1987; Faraone, Biederman, Keenan, & Tsuang, 1991; Frick, 1994; Lahey, Piacentini, et al., 1988; Stewart, deBlois, & Cummings, 1980; Tapscott, Frick, Wootton, & Kruh, 1996). These studies generally employed similar methodology. For example, they studied clinic-referred children, used structured interviews to assess antisocial disorders in both the child and the parent, and had blind assessors of the parent and child. Using this methodology, rates of parental APD in children with conduct disorders ranged from 35% to 46% compared to rates of 6% to 17% in clinic-referred children with other problems in adjustment.

These family history studies, in addition to providing an estimate of the strength and consistency of the association between parent and child antisocial behavior, provide important information for interpreting this link. For example, these studies compared the family histories of children with conduct disorders to the family histories of children with other emotional or behavioral disorders rather than comparing them to a non-referred or non-disordered control group. The use of a clinic control group provides evidence that there is some specificity in the relation between parent and child antisocial disorders, which is in contrast to findings on relation between parental depression and child adjustment (e.g., Downey & Coyne, 1990) and the relationship between parental substance abuse and child adjustment (e.g., Frick, 1993; West & Prinz, 1987). For both parental depression and parental substance abuse, offspring are at risk for many different types of adjustment problems, not just depression or substance abuse. The specificity in the link between antisocial disorders in parent and child suggests that the processes involved in the intergenerational link are factors that place a child specifically at risk for conduct disorders.

Another important issue that has emerged from the family history studies is that the link between parent and child antisocial disorders was often due to a high rate of APD in the *fathers* of *boys* with conduct disorders. One reason for this sex-specific link is that the clinic-referred samples used in the family history studies were either solely comprised of boys (Biederman, et al., 1987; Frick, 1994; Stewart, et al., 1980) or had only a very small number of girls with conduct disorders (Lahey, Piacentini, et al., 1988; Tapscott, et al., 1996). Another reason for the sex-specific link is that very few mothers in the samples met the diagnostic criteria for APD. However, when research has employed continuous measures of antisocial behavior in the mothers of children with conduct disorder, such as the number of symptoms of APD (Frick, Kuper, Silverthorn, & Cotter, 1995) or scores on personality inventories assessing antisocial behavior (Frick, Lahey, Hartdagen, & Hynd, 1989), a link between child conduct disorders and maternal antisocial behavior is also found.

One other important finding related to sex differences in the intergenerational link to antisocial disorders is the finding that mothers of children with conduct disorder not only show high rates of antisocial symptoms, but they also show high rates of somatization symptoms (Frick, et al., 1995; Lahey, et al., 1989). This finding is consistent with studies showing a link between antisocial behavior and Somatization Disorder both within individuals (Guze, Woodruff, & Clayton, 1971; Lilienfeld, Van Valkenburg, Larntz, & Akiskal, 1986; Liskow, Penick, Powell, Haefele, & Campbell, 1986) and across generations (Bohman, Cloninger, von Knorring, & Sigvardsson, 1984; Cloninger & Guze, 1975; Guze, et al., 1971; Lilienfeld, et al., 1986). Lilienfeld (1992) provided one of the best articulated theories to explain this link when he proposed that antisocial and somatization disorders share a common predisposition, most likely a common neurological substrate for behavioral disinhibition. How this predisposition is manifested (e.g., antisocial and risk-taking behaviors, negative emotionality and somatization) can be influenced by cultural factors. Due to differences in cultural prohibitions for antisocial behavior in boys and girls, Lilienfeld proposed that boys may be more likely to express the predisposition in antisocial behavior and girls are more likely to express it in somatization symptoms. Consistent with this theory, Frick, et al. (1995) reported that the somatization symptoms in mothers of children with conduct disorders were significantly correlated with a measure of behavioral disinhibition.

One final issue that is important for interpreting family history studies linking antisocial disorders in parents and children is the methodology that was used for assessing parental APD. These studies typically assessed parental antisocial disorders through the report of both biological parents if they were available. However, when they were not available, the attending biological parent (in the vast majority of cases the child's mother) reported on her own adjustment and the adjustment of the non-attending biological parent. As a result, a significant proportion of the diagnoses of APD in the fathers was based on maternal report, leaving open the possibility of reporter biases. The most feasible alternative to this methodology would be to only include parents who are available to provide a history of their antisocial behavior. Unfortunately, this methodology is also problematic since it would lead to the exclusion of the vast majority of fathers with APD who are not living in the home (Lahey, Hartdagen, et al., 1988; Tapscott, et al., 1996).

Given the problems in interpreting the results of family history studies, Tapscott, et al. (1996) attempted to gather evidence for the validity of the family history method for assessing paternal APD. They attempted to have as many fathers as possible, who were not able to provide a history on themselves in person, complete a self-report measure of antisocial behavior through the mail. Despite having a small sample (5 fathers with APD compared to 24 fathers without APD), Tapscott, et al. found that fathers with APD based on mothers' report differed significantly from fathers without APD on the measure of self-reported antisocial tendencies. These data provide at least some support for the validity of the family history methodology for assessing parental APD and suggest that the link between antisocial disorders and conduct disorders cannot solely be attributable to a biased method of assessment.

In summary, there is a fairly large and consistent literature documenting a link between parent and child antisocial disorders. The link seems to involve factors that place a child specifically at risk for conduct disorders, since children with other emotional and behavioral disorders do not have high rates of parental APD in their family history. Also, there are sex-specific differences in this link, with mothers of children with conduct disorder often showing antisocial behavior that is below a diagnostic threshold or showing high rates of somatization symptoms. Finally, the link between parent and child antisocial disorders does not appear to be an artifact of the family history methodology used.

These studies provide an important starting point for understanding the association between parent and child antisocial disorders. However, the research reviewed in this section has been descriptive; that is, it has focused on documenting the link between parent and child antisocial behavior and describing factors that influence the strength of this link. The rest of this chapter focuses on theoretical models that have been developed to explain the mechanisms involved in this intergenerational link and on data that are either consistent or inconsistent with these explanations.

MECHANISMS INVOLVED IN THE ASSOCIATION BETWEEN PARENT AND CHILD ANTISOCIAL DISORDERS

Explanations for the transmission of antisocial behavior between parent and child have typically focused on three models that are not mutually exclusive. The first model emphasizes the potential role of heredity. It focuses on predispositions that place a person at risk for showing severe antisocial behavior that are passed from parent to child through genetic mechanisms (see for example, Rutter, et al., 1990). The second model emphasizes the role of observational learning in the development of aggression and antisocial behavior. It proposes that antisocial behavior may be learned by a child through observing parental 'models' of such behavior (see for example, McCord, 1991). A third model emphasizes the disruptive effects that an antisocial parent can have on the family environment. These disruptions can interfere with the socialization of the children in the home, placing them at risk for developing conduct disorders (see for example, Patterson & Capaldi, 1991). In the following sections, we present research related to each of these models.

Behavioral Genetic Studies of Antisocial Behavior

The potential role of genetic factors in the development of antisocial disorders has been the subject of very heated debate in the scientific literature (e.g., DiLalla & Gottesman, 1991; Widom, 1991). There have been a number of published studies, using either twin or adoption methodology (see Plomin, DeFries, & McClearn, 1990), that have attempted to estimate the amount of variance in measures of antisocial, aggressive, or criminal behaviors that could be attributable to genetic factors. Mason and Frick (1994) conducted a meta-analytic review of the twin and adoption studies published between 1975 and 1991 that included measures of antisocial, aggressive, or criminal behaviors.

They found an initial pool of 70 published studies during this period. Unfortunately, many of these studies had to be excluded from the meta-analysis because of methodological limitations or because of overlapping samples.

The meta-analysis was conducted on 12 twin studies involving 3,795 twin pairs and 3 adoption studies involving 338 adoptees. To summarize data across these 15 studies, an effect size statistic, 'd', was calculated so that it would be comparable across twin and adoption studies. In twin studies, the d statistic was based on the difference between the correlations (or concordance rates) in monozygotic and dizygotic twins on antisocial measures, which is analogous to the heritability coefficient (h^2; Falconer, 1981). An analogous d statistic was calculated from adoption studies based on the difference between (a) the correlation between an adoptee's score on a measure of antisocial behavior and his or her biological parent's score on a measure of antisocial behavior and (b) the correlation between an adoptee's score on a measure of antisocial behavior and his or her adoptive parent's score on the measure. Consistent with the effect size estimates from twin studies, larger d values would indicate greater genetic influences.

Using this methodology, Mason and Frick (1994) reported an average effect size of $d = .30$ across all of the studies included in the review. This effect size is considered indicative of a 'moderate' effect in psychological research (Cohen, 1977). An effect size of this magnitude in the twin studies was equivalent to a heritability coefficient of $h^2 = .50$, indicating that approximately 50% of the variance in measures of antisocial behavior could be attributed to heredity. In this meta-analysis, several potential moderators of the effect size were tested. The two strongest moderators were the methodological rigor of the study and the severity of antisocial behavior that was measured. Studies that used more rigorous methodology (e.g., blind assessment of twins) and that investigated more severe antisocial behavior tended to have the larger effect sizes. Also, there was a trend for larger effects in adult samples ($d = .41$, $n = 9$) than in child samples ($d = .15$; $n = 10$). However, this age trend seemed to be an artifact of the tendency to use measures of less severe antisocial behavior in younger samples (e.g., number of hits to a toy doll during a play session). When the effect sizes were limited to measures of severe antisocial behavior (e.g., severe physical aggression, criminal convictions, the presence of an antisocial disorder), the mean effect sizes for child samples ($d = .45$, $n = 6$) and adult samples ($d = .43$; $n = 7$) were comparable and indicative of fairly strong genetic effects.

This meta-analytic summary of the behavioral genetic research is consistent with qualitative reviews of the literature (e.g., DiLalla & Gottesman, 1991; Rutter, et al., 1990) finding evidence for a substantial role of heredity in explaining the variance in measures of antisocial behavior. However, this interpretation needs to be made with several cautions. First, most of the estimates of genetic influences, especially those reported by Mason and Frick (1994), were based on twin studies. This is an important consideration since the estimates of genetic influences from twin studies are much more open to question than the results from adoption studies (Plomin, et al., 1990). Second, the studies included in these reviews typically did not take advantage of more sophisticated latent class modeling procedures that more clearly disentangle genotype by environment interactions (see for example, Eaves, et al., 1993). Third, neither twin nor adoption studies shed light on the physiological and temperamental processes through which heredity may play a role in placing a child at risk for an antisocial disorder, an issue that is addressed in more detail later in this chapter. Finally, even if the estimates of genetic influences are accurate (i.e., accounting for about 50% of the variance in antisocial measures), there is a substantial amount of variance that is not being explained by heredity. Therefore, it is important to view this literature as providing one important piece to a very complex puzzle.

Parental Modeling of Antisocial Behavior

The second model that has been used to explain the link between parent and child antisocial behavior proposes that children learn to act in an anti-social manner through observing their parents engage in similar behaviors. Although this explanation has great intuitive appeal, it has been difficult to test. It is also hard to reconcile this explanation with the findings that the vast major-ity of antisocial parents do not have regular contact with their children, which should limit the amount of observational learning that could take place between parent and child (Lahey, Hartdagen, et al., 1988; Tapscott, et al., 1996). Also inconsistent with this model, McCord (1991) reported that for fathers with crim-inal records who were in the home continuously (defined as no absence of greater than 6 months prior to the child's 17th birthday), the arrest rate for their sons was 46%, which was comparable to the arrest rate of 42% in sons of fathers who had been out of the home for at least this minimal period. The difference in arrest rates was quite small and, therefore, was inconsistent with a modeling explanation of the intergenerational transmission of criminal behavior.

In a test of the observational learning model, Tapscott, et al. (1996) used two different definitions of paternal contact to determine if the level of contact between father and child influenced the relation between parental APD and childhood conduct disorders. First, families were divided into those in which the father had no contact with the child after the first year of life ($n = 19$) and those in which the father had at least some contact with the child after his or her first year of life ($n = 73$). Second, the families were divided into those in which the father had frequent contact with the child, defined as having face-to-face contact with the child at least once per month within the year prior to the study ($n = 60$), and those in which the father had infrequent contact with the child, defined as being out of the home for at least the 3 years prior to the study and who had face-to-face contact with their child less than once per month in the past year ($n = 29$). The role of paternal contact in moderating the link between paternal APD and child conduct disorders for this sample of clinic-referred children is summarized in Figure 6-1. Contrary to a modeling explanation, a paternal history of APD was associated with a high rate of conduct disorder in the child, regardless of whether the father had contact with

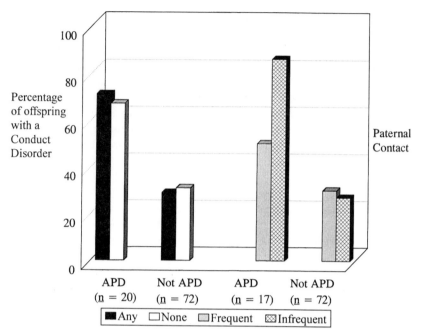

Figure 6-1   The figure illustrates the pattern of associations among a paternal history of Antisocial Personality Disorder (APD), degree of paternal contact with their child, and a diagnosis of Conduct Disorder in a clinic-referred sample. The figure is based on the percentages reported in Table 2 of Tapscott, et al. (1996).

the child since the first year of life (67%) or not (71%). Also inconsistent with this explanation, fathers with APD who had infrequent contact with their children actually had somewhat higher rates of children with conduct disorders (86%) than fathers with APD who had frequent contact with their children (50%).

   Although these findings are not consistent with the observational learning model, several limitations in this research should be noted. First, it is difficult to capture the intricate microsocial processes that can lead to observational learning with such broad measures as the degree of contact between a father and child. More sensitive measures of the child's exposure to antisocial behavior in his or her parents may provide more support for this model. Second, it is also possible that, even though a child's biological father with APD was no longer in the home, the child may still have been exposed to antisocial models. Tapscott, et al. (1996) controlled for the level of antisocial behavior in the child's mother in their analyses and found that their results could not be explained solely by the antisocial behavior of the mothers in the home. However, there was no assessment of other potential antisocial models in home, such as contact with antisocial grandparents or stepparents, that could have lead to observational learning of antisocial behavior. Despite these limitations, however, this research suggests that there is limited support for the role of observational learning in the intergenerational link to antisocial disorders.

Disruptions in Family Functioning Caused by an Antisocial Parent

The third model that has been frequently used to explain the link between parent and child antisocial disorders emphasizes the mediating role of disrupted family functioning. The clearest articulation of this model comes from Patterson and Capaldi (1991), who focused on the many stressors (e.g., major life events, daily hassles) experienced by antisocial individuals and the many family transitions (e.g., divorces and remarriages, temporary absences from the home due to incarceration) experienced by families with a parent who shows antisocial traits (see also Frick & Jackson, 1993). According to Patterson and Capaldi, these stressors and transitions play a 'disequilibrating' role in the functioning of the family; most importantly, they disrupt parents' ability to engage in effective parenting practices, such as their ability to monitor and supervise their children and to use consistent discipline practices. This model has been quite influential because most theories of the etiology of conduct disorders place a major emphasis on the role of ineffective parenting practices that lead to failures in the socialization of the child with conduct problems (Frick, 1998a; Patterson, Reid, & Dishion, 1992).

To test this model, Patterson and Capaldi (1991) conducted structural equation modeling analyses in a sample of 4th grade boys ($n = 206$) from high crime areas of a medium-sized metropolitan area. The authors used multiple indicators of parental antisocial behavior, social disadvantage, and parenting practices to test many of the predictions made from their model. As predicted, antisocial behavior in parents was significantly associated with family social disadvantage. In turn, family social disadvantage was significantly associated with dysfunctional parenting practices, such as poor discipline practices and poor monitoring. These two aspects of parenting have consistently been linked to conduct problems in children (see Frick, 1994, and Loeber & Stouthamer-Loeber, 1986, for reviews).

Although these data are consistent with many of the predictions made from the authors' model, a key limitation in these analyses is the failure to test whether or not the measures of parenting practices *mediated* the association between parental APD and childhood conduct disorders. That is, explicit in this model is the prediction that once ineffective parenting practices are controlled, the link between APD and childhood conduct disorders should become weaker (weak mediation) or non-existent (strong mediation), since the parenting practices are the proximal processes that are believed to account for this link (Baron & Kenny, 1986; Holmbeck, 1997).

Frick, et al. (1992) tested this important prediction in a sample of 177 clinic-referred boys (ages 6–13). Parental APD and childhood conduct disorders were assessed using structured diagnostic interviews and parenting practices were assessed through parental self-report on structured interviews. To test the mediational role of parenting practices, 2×2 logit-model analyses were conducted with parental APD and elevated scores on the dysfunctional parenting measures entered as the two predictors and the odds of the child having conduct disorder being the dependent measure. The results of these

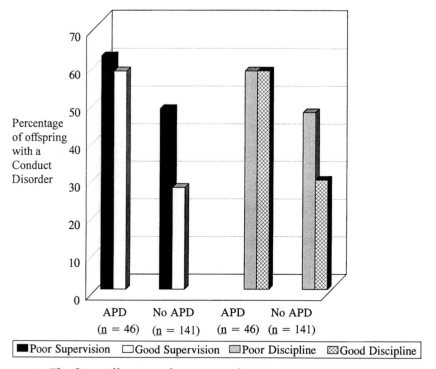

Figure 6-2   The figure illustrates the pattern of associations among a parental history of Antisocial Personality Disorder (APD), two types of dysfunctional parenting practices, and a diagnosis of child Conduct Disorder in a clinic-referred sample. The figure is based on the percentages reported in Table 2 of Frick, et al. (1992).

analyses indicated that parental APD continued to have strong effects on the odds of a child showing a conduct disorder even after controlling for levels of dysfunctional parenting. In fact, the measures of dysfunctional parenting did not contribute to the prediction of conduct disorders independent of parental APD. These results are graphically displayed in Figure 6-2 for two of the parenting constructs assessed: poor supervision and monitoring of the child and use of inconsistent discipline. The main effects for parental APD are apparent in this figure. In families with a parent with APD, there were high rates of conduct disorder in children regardless of whether or not the families showed dysfunctional parenting practices.

These analyses suggest that the association between parental APD and childhood conduct disorders can not be solely accounted for by dysfunctional parenting practices. However, there are several limitations to this study. First, although there was no main effect or interaction involving dysfunctional parenting in the 2 × 2 logit model analysis, the graphs in Figure 6-2 show that there was an increase in the rate of conduct disorder in families that exhibited dysfunctional parenting practices in families without an APD parent. This finding, while tentative, suggests that there may be two somewhat independent processes operating in predicting conduct disorder: one linking parental APD and child conduct disorders that is independent of parenting and another leading to an association between parenting practices and conduct disorder in families without parental APD. Second, the failure to find strong effects for parenting may be due to limitations in the measurement of parenting. Frick, et al. (1992) used single measures of parenting based solely on parental report rather than using multiple indicators of this important construct. Also, the dimensions of parenting practices (i.e., monitoring and supervision, inconsistent discipline) were analyzed separately, thereby ignoring potential additive effects of the different dimensions of ineffective parenting practices.

As a result of these limitations, we conducted additional analyses of the potential mediating role of parenting practices for this chapter. These analyses used 119 consecutive referrals to an outpatient child mental health clinic between the ages of 6 and 13. For these analyses, we had multiple measures of each of the relevant constructs. To measure parental APD, we used the number of adult APD symptoms and a retrospective account of the number of childhood conduct disorder symptoms for each child's biological mother and father. These were assessed using the Diagnostic Interview Schedule-Version IIIA (DIS-IIIA; Robins & Helzer, 1985). Conduct problems in the children were measured by parent and teacher report on the NIMH Diagnostic Interview Schedule for Children-Version 2.3 (DISC; Shaffer, Fisher, Piacentini, Schwab-Stone, & Wicks, 1993) and by the Aggression and Delinquency subscales of the Child Behavior Checklist-1991 (CBCL; Achenbach, 1991). To measure parenting practices, we used the Alabama Parenting Questionnaire (APQ; Frick, Christian, & Wootton, 1999; Shelton, Frick, & Wootton, 1996). The APQ was designed to assess five dimensions of parenting practices that have proven to be consistently associated with conduct problems in children: parental involvement with their children (10 items), parental use of positive reinforcement with their children (6 items), parental monitoring and supervision of their children (10 items), parental consistency in discipline (6 items), and parental use of corporal punishment (3 items). These dimensions of parenting practices were measured using three assessment formats: parental report on a questionnaire asking them to rate their typical use of each type of parenting behavior (Parent Global), child report on a questionnaire asking them to rate their parents' typical use of each type of parenting behavior (Child Global), and parental report on telephone interviews in which each parent was asked to provide the frequency with which they engaged in each parenting behavior over the 3 days preceding the interview (Parent Interview). Dysfunctional Parenting composites were formed to provide a global index of ineffective parenting practices within each method of assessment.

These measures were analyzed using the two-step approach to structural equations modeling outlined by Hatcher (1994). In the first step, the measures were tested for their usefulness in measuring the constructs of interest (i.e., parental APD, childhood conduct problems, ineffective parenting practices). Measures were deleted (i.e., Child Global report on the APQ, maternal retrospective report of her childhood conduct disorder symptoms) if they did not prove to

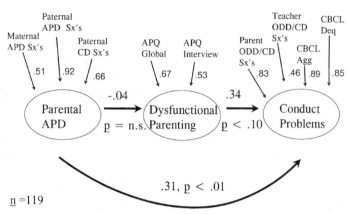

Figure 6-3 The figure summarizes the results of structural equations modeling testing the potential mediating role of dysfunctional parenting practices for explaining the association of parental Antisocial Personality Disorder (APD) and childhood conduct problems in a clinic-referred sample. CD Sx's = Conduct Disorder symptoms. APQ = Alabama Parenting Questionnaire. ODD/CD sx's = Oppositional Defiant Disorder and Conduct Disorder symptoms. CBCL = Child Behavior Checklist. Agg = Aggressive Behavior Scale. Deq = Delinquent Behavior Scale.

be reliable measures of a construct. After these tests of the measurement model, the measures were used to compare two theoretical models. One model involved dysfunctional parenting practices mediating the relation between parental APD and child conduct problems and the second model involved effects of parental APD on childhood conduct problems that were independent of parenting practices. The results of these analyses are summarized in Figure 6-3. In this figure, we provide the path coefficients for the model in which parental APD has independent effects on childhood conduct problems. It is evident from this figure that parental APD had a significant relation with conduct problems independent of dysfunctional parenting practices. The fit of this model to the data was also acceptable according to several types of fit indices (e.g., GFI = .94; NFI = .91). It is also evident from Figure 6-3 that the relation between dysfunctional parenting and conduct problems approached significance independent of parental APD.

These results are quite consistent with those reported by Frick, et al. (1992), despite using an independent sample, using different measures, and using a different analytical strategy. Both sets of finding suggest that parental APD has a substantial effect on child conduct problems independent of parenting practices, which is inconsistent with the mediational role of parenting practices in explaining the intergenerational link to antisocial behavior. Furthermore, the moderate relation between parenting practices and childhood conduct problems independent of parental APD is suggestive of at least two independent processes operating on child conduct problems. This pattern of findings is consistent with a theoretical framework in which the development of conduct problems is viewed as being the result of multiple causal pathways, each involving a distinct interaction of causal processes.

CALLOUS-UNEMOTIONAL TRAITS AND CONDUCT DISORDERS

The theoretical framework that we think helps to explain these findings is more fully developed in other publications (e.g., Frick, 1998a,b) and it will only be briefly summarized here. This framework builds on the seminal work of Moffitt (1993), Patterson, et al. (1992) and others (e.g., Hinshaw, Lahey, & Hart, 1993) who have defined two distinct groups of children with conduct disorders. One group, labeled the 'adolescent-onset' type of conduct disorder, begins showing severe antisocial behavior after the onset of puberty, and does not show high rates of neuropsychological dysfunction, cognitive impairment, or family dysfunction. This group is characterized by high rates of rebelliousness, rejection of traditional status hierarchies, and association with delinquent peers (see also Moffitt, Caspi, Dickson, Silva, & Stanton, 1996). One of the most consistent findings concerning this subgroup, however, is that they often desist in their antisocial behavior as they enter adulthood (see also Frick & Loney, 1999). The second group of children with conduct disorders is a group whose severe conduct problems emerge well before adolescence, usually with the rate and severity of conduct problems steadily increasing throughout childhood. In contrast to the adolescent-onset group, these children often show high rates of neuropsychological dysfunction, cognitive impairment, and dysfunctional family backgrounds. Furthermore, children with the childhood-onset conduct disorder often show very stable patterns of antisocial and criminal behavior that continue throughout adolescence and into adulthood (Frick & Loney, 1999).

The distinct developmental history, distinct pattern of correlations, and differential prognosis for children in these two conduct disorder groups led Moffitt (1993) to propose that there are different causal processes involved in the development of conduct problems in the two subgroups of antisocial children. The adolescent-onset pattern is conceptualized as an exaggeration of a normal developmental process resulting from a maturity gap between when adolescents reach cognitive and biological maturity and when they are permitted by society to have adult privileges and status. The antisocial behavior is a form of social mimicry of antisocial peers in a misguided attempt to gain a sense of adult status. Once adult status is provided by society, the primary motivation for the antisocial behavior is removed and the antisocial behavior decreases. In contrast, Moffitt proposes that the childhood-onset conduct disorder is the result of a transactional process between a 'vulnerable and difficult child and an adverse rearing context that evokes a series of failed parent-child encounters' (p. 682; Moffitt, 1993; see also Patterson, et al., 1992). As a result of this transactional process, the child does not become adequately socialized and then 'becomes ensnared in a lifelong pattern of antisocial behavior' (p. 683; Moffitt, 1993), such as teenage parenthood, drug abuse, school dropout, and criminal record, which further narrow his or her options for conventional behavior.

In our extension of this theory, we propose that there is yet another subdivision that can be made within the childhood-onset pathway. Our model proposes that, consistent with research on adults with APD (Hare, Hart, & Harpur, 1991), there is a subgroup of children with conduct disorders who also show a callous and unemotional interpersonal style. This style is characterized by such traits as poor empathic concern for others, an absence of guilt, use of others for own gain, and constricted emotions. These traits have been hall-marks of clinical descriptions of the 'psychopathic personality' for several decades (e.g. Cleckley, 1976; Hare, 1993). In our research we have shown that these callous-unemotional (CU) traits are at least partially independent of con-duct problems in preadolescent children (Frick, O'Brien, Wootton, & McBurnett, 1994). However, they designate a group of pre-adolescent children with con-duct disorders who show an especially severe pattern of antisocial behavior, characterized by a greater number and variety of conduct problems, more aggression, and higher rates of preadolescent police contacts (Christian, Frick, Hill, Tyler, & Frazer, 1997).

More importantly for understanding distinct causal pathways to conduct disorders, children with both conduct disorders and CU traits have several cor-relates to their antisocial behavior that distinguish them from other children with childhood-onset conduct disorder. Specifically, the conduct problems in children with CU traits seem to be more strongly related to a preference for thrill- and adventure-seeking activities (Frick, et al., 1994), a decreased sensi-tivity to punishment relative to rewards (O'Brien & Frick, 1996), and distinct neurochemical and autonomic irregularities (Goodman, et al., 1997; Lahey, Hart, Pliszka, Applegate, & McBurnett, 1993) compared to the conduct prob-lems displayed by children without these traits. In addition, the conduct prob-lems in children with CU traits are less related to intellectual impairments (Christian, et al., 1997) and children with CU traits tend to be less distressed by their behavior than children with conduct problems without these traits (Frick, 1998b).

These distinct correlates suggest that there may be different causal factors involved in the development of conduct problems in the two groups. We have proposed that children with CU traits are temperamentally at-risk for develop-ing a callous and unemotional interpersonal style (Frick, 1998b). This tempera-ment is characterized by low levels of fearful inhibitions, which is associated with autonomic irregularities, novelty seeking behavior, and decreased sensi-tivity to punishment (Gray, 1982; Kagan & Snidman, 1991). This temperament places a child at risk for problems in the development of guilt and empathy due to a failure of the child with such a temperament to experience intense internal discomfort associated with his or her misdeeds or intense internal discomfort associated with actions that harm others (Kochanska, 1993). The temperament, and resulting callous and unemotional interpersonal style, make the child less responsive to typical socializing pressures (e.g., parental socialization efforts, societal sanctions) and place the child at high risk for a severe and chronic pattern of antisocial behavior (Lykken, 1995).

How can this framework, which breaks down the childhood-onset pattern of conduct disorders based on the presence of CU traits, help to explain the rela-tions among parental APD, dysfunctional parenting practices, and childhood conduct disorders that were described previously? The relevance of this theory is due to two additional characteristics of children with CU traits. First, Christian, et al. (1997) found that when clinic-referred children (ages 6 to 13) with conduct disorders were divided into those with ($n = 11$) and without ($n = 29$) CU traits using cluster analyses, it was only those children with both conduct disorders *and* CU traits who showed high rates of parental APD. This finding is illustrated in Figure 6-4. Therefore, the link between APD and childhood conduct disorders may primarily be due to those children with conduct disorder who also show CU traits. Second, Wootton, Frick, Shelton, and Silverthorn (1997) found that in a combined sample of clinic-referred children ($n = 136$) and non-referred volunteer children ($n = 30$), conduct problems were highly related to dysfunctional parenting practices in children *without CU traits* ($n = 112$). In children high on CU traits ($n = 54$), the level of conduct problems was quite high irrespective of the quality of parenting that the child experienced. This finding is consistent with the assumption that children with CU traits, due to their lack of fearful inhibitions and their callous and unemotional interpersonal style, are not as responsive to typical socialization pressures (Frick, 1998b; Kochanska, 1993; Lykken, 1995).

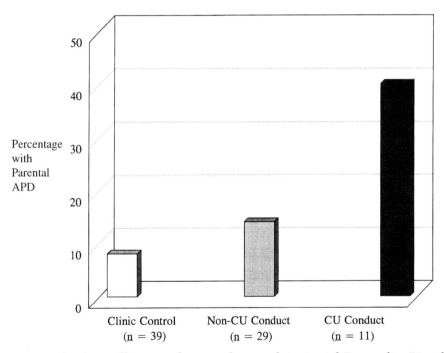

Figure 6-4 The figure illustrates the rate of parental Antisocial Personality Disorder (APD) in three of the four clusters identified in a clinic-referred sample by Christian, et al. (1997). Non-CU Conduct cluster consists of children high on conduct problems but low on callous and unemotional traits and the CU Conduct cluster consists of children high on both conduct problems and callous and unemotional traits.

These findings provide a basis for interpreting the two processes that seemed to be operating in the data illustrated in Figures 6-2 and 6-3. For children without CU traits, who are not as likely to have parents with a history of APD, dysfunctional parenting practices are significantly associated with conduct problems. In the Frick, et al. (1992) study (Figure 6-2), this would be consistent with the increase in conduct disorders in families without a parent with APD that is related to dysfunctional parenting practices. Similarly, this theory would be consistent with the structural equation modeling in Figure 6-3 in which parenting had a moderate association with conduct problems independent of parental APD. In contrast, children with CU traits who have a high rate of parental APD show conduct problems that are less strongly associated with ineffective parenting practices. Therefore, the link between parental APD and conduct disorders was largely independent of parenting practices because parental APD served as a 'marker' for the presence of CU traits. From the theory we have outlined previously, the intergenerational link could be related to a temperamental predisposition (e.g., low fearful inhibitions) to CU traits that is shared by both parent and child However, this hypothesized mediational role of low fearfulness to explain the relation between parental APD and childhood conduct disorders in children with CU traits is purely speculative at this point since it has not been tested directly.

DIRECTIONS FOR FUTURE RESEARCH

To summarize, research has consistently documented a link between antisocial behavior in parents and conduct problems in their children. It is less clear, however, what processes might account for this intergenerational link. There is evidence from behavioral genetic studies that this link may at least partially be explained by genetic influences. In contrast, there is little evidence to support the common notion that the intergenerational link can be explained by the modeling of antisocial behavior by parents of children with conduct disorder. Another common explanation, and one that fits with many comprehensive theories of conduct disorder, proposes that the link between parent and child antisocial behavior is mediated through disruptions in family functioning caused by having a parent with antisocial traits.

Although this last explanation is intuitively appealing, we have provided data that are somewhat inconsistent with this view. In several samples, we have found that parental APD has an association with conduct disorders that is independent of ineffective parenting. Furthermore, ineffective parenting seems to be more strongly associated with conduct problems in families without a family history of APD. We have interpreted these findings as being consistent with the theory that parental APD is linked primarily to a subgroup of children with conduct disorder who exhibit high rates of CU traits. In contrast, dysfunctional parenting practices are more strongly related to the development of conduct problems in children without these traits. This explanation not only fits these data well, but it is also consistent with the emerging view of conduct disorders as being the result of multiple distinct causal pathways each involving a unique interaction of causal factors. Although the model we presented is consistent with the available research, further research is needed to (a) gain confidence in this explanation through replications, (b) extend it even further for explaining the processes involved in the intergenerational link to antisocial disorders, and (c) make it more clinically useful for designing prevention and treatment strategies for children with parents who show severe antisocial behavior. There are several critical issues that must be considered in future research to achieve these important goals.

First, it has become increasingly clear that to understand the development of conduct disorders in general (e.g., Frick, 1998a; Moffitt, 1993; Patterson, et al., 1992), and to understand the link between conduct disorder and parental APD, specifically, research must be guided by the assumption that there are multiple causal pathways to the development of conduct disorders. It is almost a truism in research that multiple causal factors are involved in the development of conduct disorders. However, the dominant method of conceptualizing the multiple causal factors is through a cumulative risk model in which it is assumed that (a) causal factors operate in the same manner for all children by placing them at risk for developing conduct disorders and (b) the more factors that operate on a child, the greater the child's risk for developing conduct disorders. Such models may be helpful for some research purposes. However, this model ignores the possibility that some factors may be causal only for subgroups of children with conduct disorders and may not act in an additive fashion. For example, in the data reported in Frick, et al. (1992) and summarized in Figure 6-2, families with both dysfunctional parenting practices and a parental history of APD did not have higher rates of children with conduct disorders than families with a parental history of APD alone. Instead, children with a family history of APD had high rates of conduct disorder irrespective of the quality of parenting practices that they experienced.

Second, it is clear that future research does not need to provide further documentation that there is a link between parent and child antisocial behavior. Instead, future research needs to focus more specifically on the mechanisms involved in this intergenerational link. To do this, there needs to be continued development of clear theoretical models of these potential mechanisms, so that these models can be tested and modified based on the data. For example, the two processes we have outlined in this chapter admittedly need much further testing. Also, this two-process model is clearly too simplistic to explain all of the variance in children with conduct disorders. However, it provides an example of the type of theoretical models that are needed to guide the next generation of research in this area. These models must consider basic biological processes, temperaments that are a result of these processes, and interactions of these temperaments with the psychosocial context in which a child develops.

Third, research on criminal behavior and antisocial disorders has often focused on samples of males. As a result, there is only a limited amount of research on potential sex-specific differences in the way these behaviors may be expressed. As mentioned previously, women may express antisocial behavior either in less severe forms (e.g., Frick, et al., 1989) or in the form of somatization symptoms (Frick, et al., 1995). Similarly, girls may express aggressive tendencies less often in physical aggression and more often in relational aggression (e.g., teasing, excluding others from play) (Crick & Grotpeter, 1995). In addition, these sex-specific differences in the way antisocial tendencies are expressed may differ across the lifespan. For example, prior to adolescence, girls may show a number of the vulnerabilities to antisocial behaviors that are shown in boys (e.g., family dysfunction) but may not begin showing overt antisocial and aggressive and behaviors until they reach adolescence (Silverthorn & Frick, 1999). The way antisocial tendencies are manifested may again change in adulthood for women (Silverthorn & Frick, 1999). These issues are important in general for understanding the development of severe antisocial behavior. However, they are even more critical in studying the intergenerational link to such behavior where one needs to account for sex-specific manifestations when studying cross-generational linkages that may involve persons of both sexes (e.g., mother-son associations, father-daughter associations).

Fourth, much of the research reviewed in this chapter focused on risk factors to conduct disorders and the theoretical models that have used these risk factors to explain the link between antisocial disorders in parents and conduct disorders in their children. A critical focus that has been largely neglected in this research is a focus on the 'protective' mechanisms that might buffer against the development of antisocial behavior in a child who is predisposed to developing such behavior due to familial and temperamental risk factors. There is often a tendency to assume that, if a behavior pattern is related to a biologically based temperament, the pattern is unchangeable or best treated through biological interventions. The fallacy of this assumption is well documented in many areas of psychology (Plomin, et al., 1990). Temperaments place a child at risk for certain behavior patterns but these behavior patterns are shaped by the child's psychosocial context (Kagan & Snidman, 1991). Therefore, changes in a child's psychosocial context can clearly alter how his or her temperament is manifested.

Applying this reasoning to children with antisocial parents, if research continues to suggest that the intergenerational link is partly a function of an inherited temperamental predisposition, it becomes important to also understand what factors may help children with this temperament to channel their behavior into more prosocial avenues. One methodology for accomplishing this is to study children with the temperamental risk factor who do not develop conduct disorders to determine what factors differentiate them from children with the temperamental predisposition who go on to develop conduct disorders. Although there have been few explicit tests of such protective factors in children of antisocial parents, there are several likely candidates that can be tested. These include having a strong attachment with a parental figure (Constantino, 1996; Kochanska, 1995), having parents who emphasize positive reinforcement to socialize their children (Lykken, 1995), being involved and invested in prosocial activities (Hirschi, 1969; Wilson & Herrnstein, 1985), or being of higher intelligence (Kandel, et al., 1988). If such naturally occurring protective factors can be identified, it provides a compelling rationale for attempting prevention programs to enhance these factors when they do not occur naturally (e.g., enhance involvement with potential attachment figures, promote development of hobbies and talents, promote cognitive development).

In conclusion, the field has come a long way from early studies documenting the link between parental criminality and juvenile delinquency. We have begun to disentangle the processes involved in this intergenerational link and several key issues for future research in this area have been uncovered. Attention to these issues is critical, not only for furthering our understanding of the link between antisocial disorders in parents and their children, but for using this knowledge to design prevention programs to alter this cycle of antisocial behavior. Therefore, this is not only an intriguing body of research for social scientists, it is a body of research that can have very important and beneficial applications for society.

REFERENCES

Achenbach, T. M. (1991). *Manual for the Child Behavior Checklist/4-18 and 1991 Profile.* Burlington, VT: University of Vermont, Department of Psychiatry.

American Psychiatric Association. (1994). *Diagnostic and statistical manual of mental disorders* (4th ed.). Washington, DC: Author.

Baron, R. M. & Kenny, D. A. (1986). The moderator-mediator variable distinction in social psychological research: Conceptual, strategic, and statistical considerations. *Journal of Personality and Social Psychology, 51,* 1173–1182.

Biederman, J., Munir, K., & Knee, D. (1987). Conduct and Oppositional Disorder in clinically referred children with Attention Deficit Disorder: A controlled family study. *Journal of the American Academy of Child and Adolescent Psychiatry, 26,* 724–727.

Bohman, M., Cloninger, C.R., von Knorring, A. L., & Sigvardsson, S. (1984). An adoption study of Somatoform Disorders: III. Cross-fostering analysis and genetic relationship to alcoholism and criminality. *Archives of General Psychiatry, 41,* 872–878.

Christian, R., Frick, P. J., Hill, N., Tyler, L. A., & Frazer, D. (1997). Psychopathy and conduct problems in children: II. Subtyping children with conduct problems based on their interpersonal and affective style. *Journal of the American Academy of Child and Adolescent Psychiatry, 36,* 233–241.

Cleckley, H. (1976). *The mask of sanity* (5th ed.). St. Louis, MO: Mosby.

Cloninger, C. R. & Guze, S. B. (1975). Hysteria and parental psychiatric illness. *Psychological Medicine, 5,* 27–31.

Cohen, J. (1977). *Statistical power analysis for the behavioral sciences* (rev. ed.). New York: Academic.

Constantino, J. N. (1996). Intergenerational aspects of the development of aggression: A preliminary report. *Journal of Developmental and Behavioral Pediatrics, 17,* 176–182.

Crick, N.R. & Grotpeter, J. K. (1995). Relational aggression, gender, and social-psychological adjustment. *Child Development, 66,* 710–722.

DiLalla, L. F. & Gottesman, I. I. (1991). Biological and genetic contributors to violence—Widom's untold tale. *Psychological Bulletin, 109,* 125–129.

Downey, G. & Coyne, J. C. (1990). Children of depressed parents: An integrated review. *Psychological Bulletin, 108,* 50–76.

Eaves, L. J., Silberg, J. L., Hewitt, J. K., Rutter, M., Meyer, J. M., Neale, M. C., & Pickles, A. (1993). Analyzing twin resemblance in multisymptom data: Genetic applications of a latent class model for symptoms of Conduct Disorder in juvenile boys. *Behavior Genetics, 23,* 5–19.

Falconer, D. S. (1981). *Introduction to quantitative genetics.* London: Longman.

Faraone, S. V., Biederman, J., Keenan, K., & Tsuang, M. T. (1991). Separation of DSM-III Attention Deficit Disorder and Conduct Disorder: Evidence from a family-genetic study of American child psychiatric patients. *Psychological Medicine, 21*, 109–121.

Farrington, D. P. (1978). The family backgrounds of aggressive youths. In L. A. Hersov & M. Berger (Eds.), *Aggression and antisocial behavior in childhood and adolescence* (pp. 73–93). London: Pergamon Press.

Frick, P. J. (1993). Childhood conduct problems in a family context. *School Psychology Review, 22*, 376–385.

Frick, P. J. (1994). Family dysfunction and the Disruptive Behavior Disorders: A review of recent empirical findings. In T. H. Ollendick & R. J. Prinz (Eds.), *Advances in clinical child psychology* (Vol. 16, pp. 203–222). New York: Plenum Press.

Frick, P. J. (1998a). *Conduct disorders and severe antisocial behavior.* New York: Plenum Press.

Frick, P. J. (1998b). Callous-unemotional traits and conduct problems: A two-factor model of psychopathy in children. In R.D. Hare, D.J. Cooke, & A. Forth (Eds.), *Psychopathy: Theory, research, and implications for society* (pp. 161–187). Dordrecht, Netherlands: Kluwer Press.

Frick, P. J. & Jackson, Y. K. (1993). Family functioning and childhood antisocial behavior: Yet another reinterpretation. *Journal of Clinical Child Psychology, 22*, 410–419.

Frick, P. J. & Loney, B. R. (1999). Outcomes of children and adolescents with Oppositional Defiant Disorder and Conduct Disorder. In H. C. Quay & A. E. Hogan (Eds.), *Handbook of disruptive behavior disorders* (pp. 507–529). New York: Plenum Press.

Frick, P. J., Lahey, B. B., Hartdagen, S. E., & Hynd, G. W. (1989). Conduct problems in boys: Relations to maternal personality, marital satisfaction, and socioeconomic status. *Journal of Clinical Child Psychology, 18*, 114–120.

Frick, P. J., Lahey, B. B., Loeber, R., Stouthamer-Loeber, M., Christ, M. A. G., & Hanson, K. (1992). Familial risk factors to Oppositional Defiant Disorder: Parental psychopathology and maternal parenting. *Journal of Consulting and Clinical Psychology, 60*, 49–55.

Frick, P. J., O'Brien, B. S., Wootton, J. M., & McBurnett, K. (1994). Psychopathy and conduct problems in children. *Journal of Abnormal Psychology, 103*, 700–707.

Frick, P. J., Kuper, K., Silverthorn, P., & Cotter, M. (1995). Antisocial behavior, somatization, and sensation seeking behavior in mothers of clinic-referred children. *Journal of the American Academy of Child and Adolescent Psychiatry, 34*, 805–812.

Frick, P. J., Christian, R. C., & Wootton, J. M. (1999). Age trends in the association between parenting practices and conduct problems. *Behavior Modification, 23*, 106–128.

Glueck, S. & Glueck, E. (1968). *Delinquents and nondelinquents in perspective.* Cambridge, MA: Harvard University Press.

Goodman, J., Davidson, K. W., McGrath, P. J., Frick, P. J., Reddy, S. S. K., Jain, U., Zitner, D., & Taylor, M. (1997). Cholesterol and aggression (Letter to the Editor). *Journal of the American Academy of Child and Adolescent Psychiatry, 36*, 303–304.

Gray, J. A. (1982). *The neuropsychology of anxiety: An enquiry into the functions of the septo-hippocampal system.* Oxford, England: Oxford University Press.

Guze, S. B., Woodruff, R. A., & Clayton, P. J. (1971). Hysteria and antisocial behavior: Further evidence of an association. *American Journal of Psychiatry, 128*, 643–646.

Hare, R. D. (1993). *Without a conscience: The disturbing world of the psychopaths among us.* New York: Pocket.

Hare, R. D., Hart, S. D., & Harpur, T. J. (1991). Psychopathy and the DSM-IV criteria for Antisocial Personality Disorder. *Journal of Abnormal Psychology, 100*, 391–398.

Hatcher, L. (1994). *A step-by-step approach to using the SAS System for factor analysis and structural equations modeling.* Cary, NC: SAS Institute Inc.

Hinshaw, S. P., Lahey, B. B., & Hart, E. L. (1993). Issues of taxonomy and comorbidity in the development of Conduct Disorder. *Development and Psychopathology, 5*, 31–50.

Hirschi, T. (1969). *Causes of delinquency.* Berkeley, CA: University of California Press.

Holmbeck, G. N. (1997). Toward terminological, conceptual, and statistical clarity in the study of mediators and moderators: Examples from the child-clinical and pediatric psychology literatures. *Journal of Consulting and Clinical Psychology, 65*, 599–610.

Huesmann, L. R., Eron, L. D., Lefkowitz, M. M., & Walder, L. O. (1984). Stability of aggression over time and generations. *Developmental Psychology, 20*, 1120–1134.

Kagan, J. & Snidman, N. (1991). Temperamental factors in human development. *American Psychologist, 46*, 856–862.

Kandel, E., Mednick, S. A., Kierkegaard-Sorensen, L., Hutchings, B., Knop, J., Rosenberg, R., & Schulsinger, F. (1988). IQ as a protective factor for subjects at high risk for antisocial behavior. *Journal of Consulting and Clinical Psychology, 56*, 224–226.

Kochanska, G. (1993). Toward a synthesis of parental socialization and child temperament in early development of conscience. *Child Development, 64*, 325–347.

Kochanska, G. (1995). Children's temperament, mothers' discipline, and security of attachment: Multiple pathways to emerging internalization. *Child Development, 66*, 597–615.

Lahey, B. B., Hartdagen, S. E., Frick, P. J., McBurnett, K., Connor, R., & Hynd, G. W. (1988). Conduct Disorder: Parsing the confounded relation to parental divorce and antisocial personality. *Journal of Abnormal Psychology, 97*, 334–337.

Lahey, B. B., Piacentini, J. C., McBurnett, K., Stone, P., Hartdagen, S., & Hynd, G. (1988). Psychopathology and antisocial behavior in the parents of children with Conduct Disorder and hyperactivity. *Journal of the American Academy of Child and Adolescent Psychiatry, 27*, 163–170.

Lahey, B. B., Russo, M. F., Walker, J. L., & Piacentini, J. C. (1989). Personality characteristics of the mothers of children with Disruptive Behavior Disorders. *Journal of Consulting and Clinical Psychology, 57*, 512–515.

Lahey, B. B., Hart, E. L., Pliszka, S., Applegate, B., & McBurnett, K. (1993). Neurophysiological correlates of Conduct Disorder: A rationale and a review of research. *Journal of Clinical Child Psychology, 22*, 141–153.

Lilienfeld, S. O. (1992). The association between Antisocial Personality and Somatization Disorders: A review and integration of theoretical models. *Clinical Psychology Review, 12*, 641–662.

Lilienfeld, S. O., Van Valkenburg, C., Larntz, K., & Akiskal, H. S. (1986). The relationship of Histrionic Personality Disorder to Antisocial Personality and Somatization Disorders. *American Journal of Psychiatry, 143*, 718–721.

Liskow, B., Penick, E. C., Powell, B. J., Haefele, W. F., & Campbell, J. L. (1986). Inpatients with Briquet's Syndrome: Presence of additional psychiatric syndromes and MMPI results. *Comprehensive Psychiatry, 27*, 461–470.

Loeber, R. & Stouthamer-Loeber, M. (1986). Family factors as correlates and predictors of juvenile conduct problems and delinquency. In M. Tonry & N. Morris (Eds.), *Crime and justice* (Vol. 7, pp. 29–149). Chicago: University of Chicago Press.

Lykken, D. T. (1995). *The antisocial personalities*. Hillsdale, NJ: Lawrence Erlbaum Associates.

Mason, D. A. & Frick, P. J. (1994). The heritability of antisocial behavior: A meta-analysis of twin and adoption studies. *Journal of Psychopathology and Behavioral Assessment, 16*, 301–323.

McCord, J. (1979). Some child-rearing antecedents of criminal behavior in adult men. *Journal of Personality and Social Psychology, 37*, 1477–1486.

McCord, J. (1991). The cycle of crime and socialization practices. *Journal of Criminal Law and Criminality, 82*, 211–228.

Moffitt, T. E. (1993). Adolescence-limited and life-course persistent antisocial behavior: A developmental taxonomy. *Psychological Review, 100*, 674–701.

Moffitt, T. E., Caspi, A., Dickson, N., Silva, P., & Stanton, W. (1996). Childhood-onset versus adolescent-onset antisocial conduct problems in males: Natural history from ages 3 to 18 years. *Development and Psychopathology, 8*, 399–424.

O'Brien, B. S. & Frick, P. J. (1996). Reward dominance: Associations with anxiety, conduct problems, and psychopathy in children. *Journal of Abnormal Child Psychology, 24*, 223–240.

Osborn, S. G. & West, D. J. (1979). Conviction records of fathers and sons compared. *British Journal of Criminology, 19*, 120–133.

Patterson, G. R. & Capaldi, D. M. (1991). Antisocial parents: Unskilled and vulnerable. In P. A. Cowan & M. Hetherington (Eds.), *Family transitions* (pp. 195–218). New Jersey: Lawrence Erlbaum Associates.

Patterson, G. R., Reid, J. B., & Dishion, T. J. (1992). *Antisocial boys.* Eugene, OR: Castalia.

Plomin, R., DeFries, J. C., & McClearn, G. E. (1990). *Behavioral genetics: A primer* (2nd ed). New York: Freeman.

Robins, L. N. & Helzer, J. E. (1985). *Diagnostic Interview Schedule—Version III-A.* St. Louis, MO: Washington University School of Medicine.

Robins, L. N., West, P. A., & Herjanic, B. L. (1975). Arrests and delinquency in two generations: A study of black urban families and their children. *Journal of Child Psychology and Psychiatry, 16,* 125–140.

Rutter, M., Macdonald, H., Le Couteur, A., Harrington, R., Bolton, P., & Bailey, A. (1990). Genetic factors in child psychiatric disorders- II. Empirical findings. *Journal of Child Psychology and Psychiatry, 31,* 29–83.

Shaffer, D., Fisher, P., Piacentini, J., Schwab-Stone, M., & Wicks, J. (1993). *The NIMH Diagnostic Interview Schedule for Children—Version 2.3.* New York: Columbia University.

Shelton, K. K., Frick, P. J., & Wootton, J. M. (1996). The assessment of parenting practices in families of elementary school-aged children. *Journal of Clinical Child Psychology, 25,* 317–327.

Silverthorn, P., & Frick, P. J. (1999). Developmental pathways to antisocial behavior: The delayed-onset pathway in girls. *Development and Psychopathology, 11,* 101–126.

Stewart M. A., deBlois, C. S., & Cummings, C. (1980). Psychiatric disorder in the parents of hyperactive boys and those with Conduct Disorder. *Journal of Child Psychology and Psychiatry, 21,* 283–292.

Tapscott, M., Frick, P. J., Wootton, J. M., & Kruh, I. (1996). The intergenerational link to antisocial behavior: Effects of paternal contact. *Journal of Child and Family Studies, 5,* 229–240.

West, M. O. & Prinz, R. J. (1987). Parental alcoholism and childhood psychopathology. *Psychological Bulletin, 102,* 204–218.

Widom, C. S. (1991). A tail on an untold tale: Response to 'Biological and Genetic Contributors to Violence—Widom's Untold Tale.' *Psychological Bulletin, 109,* 130–132.

Wilson, H. (1975). Juvenile delinquency, parental criminality and social handicap. *British Journal of Criminology, 15,* 241-250.

Wilson, J. Q. & Herrnstein, R. (1985). *Crime and human behavior.* New York: Simon and Schuster.

Wootton, J. M., Frick, P. J., Shelton, K. K., & Silverthorn, P. (1997). Ineffective parenting and childhood conduct problems: The moderating role of callous-unemotional traits. *Journal of Consulting and Clinical Psychology, 65,* 301–308.

Zigler, E., Taussig, C., & Black, K. (1992). Early childhood intervention: A promising preventative for juvenile delinquency. *American Psychologist, 47,* 997–1006.

CHAPTER 7

Growing Up in an Alcoholic Family

Structuring Pathways for Risk Aggregation and Theory-Driven Intervention

Hiram E. Fitzgerald, W. Hobart Davies, & Robert A. Zucker

The University of Michigan-Michigan State University (UM-MSU) Longitudinal Study is a prospective study of children at high risk for the later development of alcoholism with high antisocial co-occurring psychopathology, as well as high risk for a wide variety of intraindividual, interpersonal, and sociocultural difficulties, including the development of other psychopathology, social complications, poor school achievement, poor physical health status, marital difficulties and divorce, lower levels of occupational achievement, and earlier death (Zucker, Fitzgerald, & Moses, 1995a).

The core model guiding the work since the study's initiation has been a risk-cumulation model of aggressive behavior, negative affect, and alcohol involvement that is both probabilistic and dynamic (Fitzgerald, Davies, Zucker, & Klinger, 1994a; Zucker, 1987, 1991; Zucker & Fitzgerald, 1991; Zucker, et al., 1995a). We propose that the developmental sequence for the emergence of such co-occurring psychopathology is regulated by familial aggressive behavior, negative affect, and alcohol use; that is embedded within a genetic vulnerability for such attributes; and then shaped by parents who model disorganized and addictive behaviors, which, in turn, serve to organize emergent intraindividual cognitive-affective schemas that are context-bound. All of these familial and intraindividual characteristics are hypothesized to be nested in social ecologies that provide maintenance structures for aggressive behavior and alcohol and other drug use (Fitzgerald et al., 2002; Zucker et al., 1995a; Zucker & Fitzgerald, 1997). This vulnerability structure increases the likelihood that the child will select peer networks that are high in aggression, negative mood, and substance use. The familial and peer structures facilitate the development of an expectancy structure about drugs that is positive toward use and relatively less negative toward abuse of alcohol and other drugs (Zucker & Fitzgerald, 1991; Zucker, Kincaid, Fitzgerald, & Bingham, 1995b). In turn, this structure promotes early onset of alcohol use, heavier drinking, alcohol abuse and problematic involvement of other drugs. Maintenance structures increase risk for clinical outcomes involving alcohol abuse/dependence with co-occurring antisociality, personality disorder, depression, and other expressions of psychopathology.

We have explored the degree to which there is risk aggregation in adults, both at the individual and familial levels. This work lead us to the concept of 'nesting structure,' and to the hypothesis that the clustering of co-active symptomatology, social dysfunction, alcoholism severity, and assortative coupling will be present in a subset of adult alcoholic families (what is referred to in the adult diagnostic literature as the subtype of antisocial alcoholism), and that this aggregation structure changes the developmental pathways supporting risk cumulation because the variable network determining the causal structure is stochastic, not hard-wired by either genetic or environmental determinism (Fitzgerald, Zucker, & Yang, 1995; Zucker, 1987, 1991; Zucker, et al., 2000).

IMPACT OF RISK LOAD ON MALE FUNCTIONING

The literature on the etiology of alcoholism provides a basis for concluding that this adult syndrome may be antedated by several child variables, including difficult temperament and problem behavior, especially externalizing behavior. In an effort to identify the earliest possible appearance of such dysregulation, Fitzgerald, et al. (1993) found that 3-year-old male children of alcoholics (COAs) were more impulsive in a delay of gratification task. Hierarchical regression analyses indicated that maternal, but not paternal, depression and lifetime alcohol problems predicted children's total problem behaviors. For example, the sons of alcoholic fathers were three times (odds ratio = 2.94) more likely to rank in the clinical range for Total Behavior Problems (TBP). A seven point difference in Stanford-Binet IQ between sons of alcoholics and sons of controls was comparable to that reported by other investigators with older subjects (Jacob & Leonard, 1986).

How does one move from the vulnerability structure to early onset of problem drinking and a longer-term trajectory, given the possibility of multiple diatheses, multiple individual risk factors, multiple environments, and the overall heterogeneity of this population (Fitzgerald, et al., 1995; Fitzgerald, Mun, Zucker, Puttler, & Wong, 2001; Zucker, et al., 1995a, 2000)? Part of the answer to this question involves the degree of fit between parent and child behavior, a topic frequently discussed within the context of child temperament.

TEMPERAMENT AND PROBLEM BEHAVIOR

A number of studies have linked difficult temperament to heightened risk for the development of alcoholism and related psychopathology (Caspi, Moffitt, Newman, & Silva, 1996; Jansen, Fitzgerald, Ham, & Zucker, 1995). Children with difficult temperament also are predisposed to a variety of behavioral disorders which, in childhood, may manifest themselves as Conduct Disorder and/or Attention-Deficit Hyperactivity Disorder, and in adulthood as Antisocial Personality Disorder and/or alcoholism (Tarter, Moss, & Vanyukov, 1996; see Table 7-1). Although the causal linkage between difficult temperament and problem behavior in childhood, and antisociality and alcohol abuse in adulthood is far from clear, the weight of the evidence suggests that a child with a difficult temperament, reared in a high risk environment, is at increased risk for the development of behavioral problems that antedate the emergence of antisocial behavior, alcoholism, or related psychopathology.

We tested several hypotheses related to temperament and problem behaviors (Jansen, et al., 1995). The first hypothesis predicted significantly more difficult temperaments in children whose Child Behavior Checklist TBP scores exceeded the clinical cutoff (98th percentile) than in children whose scores fell below the cutoff. Boys in the Clinical group had higher motor activity levels, poorer attention spans and higher levels of distractibility, were more reactive in

Table 7-1 Hypothetical developmental pathway to biobehavioral dysregulation

Age Period	Possible Expression
Core diathesis	Genetically mediated neural deficits Monoaminoergic system deficits
Prenatal	Exposure to alcohol
Infancy	Difficult temperament
Preschool	Externalizing problem behavior Social withdrawal
Childhood	Conduct problems Oppositional behavior Impulsivity Social withdrawal
Adolescence	Delinquency Substance use/abuse
Adulthood	Antisocial personality Criminality Substance use/abuse

Reprinted with permission from Fitzgerald, H. E., Puttler, L. I., Mun, E.-Y., & Zucker, R. A. (2000). Prenatal and postnatal exposure to parental alcohol use and abuse. In J. D. Osofsky & H. E. Fitzgerald (Eds.), *WAIMH handbook of infant mental health: Vol. 4. Infant mental health in groups at high risk* (pp. 121–159). New York: Wiley.

their everyday activities, and had more arrhythmic eating and sleeping patterns than did boys in the Non-Clinical group. The differences shown were robust, with all significant comparisons showing moderate to strong effect sizes. The higher levels of motor activity and distractibility, combined with poor rhythmicity and attention span in the Clinical group suggest that these boys have more difficulty with self-regulation and self-control than the boys in the Non-Clinical group. Significant predictors of boys' problem behavior scores, for both Clinical and Non-Clinical groups, concentrated on paternal perceptions of their sons' temperament, as well as the father's antisocial behavior. We also found that the relationship between difficult temperament and children's problem behavior was stronger when parental alcoholism was factored in.

Because the UM-MSU study is longitudinal, we are able to focus on such issues as the relative continuity and discontinuity of organizational processes and behaviors over the life course, including special concern for models of risk cumulation. As indicated in Table 7-2, boys rated in the clinical range for behavior problems had more difficult temperaments, were more likely to show continuity in risky behavior across the transitional period in early development than from preschool to elementary school, and were more likely to have an anti-social alcoholic father (Behling, Bingham, Fitzgerald, & Zucker, 1996; Fitzgerald, Puttler, Mun, & Zucker, 2000). In fact, the link between temperament and behavior problems is affected by the dosage of psychopathology to which the child is exposed (Mun, Fitzgerald, von Eye, Puttler, & Zucker, 2001). For preschool-age boys exposed to parents with two or more lifetime diagnoses of psychopathology (alcoholism, Antisocial Personality Disorder), high activity, high reactivity, and short attention span predicted externalizing behavior

Table 7-2 Continuity and discontinuity in Child Behavior Checklist Total Behavior Problems and difficult temperament in sons of alcoholics

	Number of Children in CBCL Rating Categories		Change in Clinical and Nonclinical Ratings			Probability of Child Rated as Having Difficult Temperament	Probability of Child Having an Antisocial Alcoholic Father
	Time 1	Time 2	T1	T2	Percentage		
Clinical	80	68	NC	NC	52	Lower	Lower
			C	C	20	Higher	Higher
			C	NC	16		
Nonclinical	135	147					
			NC	C	11	Increased	

Note: Sample = 215 Families [41 Antisocial Alcoholic Families (AAL), 90 Non-Antisocial Alcoholic Families (NAAL), and 84 Control families]. CBCL Total Behavior Problems Clinical Cutoff: >98th Percentile. NC = NonClinical Category on CBCL; C = Clinical Category on CBCL. Difficult Temperament (DT): High Activity, Low Attention span, Low Adaptability, Low Rhythmicity, and High Reactivity. Adapted from Behling, Bingham, Fitzgerald, & Zucker (1996). Reprinted with permission from Fitzgerald, H. E., Puttler, L. I., Mun, E.-Y., & Zucker, R. A. (2000). Prenatal and postnatal exposure to parental alcohol use and abuse. In J. D. Osofsky & H. E. Fitzgerald (Ed.), *WAIMH handbook of infant mental health: Vol. 4. Infant mental health in groups at high risk* (pp. 121–159). New York: Wiley.

problems, whereas withdrawal predicted internalizing problems. For boys exposed to parents with less parental psychopathology, only reactivity predicted externalizing problems. Linkages between externalizing and internalizing behavior problems were not evident when the boys were 3–5 years of age, but they were when the boys were 6–8 years of age.

Differences between the sons of alcoholic and non-alcoholic fathers provide continuing evidence of the heightened risk experienced by the sons of alcoholics. In addition, these results provide additional support for an emergent 'principle' in the general developmental psychopathology literature; namely, that an aggregate of risk factors has dramatically stronger predictive power than any single risk indicator with respect to developmental outcome (Zucker, et al., 1995a, 2000).

In these, as in other studies involving parental report of children's behavior, the question arises as to which parent has the more accurate perception of their child's behavior. Fitzgerald, Zucker, Maguin, and Reider (1994b) compared high risk mother-father concordance on ratings of the son's aggression on the Child Behavior Rating Scale (aggression scale), the Child Behavior Checklist (aggression) and the Conners Conduct Problems subscale. All correlations were different than zero, suggesting a common core to parental perceptions. As fathers spent more time alone with their sons, their perceptions of their sons moved from low order correlations with their wives' perceptions (.2's) to significantly higher levels of agreement (.6's).

Several studies document higher levels of externalizing problem behavior in COAs compared with nonCOAs (Loukas, Fitzgerald, Zucker, & von Eye, 2001; Zucker & Fitzgerald, 1991) and these behaviors are related to social support, life stress, and harsh discipline (Muller, Fitzgerald, Sullivan, & Zucker, 1994) as well as to marital conflict. Muller, et al. demonstrated that children exposed to harsh, physically punitive parenting had greater levels of aggressive behavior. This parent-to-child transmission of child maltreatment may have intergenerational roots. For example, Kirsch, Fitzgerald, and Zucker (1994) found that grandparental harshness of discipline was the strongest predictor of parental antisocial behavior, followed by socioeconomic status, and lifetime alcohol problems. Thus, for many of the children in the study, exposure to antisociality, parental aggression, and family conflict is part of a multi-generational legacy that is partially embedded within the context of low socioeconomic status (Fitzgerald & Zucker, 1995).

PARENTAL CHARACTERISTICS AND CHILD RISK

Effects of Socioeconomic Status

Pallas (1991) compiled demographic information for each of the 67 census tracts over the four county region from which the longitudinal sample was recruited. Using tract-level data as the unit of analysis, Pallas found the highest rates of alcoholic families occurred near the central part of the largest urban city in the population area. Correlations between total rates of appearance of alcoholic families and census tract level of urbanization were .34 for court-recruited alcoholics and .42 for community recruited alcoholics. Again at the tract level, both individual and family median incomes were inversely related to rates of recruitment of alcoholic families ($-.51$ and $-.44$ respectively). As predicted, there were positive correlations between rates of alcoholic families and the percentage of families living below the poverty level (.64 for the court recruited alcoholism rate, and .67 for the community-recruited alcoholism rate). Pallas also found that elevated rates of alcoholism at the census tract level corresponded with elevated rates on other indices of family stress (separation, divorce, public assistance, female heads of households, renter occupied households). Pallas' analysis suggests that at the community context level, indices of status, including family income, operate in a meaningful way to enhance or maintain the vulnerable environments in which children of alcoholics are reared. In addition, at the individual level unit of analysis, such measures, including income, occupational prestige, and education, repeatedly account for 5 to 10 % of the variance and/or emerge as significant mediators or moderators of proximal influences on child outcome (Fitzgerald & Zucker, 1995; Zucker, et al., 2000).

Parent-Child Relationship Difficulties

Whipple, Fitzgerald, and Zucker (1995) examined parent-child interaction patterns in a randomly selected subset of alcoholic and nonalcoholic families from the longitudinal study. Each parent-child dyad was observed in three standard 10-minute situations: Child-Directed Play (CDP), Parent-Directed Play (PDP), and Clean Up (CU). During the PDP and CU sessions, nonalcoholic parents were better able to keep their children on task and had greater dyadic synchrony—they were better connected and better able to read and respond to each other's cues. Children in nonalcoholic families maintained greater proximity during PDP: When the parent selected the toys, these children were better able than children of alcoholic parents to maintain physical and psychological closeness. Nonalcoholic parents facilitated self-regulation during cleanup and provided more supportive directions which increased their child's chance of success. Alcoholic parents made more demands for self-reliant behavior during CDP. Children from alcoholic families displayed an increased level of negative affect when with their fathers. It also took father-child dyads longer to clean up. These data suggest the possibility that parents, especially fathers, in alcoholic families have expectancies for child competence that are inconsistent with the developmental competencies of preschool-aged children.

Alcohol Subtypes

Our interest in subtyping and in the patterning of differences across the continuum of risk, raised the question of whether risk aggregation within alcoholic families would be even more concentrated if parental alcoholism was characterized by way of life course variations in associated co-active psychopathology. We classified alcoholic men on the basis of the presence or absence of a sustained history of antisocial behavior over their lifetime (cumulative cluster analyses); those with a patterns of alcoholism in adulthood along with a lifetime history of high antisociality were categorized as Antisocial Alcoholics (AAL), and those without this sustained history were categorized as NonAntisocial Alcoholics (NAAL) (Zucker, 1987, 1994; Zucker, Ellis, & Fitzgerald, 1994).

This classification strategy proved highly effective (see Table 7-3). For example, AALS are more likely to have a history of childhood behavior problems, illegal behavior, frequent arrests, and chronic lying (Zucker, et al., 2000), relationship disturbances (Fitzgerald, et al., 1993; Ichiyama, Zucker, Fitzgerald, & Bingham, 1996), failed relationships (Loukas, Bingham, Fitzgerald, & Zucker, 1997), depression and family violence (Ellis, Zucker, & Fitzgerald, 1997); neuroticism (Piejak, Twitchell, Loukas, Fitzgerald, & Zucker, 1996), poor

Table 7-3 Characteristics for fathers and mothers in Antisocial Alcoholic (AAL), Nonantisocial Alcoholic (NAAL) and Control families ($N = 311$)

Rating Scale	Groups							
	AAL		NAAL		Controls			
	M	SD	M	SD	M	SD	F	p
Father								
Age	31.19[ab]	5.81	33.36[a]	5.20	32.98[b]	4.56	3.83	.02
LAPS	11.59[ab]	1.88	10.13[a]	1.70	7.42[b]	1.59	122.23	.00
ASB	20.53[ab]	11.37	9.07[a]	5.08	5.29[b]	3.80	193.18	.00
EDU	12.00[ab]	1.64	13.55[ac]	2.28	14.65[bc]	2.08	28.28	.00
Wais								
PIQ	89.22[ab]	14.78	98.74[ac]	18.04	104.28[bc]	17.15	12.84	.00
VIQ	88.84[ab]	13.99	96.13[ac]	6.17	102.55[bc]	17.49	12.43	.00
IQ	86.93[ab]	13.47	96.84[ac]	15.90	109.11[bc]	14.97	20.33	.00
Mother								
Age	28.32[ab]	4.26	31.69[a]	4.49	31.53[b]	3.86	14.28	.00
LAPS	10.41[ab]	2.67	10.28[a]	2.13	9.05[b]	1.31	13.84	.00
ASB	7.41[ab]	4.32	4.76[ac]	3.60	3.38[bc]	2.49	24.21	.00
EDU	12.34[ab]	1.52	13.40[a]	2.16	13.59[b]	1.72	8.56	.00
Wais								
PIQ	107.54	18.35	114.34	19.50	114.03	19.02	2.74	ns
VIQ	85.18[ab]	12.83	91.42[a]	13.75	93.95[b]	15.94	6.55	.00
IQ	93.09[ab]	14.28	99.82[a]	14.90	101.25[b]	13.65	6.32	.00
Family								
SES	257.9[ab]	91.6	344.33[ac]	145.36	400.45[bc]	166.32	17.60	.00

Note: LAPS = Lifetime Alcohol Score, ASB = Antisocial Behavior Score, EDU = Years of Education, PIQ = WAIS Performance IQ Score, VIQ = WAIS Verbal IQ Score, and IQ = WAIS Total Score. All *df* (2, 281) or higher. .00 = *p* significant at <.01.

[a] AAL differ from NAAL. [b] AAL differ from Controls. [c] NAAL differ from Controls.

achievement and cognitive functioning (Ichiyama, et al., 1996; Zucker, et al., 1995b), and low SES (Fitzgerald & Zucker, 1995). There is also evidence of assortative mating among the AALS, suggesting that the 'nesting environment,' or contextual structure, within which high family history for alcohol offspring are reared also has a substantially higher contextual risk load (Bingham, Zucker, & Fitzgerald, 1996). Wives of AALs have higher antisociality as well as more nonantisocial psychopathology. Ichiyama, et al. (1996) found that marital relationships among the AALs were characteristized by more open expressions of hostile and disaffiliative behaviors, and greater potential for control struggles. AAL husbands were viewed as more separating and controlling toward their wives. Moreover, there is a clear relationship between level of parental aggression and violence in alcoholic families and parent-to-child aggression as well as child-to-parent aggression.

In short, AAL parents, and to a lesser extent NAAL parents, provide a rearing environment that is risky (Table 7-4) and likely to provide the maintenance structures necessary to sustain continuity of pathways leading to poor child outcomes (also see Ellis, et al., 1997; Fitzgerald, Zucker, Puttler, Caplan, & Mun, 2000).

Table 7-4 Composite indicators of risky rearing environments provided by alcoholic parents, and risky behaviors characteristic of three- to eight-year-old sons of alcoholics

---

Children's Risky Rearing Environment
Parental History of Regulatory Dysfunction
Parental History of Psychopathology
   Antisocial Personality Disorder
   Depression
Parental Relationship Disturbance
Parental Poor Value Structure
Parental Cognitive Deficiency
Family Low Socioeconomic Status
Risk-Aggregated Community

Children's Risky Behaviors
Self-Regulatory Dysfunction
Difficult Temperament
Disorganized Attachment
Externalizing Problem Behavior
Parent-Child Relationship Disturbance
Internal Models for Alcohol Use and Alcohol-Linked Behavior
Poor Value Structure
Cognitive Deficiency
High-Risk Peer Network

Reprinted with permission from: Fitzgerald, H. E., Puttler, L. I., Mun, E.-Y., & Zucker, R. A. (2000). Prenatal and postnatal exposure to parental alcohol use and abuse. In J. D. Osofsky & H. E. Fitzgerald (Ed.), *WAIMH handbook of infant mental health: Vol. 4. Infant mental health in groups at high risk* (pp. 121–159). New York: Wiley.

Impact of Parental Subtype on Child Outcomes

Cross-sectional comparisons at Time 1, as well as longitudinal analyses indicate that risky rearing environments are strongly correlated with children's risky behaviors (see Table 7-4). Children in alcoholic families had higher levels of hyperactivity (Ham, Fitzgerald, Piejak, & Zucker, 1994; Jansen, et al., 1995), earlier evidence of negative mood (Fitzgerald, et al., 1993), more problematic social relationships (Maguin, Zucker, & Fitzgerald, 1994), greater deficits in cognitive functioning (Noll, Zucker, Fitzgerald, & Curtis, 1992; Poon, Ellis, Fitzgerald, & Zucker, 2000), higher levels of aggressive behavior (Muller, et al., 1994), and more precocious acquisition of cognitive schemas about alcohol and other drugs (Zucker & Fitzgerald, 1991; Zucker, et al., 1995b).

Moreover, negative parent characteristics (aggressiveness, hyperactivity, negative mood, problematic social relationships, cognitive deficits, early onset aggressiveness, and precocious knowledge about alcohol), potentiate the appearance of child risk factors (Fitzgerald, et al., 1995; Whipple, et al., 1995; Zucker, et al., 1995a), suggesting that parental subtype may serve to differentiate child outcomes (see Table 7-5). Moreover, these outcomes may have differential impact on family functioning. Results show that during both early childhood (Time 1) and the early school years (Time 2), significant behavioral differences exist between the children from families with different alcoholic subtypes (Bingham, et al., 1996; Zucker, Ellis, Bingham, & Fitzgerald, 1996a). For example, externalizing and internalizing behaviors are greatest among the children of AAL at both assessment periods. In addition, as preschoolers, the AAL boys showed more signs of hyperactivity and scored higher on a

Table 7-5 Parent ratings of child Internalizing, Externalizing, and Total Behavior Problems on the Child Behavior Checklist (CBCL), and children's Stanford-Binet IQ among Antisocial Alcoholic (AAL), Nonantisocial Alcoholic (NAAL), and Control families ($N = 311$)

Rating Scale	Groups							
	AAL		NAAL		Controls			
	M	SD	M	SD	M	SD	F	p
Fathers' CBCL								
Internal	6.23[b]	5.00	5.74[c]	4.31	4.33[bc]	3.85	4.25	.02
External	14.37[ab]	8.05	12.20[ac]	6.21	9.70[bc]	5.77	9.44	.00
Total BP	20.60[b]	11.81	17.94[c]	9.52	14.02[bc]	8.73	8.55	.00
Mothers' CBCL								
Internal	6.44	1.09	5.22	3.82	4.69	3.65	2.33	.10
External	16.08[ab]	8.68	12.42[a]	6.77	11.09[b]	5.77	9.40	.00
Total BP	22.53[ab]	14.83	17.64[a]	9.36	15.79[b]	7.95	7.68	.00
Binet IQ	98.79[b]	14.64	103.26[c]	13.96	107.90[bc]	13.55	7.70	.00

Note: All *df* (2, 291) or higher.
[a] AAL differ from NAAL.   [b] AAL differ from Controls.   [c] NAAL differ from Controls.

measure of risky temperament than did the boys from the NAAL and control families. Other analyses indicate that these differences exist not only in the level of overall group effects but in extremes of behavior. That is, significantly more boys from AAL homes than from NAAL or control homes were classified in the clinical range on externalizing behavior problems (Behling, et al., 1996; Jansen, et al., 1995; Zucker, Ellis, Fitzgerald, Bingham, & Sanford, 1996b). Moreover, these differences are evident in multiple contexts and by observers other than parents. For example, data presented in Table 7-6 indicate that first grade teachers differentiate children of AALs, NAALs, and Controls on four of five scales assessing perceptions of children's developmental status. Although teacher ratings of child aggression, activity, likeability, and attractiveness did not differentiate among the groups, in every instance, the means were in the expected direction, with children of AALs scoring lowest. When asked to project child performance in middle school, teachers projected the poorest school performance for children of AALs (Table 7-6, Expected Outcome). Teachers also report less interest in children's school performance among AAL parents than NAALs or Controls. These results are especially interesting because teachers are completely unaware of study design and family groupings. Finally, teachers' reports are supported indirectly by findings that sons of AAL do more poorly on actual measures of academic achievement and intellectual functioning than do sons of NAAL or controls (Poon, et al., 2000).

Finally, using SEM, we have found that separate process models for the AAL, NAAL, and control families better describe the relationships among the different variables than does one overall model. This finding implies that

Table 7-6 Teachers' ratings of child behavior and development and parent interest in children's school performance among children of Antisocial Alcoholic (AAL), Nonantisocial Alcoholic (NAAL), and Control families ($N = 195$)

Rating Scale	Groups							
	AAL		NAAL		Controls			
	M	SD	M	SD	M	SD	F	p
Development								
Emotional	2.70[ab]	.75	3.20[a]	.75	3.11[b]	.78	4.97	.00
Physical	2.97[a]	.41	3.37[a]	.71	3.21	.70	4.30	.02
Social	2.77	.85	3.07	.93	3.09	.84	1.58	ns
Language	3.00[ab]	1.00	3.40[a]	.86	3.57[b]	.84	4.59	.01
Intellectual	3.16[ab]	.97	3.49[b]	.91	3.76[b]	.78	5.57	.01
Aggressiveness	2.74	.89	2.86	.93	2.83	.91	.21	ns
Activity Level	3.00	.73	3.11	.66	3.29	.85	2.02	ns
Likeability	3.74	.93	4.00	.92	4.12	.88	1.91	ns
Attractiveness	3.55	.62	3.81	.85	3.86	.83	1.65	ns
Expected Outcome	4.03[b]	1.07	3.58	1.26	3.23[b]	1.29	7.22	.01
Parent Interest	3.39[ab]	1.05	3.96[a]	.98	4.20[b]	.91	7.79	.00

Note: All *df* (2,190) or higher.

[a] AAL differ from NAAL. [b] AAL differ from Controls. [c] NAAL differ from Controls.

the pathways of influencing structure for development differ among the three groups and tentatively suggests that the mechanisms of risk development may be specific to subtypes. This suggests that there are multiple pathways within which risk aggregates, and that risk cumulation models of developmental psychopathology are best conceptualized as stemming from both continuous and discontinuous processes. For example, the different trajectories describing development of the difficult temperament-clinical problem behavior relationship (Behling, et al., 1996) supports the hypothesis that a continuity model of maladaption may fit best with AAL families, whereas a discontinuity model may provide a better fit with NAAL families.

Impact of Risk Load on Girls Functioning

With respect to issues related to the etiology of alcoholism in females, the direct connection between father's alcoholism (Chassin, Curran, Hussong, & Colder, 1996) and his violence, and the mother-to-daughter alcoholism relationship are reasonably well documented, but little is known about the causal mechanism or life-course events that mediate or moderate these relationships, especially with respect to development during preschool and childhood years. One noncontextual hypothesis to account for such variation is that the processes governing the variability are the same for girls as they are for boys, but that substantial quantitative differences in relevant parameters determine differences in outcome. Another hypothesis is that the relative importance and predictive value of different elements in the causal structure leads to a different causal matrix for girls than for boys. It is likely that both of these hypotheses are correct to a degree and to set them up as competing is to ignore the manner in which they may both operate. The analytic task therefore becomes one of determining when one causal structure fits better than the other.

One potential difference in the causal matrix for boys and girls may be the degree to which disorders of affect regulation may be symptomatic of etiology in girls relative to boys. During childhood, depressive symptoms are slightly more prevalent in boys than in girls. By mid-adolescence the pattern reverses so that by adulthood, depression is distinctively more characteristic of women than men. Nolen-Hoeksema and Girgus (1994) suggest that there is a diathesis for depression in girls that becomes manifest in relation to situation-specific challenges of adolescence, with the link between stress and context more likely to be characteristic of women than of men (Beckman, 1975). Thus, it may be that the alcohol-depression connection is to women as the alcohol-antisociality connection is to men.

Protective Factors for Females During the Early Childhood Years

Although mothers may play a protective role in the alcoholic family (Werner, 1986), little is known about the life course events of such women other than the fact that alcoholism is a recurrent theme in their family histo-ries (Russell, 1990). On the other hand, when pathology is nested within risky environments, protectiveness and risk may not represent ends of a continuum. In a study of preschool age male children of alcoholics, level of protectiveness failed to moderate the risk-damage relationship (Moses, Gonzales, Zucker, & Fitzgerald, 1993). In this study of 172 families from the first wave of the longi-tudinal study, levels of paternal alcohol problems, other parental psycho-pathology, and family environment all predicted boys' behavior problems. However, a moderating effect was observed for parental psychopathology, but not for family environment. Alcohol problems predicted behavior problems only in the presence of low levels of other psychopathology.

These findings suggest that a high incidence of parental psychopathology, in addition to alcohol problems, creates an environment so pervaded by chaos and trouble that no individual cause can be isolated, at the least, during the pre-school years and for boys. Bingham, et al. (1996) found that the children of AALs, NAALs, and Controls differed in the level of risk load they experience, with increased levels of alcohol-related psychopathology, reflected by parental alcohol typology, being positively related to the density (number of risk factors present simultaneously) and level (degree of severity) of risk factors present in their environments. As the density and level of risk factors increased, the likeli-hood for positive child development declined. In addition to their contribution to lower attained SES, the behavioral characteristics associated with the antiso-ciality and alcoholism of AALs disrupts their interpersonal interactions and rela-tionships, leads to greater alcohol consumption, increased emotional stress, and greater behavioral and emotional maladaptation (Ichiyama, et al., 1996).

Current evidence suggests that the search for protective factors should focus at the least on the density and severity of risk load, parental alcohol typology, and such intraindividual child characteristics as temperament and level of adaptive functioning (Loukas, et al., 2001). For example, daughters of AALs have lower levels of intellectual functioning than do daughters of NAALs or controls. Moreover, daughters of alcoholics (AALs or NAALs) have more CBCL total behavior problems than do controls (Puttler, Zucker, & Fitzgerald, 1996; Puttler, Zucker, Fitzgerald, & Bingham, 1998). Moreover, exposure to an alcoholic mother during the early school-age years is associated with more externalizing behavior in girls than is exposure only to an alcoholic father or exposure to both an alcoholic father and mother (Fitzgerald, et al., 2000). This finding contrasts with that reported by Mun, et al. (2001) for boys exposed to high dosages of parental psychopathology.

Effects of Marital Relationship

Analyses to date indicate that parental antisociality coupled with father's alcoholism can be linked to a trajectory of possible outcomes that involve not only a history of earlier onset of alcohol related difficulties, but also an adaptive course involving more damaged interpersonal relationships, a poorer social adaptation in both childhood and adulthood, and a concomitant cascade of other life failures that are derivative from the relationship problems. An important and well-established dimension in relationship functioning is interpersonal control. Ichiyama, et al. (1996) used Benjamin's (1993) Structural Analysis of Social Behavior (SASB) to evaluate perceptions of interpersonal control, in AALs and NAALs, and controls. Alcoholic men reported themselves to be more reckless and self destructive than nonalcoholics, and were less focused upon self-esteem and planfulness. Moreover, within the alcoholic group, AALs had a stronger propensity toward self-neglect than NAALs. Higher scores on self-neglect in the SASB system indicate a pattern of hostile independence turned inward on the self. According to Benjamin, this arena of the SASB system reflects a structure of internalized behavior indicative of being self-destructive, poorly planned and managed, impulsive, reckless, and rejecting of the self. The relationship findings indicated that AALs were more blaming and less trusting of their spouses than were NAALs and Controls. They blamed and put down their spouse, rather than themselves, and they trusted them less. These findings from Time I of the longitudinal study have explicit implications for marital stability, given the likelihood for significant separation/divorce over the course of the study (Loukas, et al., 1997).

Our results to date, therefore, have broad implications for the socialization of children of alcoholics in that fathers play a major role in the sex-role differentiation of their children (Lytton & Romney, 1991), and mothers carry major responsibility for care-provision during the early years of life. We do not know yet the extent to which father's behavior, including his interpersonal dynamics, becomes part of his son's emergent schema for what it is like to be a man, a husband, or a father, but we do know that for many boys the adage 'like father, like son' has a presence in reality (Solomon, Johnson, Zaitchik, & Carey, 1996), and that this reality appears to be taking shape as early as the preschool years.

A MODEL INTERVENTION TO AFFECT THE CO-ACTIVE PROCESS

The dynamic, co-active processes hypothesized here lead to several important tenets regarding intervention efforts with this population of risky kids growing up in risky environments. First, the multifactorial nature of the developmental phenomenon suggests that there are myriad possible foci for intervention that may have the potential for modifying or beginning to modify the developmental trajectory. For example, the child's developmental trajectory might be affected by changing any or all of the nature of the aggressive or negative interactions in the family system, improving the child's repertoire of coping responses, helping one or both parents to stop drinking, providing the child with a more appropriate adult role model on a regular basis, changing the parents' working models regarding childrearing, and providing the child with skills to help control his/her own impulsive or uninhibited behavior (Loukas, et al., 2001). Systemic principles dictate that interventions are most likely to create a change which is maintained and enhanced over time when they are targeted directly at aspects of the system which contribute to the genesis and maintenance of multiple negative outcomes (e.g., the aversive communication styles in the family), rather than isolating specific behavior problems for attention (impulsive behavior) or attempting change by working with only the child while ignoring the rest of the system. The majority of empirical attempts at intervention in this population have been focused on school-aged children and older, and have virtually ignored the family system (see review by Williams, 1990).

The intervention effort must also remain aware of the impressive developmental inertia of the system which will need to be overcome in order to see impact on the developmental trajectory of the child. Many of the identified risks are relatively immutable (e.g., temperament) or represent behavioral or interactional patterns which have developed and been reinforced over a much larger percentage of the life course than the interventions could ever attempt. Similarly, while there may be some changes that could be made which would reverberate in impacting several different life areas (a parent stopping drinking), there will always be many of the maintenance structures which are unaffected by even an aggressive systemic intervention. The developmental inertia is supported by the cognitive and emotional barriers which accompany all psychological interventions, ranging from myths and misconceptions about 'who' enters behavioral treatment, 'what' happens once you get there, and the reality that successful treatment is invariably hard work which runs the risk of causing unforeseen disruptions in other areas of the family system.

We present below a model intervention, the Michigan State University Multiple Risk Child Outreach Program (Zucker, Maguin, Noll, Fitzgerald, & Klinger, 1990), undertaken with awareness of many of the interconnecting risk factors present in the lives of these children and families. Families in this project were from the first wave (preschool-aged sons, mean age = 4.4 years) of the UM-MSU Longitudinal Study. Of the many potential targets, the conceptual focus chosen was aggressive and antisocial behavior in the child, and coercive interactions throughout the system, but especially within the parenting alliance. This focus reflects the realities that (a) antisocial behavior and aggression are a common finding for this population even at this age; (b) as such, parents are often already dealing with behavior management issues, or anticipating from earlier experiences that it will be part of being a parent, and so this may be a focus which engenders a greater degree of parental interest, motivation, and participation; (c) that antisociality is believed to be an important mediating factor between the earlier temperamental and behavioral challenges these children face and later alcoholism and co-active psychopathologies; (d) that coercive and aggressive interactions within the marital and parenting alliances serve as models for antisocial behavior in the child and undermine attempts by the parents to shape prosocial behaviors; and (e) a well-developed literature is available in this area to guide the structure of the intervention.

Description of the Intervention

The intervention regimen has been described in detail elsewhere (Maguin, et al., 1994; Nye, Zucker, & Fitzgerald, 1995; Zucker, et al., 1988). We will provide an overview of the content and structure here. After completion of the standard data collection visits, 65 families were randomized into treatment participation or a no-treatment control group. Participant families were further randomized into both-parents-participate ($n = 22$) and mother-only ($n = 20$) groups. The intervention was described as an educational intervention designed to 'enhance parent-child communication and improve parent-child relationships' since families were not necessarily identifying the target child as clinically in need of services. Families were required to remain intact in order to remain in the intervention. The protocol was a modification of the Social Learning Therapy protocol from the Oregon Social Learning Center to modify antisocial behavior in socially aggressive children (Patterson, Reid, Jones, & Conger, 1975).

Sessions were held weekly for 3 to 4 months during the skill acquisition phase, with one or two between session phone calls to support the practice and implementation of skills. This was followed by biweekly sessions for 6 months to reinforce the skills and deal with other issues that had arisen. Thus, the intervention typically consisted of 28 sessions over a 10-month period. The standard order of skill building was (a) tracking the child's behavior; (b) rewarding prosocial behavior (star charts and social reinforcement); (c) non-physical discipline (time out); and (d) marital communication skills. Families were encouraged to come into a clinic at a University based health center, but the option remained open to hold sessions in the family's home based on their preference, or clinical judgment that the treatment could be sustained better if carried out at home. Therapists were all advanced graduate students in clinical psychology or experienced clinical social workers who underwent 20 hours of training in the techniques of the intervention, and who had experience working with this or similar populations. Cases were supervised by one of two doctoral level psychologists with extensive experience in the area. To maximize consistency in the intervention, supervision was conducted in teams of three therapists, and the supervisors rotated between teams every 2 years.

Results to Date

Maguin, et al. (1994) have demonstrated that, at least over the period of time when the intervention is actively being completed, the intervention reduced antisocial behavior and increased prosocial behavior compared to the no-treatment control group. Children whose parents received the intervention in the two-parent condition showed greater increases in prosocial behavior than the children in the mother-only condition. This is partially confounded because the families in the two-parent condition showed a lower rate of completion of the program (55% vs. 85% for mother-only families) (Nye, et al., 1995), so the remaining families may represent a more motivated group.

The data suggest that improvements in child behavior are seen primarily during the early phases of the intervention, when the treatment is exclusively child focused and the schedule of sessions is more intensive (Zucker, et al.,

1990). Positive behavior change occurred only in that group of families where the mother not only completed the early sessions of the protocol, but showed high levels of investment in the process (Nye, et al., 1995).

It has been shown that the intervention can affect relevant behavioral symptomatology, but we do not yet know whether this intervention with these specific components delivered at this developmental time will be successful in leading to sustained systemic changes with subsequent alteration of the child's developmental trajectory. Early results do suggest that a longer period of maintenance support (perhaps much longer) will be necessary to maintain and extend progress. The appropriate developmental period to apply the intervention remains an important theoretical and empirical question, which can be restated as whether the intervention should be one of primary/secondary prevention in the preschool years (i.e., before the target children are showing clinical levels of behavioral difficulty) or one of secondary/tertiary prevention during the primary school grades (when most of these children will begin being labeled by schools and social institutions as having problems and behavior management at home becomes more problematic) (Zucker & Bermann, 1994). This question explicitly trades off issues of parental motivation driven by the level of problems they face, with the easier task of correcting problems before they have picked up more developmental momentum.

Applicability to minority populations is another important question that has started to be addressed through the University of Michigan Project on Family Intervention with Substance Abusing Families (Zucker & Bermann, 1994). This pilot program attempted to extend the intervention model to an African-American and Latino population with parents experiencing substance abuse problems, and also changed the developmental target for intervention to 6 to 11 year old children.

Lessons from the pilot work (Zucker & Bermann, 1994) suggested that these families presented with a more diverse range of family structures, and were grappling with a more debilitating array of life stresses ranging from basic family resources to legal system involvements that often necessitated a 'crisis management' approach from the therapists. Similarly, it was more often the case that issues related directly to the substance abuse needed to be directly addressed before the families could engage around the intervention protocol. These differences, no doubt, are associated both with the relative social standing of the different ethnic groups and the later developmental time period selected for the intervention with minority families. However, the pilot work also concluded that once the barriers presenting from the family context are neutralized, and if the developmental target is appropriately titrated, the intervention regimen showed promise.

All of these data speak to the difficulties of attempting to influence the powerful developmental inertia that these families have built up over years and generations. However, the developmental and systems models make clear that intervention attempts which deal with the child individually, which focus only on issues related to alcohol use (or any other isolated behavioral symptom), or which are targeted at the preadolescent period or later are almost certain to fail.

ACKNOWLEDGMENTS

Preparation of this work was supported in part by the National Institute on Alcohol Abuse and Alcoholism Grant AA07065 to R. A. Zucker and H. E. Fitzgerald. Correspondence concerning this chapter should be addressed to H. E. Fitzgerald, Assistant Provost University Research, 22 Kellogg Center, Michigan State University, East Lansing, MI, 48824. Electronic mail may be sent via Internet to fitzger9@msu.edu.

REFERENCES

Beckman, L. J. (1975). Women alcoholics: A review of social and psychological studies. *Journal of Studies on Alcohol, 36*, 797–824.

Behling, L. A., Bingham, C. R. Fitzgerald, H. E., & Zucker, R. A. (1996). Pathways into risk: Continuity and discontinuity in the difficult temperament-problem behavior relationship in sons of alcoholics. *Alcoholism: Clinical and Experimental Research. Supplement: NIAAA/ISBRA Abstracts, 20*, 81A.

Benjamin, L. S. (1993). *Interpersonal diagnosis and treatment of personality disorders.* New York: Guilford Press.

Bingham, C. R., Zucker, R. A., & Fitzgerald, H. E. (1996, August). *Risk load and problem behavior of children of alcoholics.* Poster presented at the meeting of the International Society of Behavioral Development, Quebec City, Quebec.

Caspi, A., Moffitt, T. E., Newman, D. L., & Silva, P. A. (1996). Behavioral observations at age 3 years predict adult psychiatric disorders. *Archives of General Psychiatry, 53*, 1033–1039.

Chassin, L., Curran, P. J., Hussong, A. M., & Colder, C. R. (1996). The relation of parent alcoholism to adolescent substance use: A longitudinal follow-up study. *Journal of Abnormal Psychology, 105*, 70–80.

Ellis, D. A., Zucker, R. A., & Fitzgerald, H. E. (1997). The role of family influences in development and risk. *Alcohol Health and Research World, 21*, 218–226.

Fitzgerald, H. E. & Zucker, R. A. (1995). Socioeconomic status and alcoholism: structuring developmental pathways to addiction. In H. E. Fitzgerald, B. M. Lester, & B. Zuckerman (Eds.), *Children of poverty* (pp. 125–147). New York: Guilford Press.

Fitzgerald, H. E., Sullivan, L. A., Ham, H. P., Zucker, R. A., Bruckel, S., & Schneider, A. M. (1993). Predictors of behavioral problems in three-year-old sons of alcoholics: Early evidence for onset of risk. *Child Development, 64*, 110–123.

Fitzgerald, H. E., Davies, W. H., Zucker, R. A., & Klinger, M. (1994a). Developmental systems theory and substance abuse: A conceptual and methodological framework for analyzing patterns of variation in families. In L. L'Abate (Ed.), *Handbook of developmental family psychology and psychopathology* (pp. 350–372). New York: Wiley.

Fitzgerald, H. E., Zucker, R. A., Maguin, E., & Reider, E. E. (1994b). Time spent with child and parental agreement about preschool children's behavior. *Perceptual and Motor Skills, 79*, 336–338.

Fitzgerald, H. E., Zucker, R. A., & Yang, H.-Y. (1995). Developmental systems theory and alcoholism: Analyzing patterns of variation in high risk families. *Psychology of Addictive Behaviors, 9*, 8–22.

Fitzgerald, H. E., Puttler, L. I., Mun, E.-Y., & Zucker, R. A. (2000). Prenatal and postnatal exposure to parental alcohol use and abuse. In J. D. Osofsky & H. E. Fitzgerald (Eds.), *WAIMH handbook of infant mental health: Vol. 4. Infant mental health in groups at high risk* (pp. 123–160). New York: Wiley.

Fitzgerald, H. E., Zucker, R. A., Puttler, L. I., Caplan, H. M., & Mun, E.-Y. (2000). Alcohol abuse/dependence in women and girls: Aetiology, course, and subtype variations. *Alcoscope: International review of alcohol management, 3*(1), 6–10.

Fitzgerald, H. E., Zucker, R. A., Mun, E. Y., Puttler, L. I., & Wong, M. M. (2002). Origins of addictive behavior: Structuring pathways to alcoholism during infancy and early childhood. In H. E. Fitzgerald, K. Karraker, & T. Luster (Eds.), *Infant development: Ecological perspectives* (pp. 221–252). New York: Routledge Falmer.

Ham, H. P., Fitzgerald, H. E., Piejak, L. A., & Zucker, R. A. (1994). Attention Deficit-Hyperactivity Disorder and related conduct problems: Explaining behavioral dysregulation in preschool-age sons of male alcoholics [Abstract]. *Alcoholism: Clinical and Experimental Research, 18*, 472.

Ichiyama, M. A., Zucker, R. A., Fitzgerald, H. E., & Bingham, C. R. (1996). Articulating subtype differences in self and relational experience among alcoholic men via structural analysis of social behavior. *Journal of Consulting and Clinical Psychology, 64*, 1245–1254.

Jacob, T. & Leonard, K. (1986). Psychosocial functioning in children of alcoholic fathers, depressed fathers, and control fathers. *Journal of Studies on Alcohol, 47*, 373–380.

Jansen, R. E., Fitzgerald, H. E., Ham, H. P., & Zucker, R. A. (1995). Difficult temperament and problem behaviors in three-to five-year-old sons of alcoholics. *Alcoholism: Clinical and Experimental Research, 19*, 501–509.

Kirsch, E. A., Fitzgerald, H. E., & Zucker, R. A. (1994). *Childhood contextual markers of adult antisocial behavior, lifetime problems with alcohol, and depression.* Paper presented at the annual meeting of the American Psychological Association, Los Angeles.

Loukas, A., Bingham, C. R., Fitzgerald, H. E., & Zucker, R. A. (1997). Antisocial comorbidity, depression, and stress: Prospective predictors of divorce/separation in alcoholic and nonalcoholic families [Abstract]. *Alcoholism: Clinical and Experimental Research, 21*(3), 99A.

Loukas, A., Fitzgerald, H. E., Zucker, R. A., & von Eye, A. (2001). Parental alcoholism and co-occurring antisocial behavior: Prospective relationships to externalizing behavior problems in their young sons. *Journal of Abnormal Child Psychology, 29*, 91–106.

Lytton, H., & Romney, D. M. (1991). Parents' differential socialization of boys and girls: A meta-analysis. *Psychological Bulletin, 109*, 267–296.

Maguin, E., Zucker, R. A., & Fitzgerald, H. E. (1994). The path to alcohol problems through conduct problems: A family based approach to very early intervention with risk. *Journal of Research on Adolescence, 4*, 249–269.

Moses, H. D., Gonzales, F., Zucker, R. A., & Fitzgerald, H. E. (1993). Predictors of behavior problems in preschoolers at risk for later alcohol abuse [Abstract]. *Alcoholism: Clinical and Experimental Research, 17*, 488.

Muller, R., Fitzgerald, H. E., Sullivan, L. A., & Zucker, R. A. (1994). Social support, child belligerence, and child maltreatment: A study of an alcoholic population. *Canadian Journal of Behavioural Science, 26*, 438–461.

Mun, E. Y., Fitzgerald, H. E., von Eye, A., Puttler, L.I., & Zucker, R. A. (2001). Temperament characteristics as predictors of externalizing and internalizing child behavior problems in the contexts of high and low parental psychopathology. *Infant Mental Health Journal, 22*, 393–415.

Nolan-Hoeksema, S., & Girgus, J. S. (1994). The emergence of gender differences in depression during adolescnece. *Psychological Bulletin, 115*, 424–443.

Noll, R. B., Zucker, R. A., Fitzgerald, H. E., & Curtis, W. J. (1992). Cognitive and motoric functioning of sons of alcoholic fathers and controls: The early childhood years. *Developmental Psychology, 28*, 665–675.

Nye, C. L., Zucker, R. A., & Fitzgerald, H. E. (1995). Early intervention in the path to alcohol problems through conduct problems: Treatment involvement and child behavior change. *Journal of Consulting and Clinical Psychology, 63*, 831–840.

Pallas, D. (1991). *The ecological distribution of alcoholic families: A community study in mid-Michigan.* Unpublished Master's Thesis, University of Wisconsin, Oshkosh, WI.

Patterson, G. R., Reid, J. B., Jones, R. R., & Conger, R. E. (1975). *A social learning approach to family intervention: Vol. 1. Families with aggressive boys.* Eugene, OR: Castalia.

Piejak, L. A., Twitchell, G. R., Loukas, A., Fitzgerald, H. E., & Zucker, R. A. (1996). Parental alcoholism, personality characteristics and antisociality: Influences on child behavior problems [Abstract]. *Alcoholism: Clinical and Experimental Research, 20*, 473.

Poon, E., Ellis, D. A., Fitzgerald, H. E., & Zucker, R. A. (2000). Cognitive functioning of sons of alcoholics during the early elementary school years: Differences related to subtypes of familial alcoholism. *Alcoholism: Clinical and Experimental Research, 24*, 1020–1027.

Puttler, L. I., Zucker, R. A., & Fitzgerald, H. E. (1996). Outcome differences among female COAs during early and middle childhood years: Familial subtype variations [Abstract]. *Alcoholism: Clinical and Experimental Research, 20*, 473.

Puttler, L. I., Zucker, R. A., Fitzgerald, H. E., & Bingham, C. R. (1998). Behavioral outcomes among children of alcoholics during the early and middle childhood years: Familial subtype variations. *Alcoholism: Clinical and Experimental Research, 22*, 1962–1972.

Russell, M. (1990). Prevalence of alcoholism among children of alcoholics. In M. Windle & J. S. Seales (Eds.), *Children of alcoholics: Critical perspectives* (pp. 9–38). New York: Guilford Press.

Solomon, G. E. A., Johnson, S. C., Zaitchik, D., & Carey, S. (1996). Like father, like son: Young children's understanding of how and why offspring resemble their parents. *Child Development, 67*, 11–171.

Tarter, R. E, Moss, H. B., & Vanyukov, M. M. (1996). Behavioral genetics and the etiology of alcoholism. In H. Begleiter & B. Kissin (Eds.), *The genetics of alcoholism. Alcohol and alcoholism* (Vol. 1, pp. 294–326). New York: Oxford University Press.

Werner, E. E. (1986). Resilient offspring of alcoholics: A longitudinal study from birth to age 18. *Journal of Studies on Alcohol, 47*, 34–40.

Whipple, E. E., Fitzgerald, H. E., & Zucker, R. A. (1995). Parent–child interactions in alcoholic families: Implications for psychological child maltreatment. *American Journal of Orthopsychiatry, 65*, 153–159.

Williams, C. N. (1990). Prevention and treatment approaches for children of alcoholics. In M. Windle & J. S. Searles (Eds.), *Children of alcoholics: Critical perspectives* (pp. 187–216). New York: Guilford Press.

Zucker, R. A. (1987). The four alcoholisms: A developmental account of the etiologic process. In P. C. Rivers & R. A. Diensthier (Eds.), *Alcohol and addictive behavior. Nebraska Symposium on Motivation, 1986: Vol. 34* (pp. 27–83). Lincoln, NE: University of Nebraska Press.

Zucker, R. A. (1991). The concept of risk and the etiology of alcoholism: A probabilistic-developmental perspective. In D. J. Pittman & H. R. White (Eds.), *Society, culture, and drinking patterns reexamined* (pp. 513–532). Piscataway, NJ: Rutgers Center of Alcohol Studies.

Zucker, R. A. (1994). Pathways to alcohol problems and alcoholism: A developmental account of the evidence for multiple alcoholisms and for contextual contributions to risk. In R. A. Zucker, J. Howard, & G. M. Boyd (Eds.). *The development of alcohol problems: Exploring the biopsychosocial matrix of risk* (pp. 255–289) (NIAAA Research Monograph No. 26). Rockville, MD: U.S. Department of Health and Human Services.

Zucker, R. A. & Bermann, E. (1994). *The MSU/U of M Family Intervention Program: Final report 1992–1994.* Unpublished manuscript, University of Michigan, Ann Arbor, MI.

Zucker, R. A. & Fitzgerald, H. E. (1991). Early developmental factors and risk for alcohol problems. *Alcohol Health & Research World, 15*, 18–24.

Zucker, R. A. & Fitzgerald, H. E. (1997). *Risk and coping in children of alcoholics: Years 11–15 of the Michigan State University-University of Michigan Longitudinal Study.* Unpublished grant proposal, NIAAA 07065.

Zucker, R. A., Maguin, E. T., Noll, R. B., Fitzgerald, H. E., & Klinger, M. T. (1990, August). *A prevention program for preschool children of alcoholics: Design and early effects.* Paper presented at the meeting of the American Psychological Association, Boston.

Zucker, R. A., Ellis, D. A., & Fitzgerald, H. E. (1994). Developmental evidence for at least two alcoholisms: I. Biopsychosocial variation among pathways into symptomatic difficulty. *Annals of the New York Academy of Science, 708*, 134–146.

Zucker, R. A., Fitzgerald, H. E., & Moses, H. (1995a). Emergence of alcohol problems and the several alcoholisms: A developmental perspective on etiologic theory and life course trajectory. In D. Cicchetti & D. Cohen (Eds.), *Manual of developmental psychopathology: Vol. 2: Risk, disorder, and adaptation* (pp. 677–711). New York: Wiley.

Zucker, R. A., Kincaid, S. B., Fitzgerald, H. E., & Bingham, C. R. (1995b). Alcohol schema acquisition in preschoolers: Differences between COAs and Non-COAs. *Alcoholism: Clinical and Experimental Research, 19*, 1011–1017.

Zucker, R. A., Ellis, D. A., Bingham, C. R., & Fitzgerald, H. E. (1996a). The development of alcoholic subtypes: Risk variation among alcoholic families during the early childhood years. *Alcohol Health & Research World, 20*, 46–54.

Zucker, R. A., Ellis, D. A., Fitzgerald, H. E., Bingham, C. R., & Sanford, K. (1996b). Other evidence for at least two alcoholisms: II. Life course variation in antisociality and heterogeneity of alcoholic outcome. *Development and Psychopathology, 8*, 831–848.

Zucker, R. A., Fitzgerald, H. E., Refior, S. K., Puttler, L. I., Pallas, D. M., & Ellis, D. A. (2000). The clinical and social ecology of childhood for children of alcoholics: Description of a study and implications for a differentiated social policy. In H. E. Fitzgerald, B. M. Lester, & B. Zuckerman (Eds.), *Children of addiction* (pp. 109–141). New York: Garland.

CHAPTER 8

Helping Children with Fetal Alcohol Syndrome and Related Conditions

A Clinician's Overview

HEATHER CARMICHAEL OLSON

This chapter presents an overview of the possible consequences for children born affected by maternal drinking during pregnancy, and discusses diagnosis, assessment, and intervention issues. A case history of Josie, a girl with FAS, is included in this chapter, and traces her story from birth to the start of middle school. Alcohol is a neurobehavioral teratogen—an agent that can cause defects in the structure and function of the developing central nervous system (CNS). Prenatal exposure to alcohol can interfere with the developing brain at many levels, altering its coordinated developmental schedule. As a result, alcohol exposure before birth can have long-term consequences for learning and behavior, and can potentially create lifelong disabilities. Alcohol effects are wide-ranging, occurring along a continuum. The most obvious impact is known as 'fetal alcohol syndrome' (FAS), while the partial expression of these problems has traditionally been known as 'fetal alcohol effects' (FAE) or, more recently, given labels such as 'alcohol-related neurodevelopmental disorder' (ARND).

This wide range of developmental disabilities, called here 'FAS and related conditions,' requires new thinking about diagnosis, assessment, and intervention. While surprisingly common, these disabilities can remain somewhat 'hidden' because they have not yet been well-described, and are still hard to easily and reliably diagnose. The problems of young alcohol-affected children may not be easily recognized at established timepoints for screening (such as at birth or kindergarten entry), or at the usual times for intake into early intervention. Alcohol-affected children's problems typically grow more obvious later in life, when diagnosis may be more reliably accomplished. Unfortunately, as children grow older, intervention can be harder to mobilize.

Research data from the reports of caregivers reveal that alcohol-affected individuals, from preschool through adulthood, often have complex and variable cognitive and learning deficits, and diverse difficulties in lifestyle and adaptive behavior (including a wide range of mental health problems) (Streissguth, Barr, Kogan, & Bookstein, 1996). Treatment issues differ depending upon whether an alcohol-affected child lives in adoptive or foster care, or in a birth family in recovery (or one in which the parents are still drinking). Ongoing and comprehensive intervention, though often needed, is frequently unavailable, and established or programmatic treatment strategies may not work in predictable ways. Each alcohol-affected client needs treatment planning that is individualized. Unfortunately, systematic research is not yet available to assist care providers in choosing treatment techniques. Because FAS and related conditions are preventable disabilities, intervention may need to expand beyond the child to focus on the larger family, requiring treatment providers to deal with new service systems and clinical issues. To accomplish prevention, providers may need to reach out to offer services to the birth mother, if she is still drinking—and beyond that treatment could extend to other affected siblings or to the larger family, if alcoholism is an intergenerational family problem. Assistance to families will differ depending upon whether the child lives with the birth parents (and if they are in recovery or still drinking), or whether the child is in foster or adoptive care. Clearly, clinicians working with FAS and related conditions often face complex treatment situations, as do the families. This chapter is designed to help clinicians better respond to this important set of developmental disabilities.

DIAGNOSIS, TERMINOLOGY, AND INCIDENCE

FAS is generally associated with heavy maternal alcohol use throughout pregnancy. Diagnosis is made by confirming the presence of a characteristic set of craniofacial abnormalities, pre- and/or postnatal growth deficiency, and evidence of CNS dysfunction (see Figure 8-1). In addition, individuals with FAS may show a wide range of non-specific physical abnormalities. Differential diagnosis is important to distinguish alcohol-related problems from syndromes that feature growth deficiencies and facial anomalies similar to those in FAS (e.g., fetal hydantoin syndrome), and from various genetic disorders and congenital syndromes that also show a complex pattern of cognitive and behavioral deficits. (For a complete diagnostic discussion, and a presentation of the debate and need for consistent clinical terminology, see *Fetal Alcohol Syndrome: Diagnosis, Epidemiology, Prevention, and Treatment*, published in 1996 by the Institute of Medicine (IOM).)

A history of confirmed prenatal alcohol exposure is usually essential to diagnosing teratogenic alcohol effects. However, it is possible to diagnose the full syndrome without confirmed maternal drinking—if the characteristic clinical expression is complete (and there is no confirmed *negative* exposure history). A relevant history of maternal exposure involves 'a pattern of excessive

Figure 8-1 Photograph of a sibling pair of children (male with FAS and female with ARND). The degree of facial dysmorphology seen in individuals with the full syndrome varies and, in general, the greater the extent of facial dysmorphology, the greater the level of cognitive impairment. In some individuals, the facial anomalies may not be noticed by a casual observer. The characteristic pattern of facial anomalies includes features such as short palpebral fissures (eye slits) and abnormalities in the premaxillary zone (e.g., flat or thinned upper lip, flattened philtrum, and flat midface.) Individuals with ARND do not show this characteristic set of facial features. ARND is currently defined as 'evidence of CNS neurodevelopmental abnormalities' and/or 'evidence of a complex pattern of behavior or cognitive abnormalities that are inconsistent with developmental level and cannot be explained by familial background or environment alone' (IOM, 1996; pp. 4–5). Individuals with both FAS and ARND can show behavior and learning problems. This photograph shows a heavily alcohol-exposed brother and sister. The older brother has full FAS, with mild mental retardation that was evident early in life and multiple behavior problems that are relatively manageable. He has always received special education services. His younger sister, who had a much more complicated and traumatic early life, has been diagnosed with ARND. Her IQ is in the average range, but as she has grown older she has shown evidence of subtle learning disabilities, lowered academic achievement, very high activity level and mood regulation problems, and has received psychiatric diagnoses of Post-Traumatic Stress Disorder and Generalized Anxiety Disorder. Management of her many behavioral issues is very complex.

intake characterized by substantial, regular intake or heavy episodic drinking' (IOM, 1996; p. 6), and one diagnostic system raises special concern about an exposure pattern that results in generally high peak blood alcohol concentrations delivered at least weekly in early pregnancy (Astley & Clarren, 1999). Clinicians should remember that diagnosis depends upon whether maternal alcohol use can be demonstrated *during pregnancy*, not necessarily later in the child's life.

Alcohol teratogenesis produces a continuum of effects, as revealed by a great deal of animal and epidemiological research. Therefore, it is accepted that many individuals prenatally exposed to high levels of alcohol will show some of the features of FAS, but not meet criteria for the full syndrome. For this group, the label of FAE has been used in much of the research and public discussion so far, and indicates that prenatal alcohol exposure is suspected as a cause of observed anomalies, but further confirmation is needed (NIAAA, 1997). However, FAE has not been well-described, and may not be a useful term outside animal or human population research in which maternal alcohol consumption is the independent variable under study (Aase, Jones, & Clarren, 1995). More useful to clinicians are diagnostic terms that refer to categories in which some of the features of FAS occur, and for which research has linked maternal alcohol ingestion to observed outcomes that are part of the category definitions. One category suggested by the IOM report (1996) is ARND (see Figure 8-1). Used when there is confirmed prenatal alcohol exposure, the diagnosis of ARND is currently defined as 'evidence of CNS neurodevelopmental abnormalities' and/or 'evidence of a complex pattern of behavior or cognitive abnormalities that are inconsistent with developmental level and cannot be explained by familial background or environment alone' (IOM, 1996; pp. 4–5). Systematic approaches to making alcohol-related diagnoses are evolving; One method was developed by Astley and Clarren (1999), and is available in the *Diagnostic Guide for Fetal Alcohol Syndrome and Related Conditions: The 4-Digit Diagnostic Code (second edition).* No matter what diagnostic system is used, a clinically important (even essential) addition to the diagnostic label is a clear presentation of the client's distinctive, individual pattern of deficits and strengths via an assessment that describes cognitive, behavioral, and (especially) functional skills.

Literature on the prevalence and epidemiology of FAS is far from consistent or conclusive. Passive surveillance systems, such as birth defects registries, generate figures that are too low because alcohol effects often are not evident at birth. Extrapolations from research studies suggest that the incidence of FAS ranges from 0.5 to 3.0 per thousand births in most populations, with some communities having much higher rates (IOM, 1996). Estimates vary depending on socioeconomic and ethnic factors. A commonly cited estimate of 1.9 per thousand births suggest that the incidence rate of FAS is considerably higher than that of Down syndrome or spina bifida (Streissguth, 1997). While difficult to evaluate, a recent congressional report indicates that, among heavy drinkers, 4.3% of children born annually have FAS (NIAAA, 1997), although not all children of mothers who are heavy drinkers will be born with the full syndrome. The IOM report (1996) states that the full range of alcohol-related disabilities, including FAS and other diagnosable alcohol-related birth defects or ARND designations, may occur on average in as many as 6 per thousand births. At present, clinicians should note that all estimates are considered conservative, and will be verified when diagnostic and surveillance methods improve.

While FAS is a clinically recognizable syndrome, the diagnosis cannot be made on the basis of any single distinctive feature or biochemical, chromosomal, or pathological test. In some cases, usually when babies are more severely affected, trained observers can make the diagnosis in infancy, but the characteristic facial dysmorphology is subtle and not always recognized in infants. When babies are referred, it is often because of the infant's growth problems or concern about maternal drinking behavior. It appears that an alcohol-related diagnosis is frequently made during the school years. Current data from a statewide system of FAS diagnostic clinics indicate that the average age of diagnosis of FAS is 8.9 years, and that 59% of all patients seen for alcohol-related diagnoses are between 5 and 14 years old (FAS Diagnostic and Prevention Network (DPN), 2000). The cognitive and social deficits seen in many alcohol-affected individuals become more apparent after infancy, the facial anomalies are most clearly detectable during childhood and, in some cases, growth retardation also becomes more noticeable at that time (Aase, 1994). It is quite possible for alcohol-affected individuals to go unrecognized until later life, and the diagnosis may be harder to make in adolescence and adulthood. Growth retardation often disappears at older ages (although head circumference does not tend to normalize with age (NIAAA, 1997)) and, given the midface development that occurs after puberty, the characteristic facial features may not be obvious in the alcohol-affected teenager or adult.

EVIDENCE OF CENTRAL NERVOUS SYSTEM (CNS) DYSFUNCTION AS 'PRIMARY DISABILITIES' IN LEARNING AND BEHAVIOR, AND RESULTING 'SECONDARY DISABILITIES' IN LIFESTYLE AND DAILY FUNCTION

It is the CNS dysfunction caused by prenatal alcohol exposure, not the facial dysmorphology or growth issues, that has the most serious consequences for the affected individual and her family. CNS dysfunction underlies the problem behavior that often leads to trouble in daily life. Early case reports on patients with FAS revealed clear deficits in adaptive function, including unusual or inappropriate social behaviors. The most commonly reported neurobehavioral disorders included diminished cognition, severe learning disabilities, hyperactivity, attention and memory deficits, and speech/language disorders (Rosett & Weiner, 1984; Streissguth, Aase, Clarren, LaDue, Randels, & Smith, 1991). Yet pioneering autopsy studies of patients with FAS revealed no constant, specific type of malformation or developmental disorder, and neurobiological research showed great diversity in teratogenic alcohol damage. This led researchers to speculate that alcohol-related CNS dysfunction would vary a great deal across individuals, with difficult patterns to define, but typically resulting in persistent deficits that could change form over the lifespan. Streissguth (1997), an expert on FAS, comments that 'although people with FAS/FAE exhibit some common characteristics, largely as a result of the brain damage they sustained before they were born, it is important to recognize their individuality, their uniqueness, and their own tempos and temperaments as well' (p. 127).

Evidence of CNS Dysfunction in 'Primary' Disabilities

There is a slowly accumulating body of data showing 'primary' disabilities in cognition and behavior, resulting from damage to the CNS, among alcohol-affected individuals. Informed by theoretical models of cognitive function and recent neuroimaging evidence, researchers have suggested that specific brain regions may be especially sensitive to the teratogenic effects of alcohol, and certain behavioral functions especially compromised. This remains open to debate, however, because of the diffuse and wide-ranging effects of alcohol's teratogenicity. In research to date, some patterns of CNS dysfunction can be discerned, but as yet there is no consensus. Existing data often come from mixed groups of clients with FAS and what has been termed FAE, so findings must be interpreted carefully. Clinicians should remember that while a teratogenic etiology is usually assumed for patterns of CNS dysfunction in alcohol-affected clients, the relationship between specific neurological damage and particular behaviors or patterns of behavioral development has not yet been well established (IOM, 1996). However, the clinical literature fits well with a body of experimental animal studies and epidemiological human data that do reveal patterns of alcohol teratogenesis (Driscoll, Streissguth, & Riley, 1990).

Only a small percentage of affected individuals show the full FAS, with obvious signs of brain damage such as seizures or microcephaly (Astley & Clarren, 1999; IOM, 1996). Across individuals, the CNS dysfunction associated with the impact of prenatal alcohol exposure varies in type of impairment and degree of severity. While overall intelligence can be compromised (Mattson & Riley, 1998), mental retardation is not always a defining characteristic of FAS, and is certainly not a defining characteristic of what might be called ARND. In clinical research on over 400 affected individuals by Streissguth, et al. (1996), for example, the average IQ of individuals with FAS actually fell within the borderline range (mean = 79), although with a broad range from 29 to 120. Importantly, the mean IQ of those with what was termed FAE was in the average range. Recent intake data from a diagnostic clinic network revealed that of 257 children with confirmed prenatal alcohol exposure who were referred for an evaluation of FAS/ARND, 72% had IQ scores in the normal range, but *all* had evidence of some type of cognitive/behavioral dysfunction (FAS DPN, 2001). Clearly, performance on an IQ test often does not adequately capture the full range of deficits (or the extent of functional compromise) arising from the teratogenic effects of alcohol.

Regardless of level of IQ, most individuals exposed to alcohol before birth do show a range of identifiable cognitive deficits—at a rate greater than that expected given their intellectual level (Kerns, Don, Mateer, & Streissguth, 1997). These deficits often occur across multiple domains of functioning, with different cognitive/behavioral profiles, and may not fit the definitions that will make an alcohol-affected individual eligible for special education, funding through developmental disabilities, or necessary social services. Because of the variability of alcohol-related damage, a wide-ranging assessment battery is necessary. But what *are* the functions potentially affected by prenatal exposure to alcohol? One clinically useful answer to this question is to think of alcohol-affected individuals as having 'primary disabilities' in the broadly-defined domains of: (a) neuromotor skills, sensory processing, and sensory-motor integration; (b) cognition and learning; and (c) speech and language.

In the neuromotor domain, recent clinical data suggest an increased prevalence of soft neurological signs among individuals with evidence of significant prenatal alcohol exposure (FAS DPN, 2001). Prenatal alcohol exposure appears to impact the developing motor system, with potential effects on multiple dimensions of motor function (Mattson & Riley, 1998). Alcohol-affected individuals also show deficits in sensory processing and sensory-motor integration. In fact, Streissguth (1997) highlights difficulty in modulating incoming stimuli as a hallmark feature of fetal alcohol effects, presumably across the lifespan. When compared with controls, for example, young children characterized as having FAS/FAE exhibited significantly more problems with touch, movement, visual and auditory stimuli, and taste/smell—and showed more problems in activity level, disorganization, and feeding and sleeping (all presumed as manifestations of poor sensory processing) (Morse & Cermak, 1994). Children with FAS commonly show impaired visual acuity and nearsightedness, with evidence from animal studies implicating alcohol as the causative factor (NIAAA, 1997), and also show high rates of central and peripheral hearing disorders (Church & Kaltenbach, 1997).

In the domain of cognition and learning, researchers working with patients with FAS/ARND have found deficits in complex visual-spatial skills, learning, and memory, impaired verbal learning with relatively unimpaired retention, and deficits in speed of central processing of information (e.g., Carmichael Olson, Feldman, Streissguth, Sampson, & Bookstein, 1998; Mattson, Riley, Delis, Stern, & Jones, 1996). In addition, academic achievement is often compromised (Mattson & Riley, 1998). Hyperactivity, often seen in younger alcohol-affected children, appears to evolve in adolescence into problems of distractibility and difficulties in cognitive and behavioral control (NIAAA, 1997). In particular, deficits in 'executive functioning' have consistently been identified among alcohol-affected individuals in the school-age years and adulthood, using tests of problem-solving, concept formation, planning ability, working memory, inhibitory control, and self-regulation (e.g., Carmichael Olson, Feldman, et al., 1998; Jacobson & Jacobson, 1997; Kodituwakku, Handmaker, Cutler, Weathersby, & Handmaker, 1995; Mattson, Goodman, Caine, Delis, & Riley, 1999). Executive functioning can be thought of in a global sense as regulation of novel, adaptive behavior, and shows protracted development over childhood and into early adulthood, becoming more prominent and necessary to successful performance on the tasks of daily life beginning in the school years. There is evidence that specific executive function skills, especially those involving inhibitory control, are powerful predictors of children's later behavioral development (Nigg, 2000; Nigg, Quamma, Greenberg, & Kusche, 1999) and adaptive functioning (Price, 2000). Deficits in executive functioning are related to enduring deficiencies in attention, often viewed as hallmark features of prenatal alcohol exposure (Riley & Mattson, 1997). Deficits in visual attention have been identified in children and adults (Carmichael Olson, Feldman, et al., 1998; Coles, Platzman, Raskind-Hood, et al., 1997; Kerns, et al., 1997), as have deficits in auditory attention using complex tasks with alcohol-affected adolescents and adults (Connor, Streissguth, Sampson, Bookstein, & Barr, 1999; Kerns, et al., 1997).

In the speech-language domain, a high prevalence and wide variety of deficits have also been documented among alcohol-affected individuals (Church, Eldis, Blakely, & Bawle, 1997), with relatively more deficits on measures of complex language functions. Clinicians have described individuals with FAS as showing a discrepancy between somewhat better verbal fluency and vocabulary, compared to a relatively poor ability to communicate and function in social situations (Carmichael Olson, 1994). Indeed, recent research on FAS has identified an apparent disruption in the development and use of the social-communicative functions of language, which 'allow people to exchange information, initiate and develop social relationships, cope with changing environmental demands, and assert one's needs, desires, and preferences' (Coggins, Friet, & Morgan, 1997; p. 2). These authors speculate that individuals with FAS do not seem to skillfully use their presumed language competence in the service of logical judgment, critical thought, and social problem solving.

Adaptive Behavior Problems

Unlike those with obvious physical handicaps, the broad range of often 'hidden' neuromotor, sensory, cognitive, and speech-language deficits among alcohol-affected individual—coupled with society's difficulty in recognizing these deficits—typically leads to debilitating problems in social adaptation and behavior. Adaptive behavior problems have consistently been noted in the clinical literature and systematic research (Streissguth, et al., 1991, 1996; Thomas, Kelly, Mattson, & Riley, 1998), including deficits in communication, daily living skills, and socialization. These problems go beyond what can be expected based solely on IQ. For both those with FAS and what was termed FAE, for example, Streissguth, et al.'s (1996) data showed significant shortfalls relative to IQ for adaptive behavior scores (drawn from a caregiver interview).

'Secondary' Disabilities

An interesting line of research has focused on 'secondary disabilities,' such as school disruption, mental health problems, or trouble with the law, that tend to develop in the lifestyle and daily function of many clients characterized as having FAS or FAE (Streissguth, et al., 1996). These secondary disabilities may be more appropriately treated if they are understood as an outgrowth of the client's 'primary' deficits in cognition, communication, and learning that can impact social competence. Secondary disabilities may also occur less often if the primary deficits are addressed sufficiently early in life.

To assess secondary disabilities, caregiver interview data covering the client's life history were obtained for 415 individuals with FAS or FAE, aged 6 to 51. These clients were typically referred for diagnostic evaluation because of cognitive and/or behavioral problems in the presence of prenatal alcohol exposure, and there was no comparison group. Many of these clients had disruptive environmental influences in their lives (Streissguth, et al., 1996). Findings revealed a high prevalence of problems in lifestyle and daily functioning across the lifespan. In the full sample, 94% of the clients were reported to show mental health difficulties and/or involvement in treatment, the prevalence of these problems was high no matter what the client's age, and 7 years was the median age of onset (Streissguth, 1997). Children with FAS/FAE showed concerning prevalence rates of other secondary disabilities: disruptions in school (16%); trouble with the law (14%); confinement for inpatient treatment or incarceration (9%); and inappropriate sexual behavior (30%). Combining figures for alcohol-affected adolescents and adults, reports of a history of disrupted school experiences, trouble with the law, a confinement experience, and inappropriate sexual behavior ranged from 49% to 60%, with 35% of these patients reported to have a history of alcohol/drug problems. Interestingly, for these secondary disabilities, patients 12 and older with a label of FAE showed higher rates in all categories than did those diagnosed with FAS.

Maladaptive behavior, and a variety of mental health and psychiatric conditions, have been noted among alcohol-affected individuals of all ages (Famy, Streissguth, & Unis, 1998; Roebuck, Mattson, & Riley, 1999). A clinical follow-up of 158 children with FAS, many with borderline IQ or below, showed a high rate of psychiatric and developmental disorders. For subjects in preschool and middle childhood, a leading diagnosis was 'hyperkinetic disorders,' with 'eating disorders' and 'enuresis' also relatively common during preschool, and the rates of these and most other problems increasing over time. From middle childhood through adolescence, what were termed 'emotional disorders,' 'habits/stereotypies,' and 'hyperkinetic disorders' occurred most often. Both parents and teachers completed behavioral checklists for school-aged children, with peaks on scales measuring problems of attention deficits and social relationships (Steinhausen & Spohr, 1998). Caregiver interview data has revealed that the three most frequent mental health problems in the history of alcohol-affected individuals were attentional deficit, depression, and suicide threats (Streissguth, et al., 1996).

In clinical samples such as these, clients are typically referred because of problems in behavior or adaptive function, so these data may show selective bias. In addition, the clinical samples studied so far may have had less opportunity for appropriate intervention than is now available. An initial report on one small sample of prospectively followed children characterized as having FAS/FAE did not reveal behavior or emotional problems at the rather early age of 7 years (Coles, Platzman, & Brown, et al., 1997). Further follow-up of these children and other prospective samples will be important in order to establish whether this pattern holds into the years in which psychopathology is more likely to occur.

THE BASIS FOR ALCOHOL EFFECTS

The IOM (1996) has presented a theoretical, multifactorial model of influences that can affect the expression of prenatal alcohol exposure, reproduced here as Figure 8-2 (and meant only as a partial list). As this model indicates, 'expression of adverse effects in the offspring from birth to adulthood can be influenced by factors that include the critical period during pregnancy when exposure occurs, the pattern and amount of maternal alcohol intake, and a host of biological and environmental variables that can possibly impact both the pre- and postnatal periods' (IOM, 1996; pp. 47–48). The many factors that can potentially mediate the impact of alcohol on outcome explain why there is such diversity in the individual expression of prenatal alcohol exposure.

Effects of Dose, Pattern, and Timing of Alcohol Exposure

Like other teratogens, the impact of alcohol depends on the amount, timing, pattern, and conditions of prenatal exposure. Cognitive and behavioral effects can occur even in the absence of obvious dysmorphology or abnormal growth, and some functional deficits may be detected only under challenging or stressful conditions (Riley, 1990). The CNS is sensitive to alcohol exposure during a prolonged developmental period, and thus can be affected even when exposure occurs only during the later part of pregnancy (NIAAA, 1997). In general, the specific type of birth defects produced depends on the system(s) in the fetus undergoing development at the time of exposure. Greater levels of exposure have been associated with more serious deficits, although subtle developmental consequences have been found in human and animal offspring after exposure to moderate doses of alcohol. Animal research has shown that alcohol is most damaging to the brain and severity of deficits are increased when consumption is concentrated in a short period of time; peak blood alcohol level is one critical factor in subsequent offspring effects (Band & West, 1996).

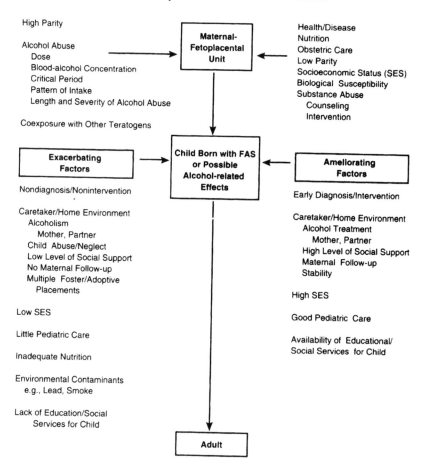

Figure 8-2 Theoretical influences on the expression of prenatal alcohol exposure. Reproduced with permission from *Fetal alcohol syndrome: Diagnosis, epidemiology, prevention, and treatment.* Copyright 1996 by the National Academy of Sciences. Courtesy of the National Academy Press, Washington, D.C.

Impact of Other Prenatal Influences

Not all alcohol-exposed individuals show deficits, and there are marked individual differences in vulnerability according to the conditions of exposure, as well as the influence of other biological and environmental factors. Twin studies show that alcohol's teratogenic effects can be modified by genetic differences in fetal susceptibility and resistance (Riikonen, 1994). Put briefly, some maternal characteristics apparently related to a greater chance of delivering a child with FAS are older age, higher parity, smoking, severity of alcoholism, fetal undernutrition, and perhaps poverty (Abel & Hannigan, 1996; Jacobson, Jacobson, & Sokol, 1996; Jacobson, Jacobson, Sokol, & Ager, 1998; NIAAA, 1997; Whitty & Sokol, 1996). Questions of differences by ethnicity and the interactions of maternal gestational use of alcohol and other drugs are also being investigated. Now being intensively studied are women who have already produced a child with FAS. It appears this is a very heterogeneous group, with many similarities to the larger population of substance-abusing women. Their histories include high rates of childhood maltreatment and mental health problems (Astley, Bailey, Talbot, & Clarren, 2000).

Impact of Postnatal Factors and a Diathesis-Stress Perspective

A 'diathesis-stress perspective' on development suggests that problems will emerge when an individual who is constitutionally vulnerable is exposed to a sufficient level and/or type of stressors. This perspective also implies that it may be possible to protect vulnerable persons from stressors that can mediate poor outcome. Taking this perspective, it is clinically important to identify vulnerabilities (whether biological and/or psychological), as well as environmental stressors and protective factors, among affected individuals. It is also important to understand the mechanisms by which stressors bring on problems in those who are vulnerable. It should also be useful to study the lives of those resilient to alcohol effects for further insight into protective influences (Weinberg, 1997), and to study outcome in groups at high risk for alcohol effects to identify markers for vulnerability.

Figure 8-2 displays presumed postnatal 'exacerbating' and 'ameliorating' factors. These postnatal factors, although generally known to impact developmental outcome, have not been adequately studied in alcohol-affected individuals. Stressors, such as problematic caregiving environments, do appear likely to occur in this population—perhaps more often than with other disabilities. For instance, alcohol-affected children must often deal with loss of their biological parents and shifts in home placement (IOM, 1996), or with life with a substance-abusing parent (who may also struggle with mental health problems).

Researchers studying over 400 clients characterized as having FAS/FAE examined a set of risk and protective factors potentially associated with occurrence of later lifestyle problems (or secondary disabilities). Eight protective factors emerged that almost uniformly were related to reduced odds that six major types of secondary disabilities would occur. According to these data, it appears protective for an individual with FAS/FAE to live in an adequate, stable, nurturant, or good quality home during an important time (or the majority) of life, to remain safe from personal violence, to apply and be eligible for social services because of developmental disabilities, to receive an early diagnosis (before age 6) and, interestingly, to have a diagnosis of FAS rather than a label of FAE. A diathesis-stress perspective suggests that the clinician should use treatments that can increase the presence or power of these protective influences in the lives of alcohol-affected individuals. Yet clinicians should remember that alcohol-affected individuals can still show clear disabilities even when raised in positive circumstances. For example, a recent follow-up study of alcohol-exposed adoptees showed they clearly had more mental health and substance abuse problems as adults than did non-alcohol-exposed adoptees (whether or not these these non-exposed adoptees had grown up with environmental risks) (Cadoret & Riggins-Caspers, 2000).

In speculating on how later psychopathology can begin, some clinical observers have emphasized the early relationship between parent and alcohol-affected child. Irritability and difficulties in behavioral regulation, activity, feeding, and sleeping among alcohol-affected infants may impair the process of bonding between parent and child, whether in a birth, foster, or adoptive home. For example, in programmatic research O'Connor and her colleagues found that birth mothers reporting moderate to high levels of alcohol consumption during pregnancy had infants displaying more negative affect in interaction with their mothers than did babies with less prenatal exposure. These more heavily drinking women engaged in less optimal interaction with their babies, the mother-infant pairs more often showed less secure attachment relationships, and the heavily exposed children showed higher self-reported depression at ages 5 to 6 years (O'Connor, 1996; O'Connor & Kasari, 2000). A disordered parent-child attachment lays the groundwork for disruption in a child's later behavior and relationships, and in what are called the child's 'internal working models' of social relationships. It is likely that the alcohol-affected child's emerging cognitive deficits can compound these problems over time. Expert clinicians have speculated that what are called 'attachment disorders' may occur with increased frequency among alcohol-affected children—in part due to abuse and neglect (when these have taken place), and in part because alcohol-related primary disabilities could interact with the environmental conditions that underlie this kind of psychopathology.

Thinking through how secondary disabilities emerge in individuals with FAS and related conditions over the lifespan, Streissguth's (1997) comments suggest the following process. Prenatal alcohol exposure (coupled with and modified by other prenatal factors) induces CNS dysfunction, shown in characteristics such as attentional deficits or memory problems, and perhaps altered reactivity to stress. This leads to observable dysfunctional behaviors (such as distractibility, evidence of mood swings, or not learning from experience) and real-world consequences (such as not completing goals and being criticized). Over time, a pattern of failure provokes increasing negative thoughts, attributions, and emotions in the alcohol-affected individual. These can underlie further behavioral problems, with resulting consequences in the real world, and a further rise in negative emotions. Unfortunate real-life outcomes develop, such as mental health problems, trouble in school or work, and/or substance abuse. Caregivers raising these affected individuals may respond in ways that do not work if they do not understand that the individual's maladaptive behavior arises at least partly from CNS dysfunction—but see it as coming primarily from causes such as lack of motivation or improper parenting. Frustrated caregivers may feel negatively about the affected individual, or about themselves, and these emotions can build over time. Living in an environment that lacks protective factors can worsen this growing cycle of problems.

At this stage, there is incomplete understanding of what stressful events usually occur in the lives of alcohol-affected individuals. These stressors may differ from those important in the lives of individuals with other developmental disabilities, because FAS and related conditions are relatively 'hidden' disabilities that are not well understood, and sometimes denied because of the stigmas attached to problem alcohol use. In today's world, alcohol-affected individuals are often expected to function independently when they cannot successfully do so, and families are expected to handle problems for which they may not be well-equipped. Such expectations may actually act as stressors, prompting the use of poor coping strategies (such as substance use). With increased societal understanding, and availability of appropriate services, such stressors may lessen in intensity, and child and family outcome may improve.

A Case History of a Girl with FAS (and Some Positive Comments!)

So far, this chapter has focused on discussing the problems of those with fetal alcohol effects, but parents and professionals caring for these individuals often speak of the value and joy these children and adults have added to their lives. A poll of parents involved in an internet discussion group, FASLink, yielded many positive comments about their children: *'FAS = funny and sweet,' '[my child has] an amazing ability to bounce back from failure, rejection and disappointment*, and *'he has given me unconditional love!'*. Streissguth (1997) describes the socially engaging, bright-eyed manner of many toddlers and preschoolers with FAS/FAE, and the developmental strides these youngsters may make upon arriving in a nurturing, stimulating home after early abuse and neglect. But true to her lifespan approach to FAS, Streissguth reminds clinicians that the behavioral picture can change. As the child matures, the positive may endure but difficulties can emerge. To achieve the best possible outcome, Streissguth stresses the importance of focusing on emotional well-being as a goal, and providing careful, individualized intervention and planning over time.

The experiences of families and professionals working with alcohol-affected children include many engaging, humorous, poignant, courageous, and optimistic tales, even though these stories also acknowledge the families' struggles with daily life. What follows is a case history of Josie, a girl with FAS, to give the reader a personal view of this disability and bring alive the discussion of diagnostic and treatment issues that follows.

An engaging, attractive, and energetic girl, Josie is now 12 years old. Her facial features are characteristic of FAS but over time have not alerted observers to a developmental disability, so that her alcohol-related problems remain somewhat 'hidden.' Josie has a history of developmental delay, notable memory deficits, persistent and pronounced temper tantrums as a toddler and preschooler, and an enduring pattern of impulsivity and mood lability. Her IQ has consistently been tested within the average range, with assessment at age 10 yielding a Full-Scale IQ score of 97. She lives with her adoptive family, who has cared for her since the age of 7 months. Josie's adoption came about largely because of parental termination of rights due to her mother's polydrug use. Josie's grandmother (with whom Josie was placed after birth) actually sought out this adoptive mother, who directed a daycare, because of her childrearing skill and patience, and the stable, consistent, and nurturant home this adoptive family could provide. Josie's mother relinquished her parental rights, as she did with her other children. Since that time, she has sought recovery and married, but has not had other children. Josie has not been in contact with her biological family since the age of 4.

Because her mother's prenatal drug use was well-known, Josie was evaluated at 3 years of age for fetal alcohol and drug effects, and was given a diagnosis of FAS by a physician specializing in birth defects—a service not commonly available at the time. Josie's early health problems, including persistent respiratory difficulties and ear infections, were initially thought by parents and teachers to explain her slowed developmental progress. At the age of 3, Josie was placed by her determined and knowledgeable adoptive family in a day treatment program for children with behavior and emotional problems, because of her prenatal drug exposure, possible hyperactivity, and history of difficult behavior in daycare. Placement in a day treatment program meant the staff was well-trained, therapeutic childcare techniques were used, and the teacher-child ratio was 1:2. But there were also drawbacks to this setting; for example, Josie initially imitated many of the deviant behaviors of her classmates. In preschool, Josie already showed great scatter in her abilities, often regressed or forgot skills, and did not learn in altogether predictable ways. School staff and family worked closely together to create a treatment plan that worked but could be changed on short notice given Josie's inconsistencies. The diagnosis of FAS was of benefit in helping teachers shape the classroom environment to facilitate Josie's development, by avoiding overstimulation and behavioral breakdowns, and setting realistic expectations. The teachers learned to let Josie know what was expected of her, rather than to discipline her for misbehavior. Josie's behavior improved dramatically, and her achievement, language skills, and learning rate were seen as close to age-appropriate during her later preschool years.

In the transition to the public schools, Josie qualified for special services based on her history of developmental difficulties, prior day treatment intervention, and FAS and ADHD diagnoses (the latter given to her at about age 5, but altered to Attention Deficit Disorder (ADD) when she reached age 9). With her parents as advocates, she was placed in a high quality school, and served using an inclusion model with resource room assistance. Her school psychologist was particularly knowledgeable about fetal alcohol effects, which helped to ensure appropriate, customized classroom intervention, and to maintain Josie's eligibility for special services even when improving academic progress meant that she did not easily fit within accepted service guidelines. Follow-up testing at age 8 through a local FAS diagnostic clinic provided data additional to that gathered by standard school assessment to help the multidisciplinary team hone Josie's goals.

Outside the school setting, multiple interventions were employed during these middle childhood years. Ritalin was prescribed and had a positive impact on behavior, which has maintained over time. Josie's family found they had to be more creative than with their previous children in developing interventions and coming up with meaningful behavioral consequences. They realized that what is motivating to Josie cannot be long-term or abstract; for example, she cannot be told to do her homework because she will then get good grades, but will be motivated by the idea that she will be the first one done, or that her teachers or peers will think well of her if she completes her work. Over time, her family learned to use relaxation techniques (such as saying: 'Breathe deep!'), which Josie actually began to use with classmates to help them stay calm. Josie's parents kept her enrolled in extracurricular activities that capitalized on her high energy level and built positive self-esteem. Yet minor and annoying behavior problems, arising in part from Josie's underlying CNS dysfunction, continued at home and at school. Josie continued to be highly active, was seen as 'bossy' by her peers, and had few friends. She was occasionally caught lying, or impulsively taking things that did not belong to her. She provoked her parents by crying out that she was being hurt (although no one was touching her) while at the grocery store. In first and second grades, she took certain ideas too literally; for example, unlike her classmates, she grew quite fearful that leprechauns might really appear on St. Patrick's Day when (for fun) her teachers pretended this was a possibility. Throughout these years, the FAS diagnosis helped her parents and teachers stay calm and understand why these odd behaviors might happen and why they might be difficult to change. Interestingly, Josie's ability to organize objects and plan, when playing board games or completing puzzles, was above average; she could win in a Chinese Checkers game even when vying with an adult. But her ability to organize herself, regulate her behavior and mood, succeed in social situations, and function independently have continued well below expectations for a child of her age and intellectual level.

Follow-up testing through an FAS diagnostic clinic at age 10 revealed some important, if subtle, deficits. A developmental neuropsychological assessment indicated that Josie had problems in auditory attention, verbal fluency, and sensory-motor integration, but strengths in executive functioning and visual-spatial function. (This is an unusual pattern according to the current research consensus, but only serves to show how variable the CNS dysfunction in this population can be.) These test findings may help maintain Josie's eligibility for special services as she moves on in school, and do suggest strategies to support learning. Specialized assessment of social communication, including underlying social-cognitive skills (such as what is called 'mental state reasoning'), indicated that Josie had difficulty assuming the perspective of another person and communicating effectively with her peers. These difficulties may contribute to her ongoing failure in social situations.

Intervention carried out so far with Josie may help to limit the potential cycle of dysfunctional behavior and negative emotions that FAS expert Streissguth has described. Thinking ahead is helpful too. More than with her *previous children, Josie's adoptive mother has for several years been planning the transition to middle school, with her greatest concern centering on how peers may view Josie and how, in turn, she may be influenced by them and come to choose her peer group. According to Josie's mother, there is apprehension about adolescence for any parent, but for children with alcohol effects there seem to be many 'horror stories;' she tries to have confidence and hope, and to remember how successful Josie has been so far—but she still has fears. Josie's mother continues to keep her daughter involved in positive activities such as soccer, piano, and perhaps soon a church group and therapeutic horseback riding. From a very young age, Josie's adoptive mother has consciously tried to educate her daughter about drugs, but worries about how Josie will make the transition from the 'concrete' idea that all smoking and drinking are bad, to more abstract realizations that these occur in society, and that she could engage in these behaviors but should not. Now that Josie is about to enter middle school, her parents have examined all possible schools in order to place her where she will fare best. Josie's mother says she hopes her daughter will be successful and wants to set up the right kind of environment for her, but is uncertain—as she visualizes the future—just what that environment will be.*

ISSUES FOR CLINICAL PRACTICE

The Diagnostic Process

Clinicians sometimes question the benefit of alcohol-related diagnoses in the belief that even without such labels problems can be adequately treated as they arise (Morse & Weiner, 1996). Yet as Josie's case history shows, an accurate alcohol-related diagnosis can have many benefits. A diagnosis can provide one important explanation for difficult behavior, and so lay the groundwork for more realistic expectations, make clear that secondary disabilities arise from primary cognitive and language problems, and help clinicians select appropriate behaviors to target for intervention. A diagnosis can help explain why medication response has been ineffective (when administered for clear target symptoms), or why problems have been resistant to psychosocial interventions that are typically effective. As a result, a diagnosis can prompt consideration of alternate treatments and/or provide eligibility for additional services or funding. An alcohol-related diagnosis can also lead to addiction treatment for the birth mother, when she can be identified and is willing to be involved, and thus to prevention of births of more children with FAS. Anecdotal observations suggest that the benefits of a diagnosis usually outweigh concerns that the label will stigmatize the client or the birth mother, create self-fulfilling prophecies, or provide an inappropriate excuse for antisocial behavior. Clinical experience shows that birth, adoptive, and foster parents all find the diagnosis useful. So far, however, there is limited empirical evidence on diagnostic utility. Data show only that early diagnosis of what has been termed FAS/FAE is associated with less frequent occurrence of later secondary disabilities (Streissguth, et al., 1996).

In clinical settings, it is essential to gather a comprehensive history of prenatal alcohol and other exposures, and to be alert for signs of facial anomalies, a history of growth impairment, and evidence of CNS dysfunction. Practical tools are being developed to screen for individuals who should be assessed further for alcohol-related diagnoses. For example, computerized morphometric analysis of facial photographs can identify a set of facial features best differentiating between children with and without a diagnosis of FAS with high sensitivity and specificity (unaffected by race, gender and age through 10 years) (Astley & Clarren, 1995). Behavioral checklists are also under development (Streissguth, Bookstein, Barr, Press, & Sampson, 1998).

A directory available through the Maternal and Child Health Clearinghouse has identified diagnostic expertise in virtually all 50 states (Morse & Barnwell, 2000). Even so, diagnostic services are still not widely and readily available. The process of diagnosis requires participation of qualified medical professionals with specific training in diagnosing alcohol effects, and with this complex population effective diagnosis and referral seems best implemented using a team approach (Li & Pearson, 1996). One promising team model is the Washington State FAS Diagnostic and Prevention Network (FAS DPN), a statewide system of diagnostic clinics staffed by multidisciplinary developmental assessment teams with specialized training in alcohol effects (Clarren, Carmichael Olson, Clarren, & Astley, 2000). The state of Alaska has also reported on the benefits of a statewide FAS diagnostic system (Li & Pearson, 1996).

Assessment of CNS Dysfunction

To confer an alcohol-related diagnosis and make appropriate referrals, the impact of prenatal alcohol exposure on brain structure and function must be evaluated, and ongoing follow-up evaluation can help shape a child's intervention program over time. Given the widely variable patterns of CNS dysfunction associated with prenatal alcohol exposure, the assessment process requires informed clinical judgment and a range of techniques. Diagnostic assessment guides are available (e.g., Astley & Clarren, 1999; Carmichael Olson, Clarren, Beck, Lewis, & Jirikowic, 1998; Coggins, 1998). Assessment techniques include caregiver interview and observations designed to assess behavior that suggests the presence of neurological impairment. Measurements of head circumference, data from neuroimaging or evaluation of neurophysiological function, and assessment of neurological status can provide evidence of hard or soft neurological signs. Evaluation of sensory-motor integration and neuromotor status provide information on outcome domains often affected by alcohol in younger clients. Psychiatric assessment and/or psychometric testing can provide information on affected domains and document co-occurring psychiatric conditions. For clients of preschool age or older, a standard psychological evaluation provides useful data, including measures of IQ, preacademic or academic achievement, adaptive function, and maladaptive behavior. Beyond this basic test battery can be added (as needed and developmentally appropriate) neuropsychological measures that assess processing speed and attention, memory, executive functions, and social-communicative competence.

Intervention Strategies

Early Diagnosis, Early Intervention, and the Potential for Change in Later Life

Early intervention has been generally shown to be effective for children with disabilities or environmental deprivation. Although there is as yet no systematic human research focused on the effectiveness of early intervention for alcohol-affected children, there are animal data suggesting that early handling or post-weaning environmental enrichment can alter or attenuate some but not all alcohol-induced deficiencies (Hannigan, Berman, & Sajac, 1993; Weinberg, Kim, & Ju, 1995). Given the plasticity of the young brain and the potential for early intervention to effect actual neurological change, treatment early in life might minimize alcohol's adverse impact on the CNS. Early intervention might also reduce the impact of stressors on a child made constitutionally vulnerable by prenatal alcohol exposure. For example, early intervention could improve the postnatal environment by helping caregivers respond more appropriately to the alcohol-affected child, perhaps enhancing the quality of the essential caregiver-child attachment relationship and laying a more secure foundation for later development. As described in the case history, Josie received early intervention which was thought to be very helpful.

Unfortunately, clinical observations suggest that 'diagnosis becomes increasingly less effective in improving outcomes if left unrecognized into adolescence and beyond' (IOM, 1996; p. 80). In research so far (with clearly affected clients), compensatory influences have been less important than originally expected for outcome in adolescence and young adulthood (Spohr, 1996). A small study of children born to alcoholic mothers suggests that early foster parenting did not eliminate the harmful effects of prenatal exposure by early adolescence, though some improvement was noted (Aronson & Hagberg, 1998). Yet if early intervention does not occur, alcohol-affected individuals should not be viewed as beyond help. Anecdotal data, and suggestive animal evidence, show that, with provision of appropriate family and community supports, there remains potential for improvement even if intervention begins after early childhood (Kleinfeld, Morse, & Westcott, 2000; Klintsova, Matthews, Goodlett, Napper, & Greenough, 1997).

Intervention at Multiple Levels Across the Lifespan

Josie's case history shows that clients with FAS and related conditions have a wide range of needs. 'Multi-level intervention' and a 'partnership of services' are needed for alcohol-affected individuals across the lifespan, including reliable and available diagnostic services, and appropriate, individualized medical, mental health, educational/vocational, and social services (Carmichael Olson, 1994; Kleinfeld, et al., 2000; Smith & Coles, 1991). Systems to provide alcohol treatment and recovery support, respite care and family crisis services, post-adoption support services, and long-term, consistent family support and consultation are especially needed, but are often inadequate. Family support is essential to prevent disruption of home placements for alcohol-affected children. Parent support groups and advocacy hotlines can provide help in these areas, and clinical observations support the value of these resources—which are springing up nationwide (Weiner & Morse, 1994). There are a growing number of self-help books, newsletters and videotapes, and internet sites and list-servs available to assist clients and their families. Support and ongoing consultation can also be obtained from professionals who understand alcohol-related diagnoses specifically and developmental disabilities in general, behavioral treatment and the possibilities of medication, how to access the full range of service systems, and how to be an effective advocate. The national directory available through the Maternal and Child Health Clearinghouse has identified providers with expertise in alcohol effects (Morse & Barnwell, 2000).

Clinicians working with older alcohol-affected individuals must face one of the central treatment problems for this group: Because the disabilities of these clients are not yet well recognized, services are often unavailable. Parents, like Josie's, must wrestle with this dilemma as their children grow up. Current guidelines for gaining access to SSI funding, DDD eligibility, and entry into special education or vocational rehabilitation programs often fail to capture the deficits of those with FAS and related conditions—who therefore may not qualify. Appropriate services may not even exist and yet are desperately needed. These include long-term group homes for individuals who are not significantly mentally retarded and/or have mental illness or correctional involvement (but are not appropriately served in jails or inpatient mental health facilities), specialized therapy for inappropriate sexual behavior, and parenting support programs for disabled alcohol-affected parents. Special services are needed for alcohol-affected women of childbearing age to accomplish both intervention and FAS prevention. Lack of services is a real problem for a population that frequently shows secondary disabilities. Clinicians may have to develop new programs or work toward changing eligibility criteria for existing services. Yet even when services do exist and alcohol-affected clients qualify for them, such services are rarely centralized and coordinated in the manner required by clients with multiple needs. Instead, it seems inevitable that these clients and their families will be served by many different elements of the service system, and clinicians must work to ensure coordination of all service elements and hold clinical services to the principles of individualized and tailored care. Another reality is that older alcohol-affected individuals may have legal, correctional, or judicial involvement. Clinicians may be asked to provide expert testimony, perform specialized psychological or psychiatric assessment for competency, diminished capacity, and decline/remand determinations (LaDue & Dunne, 1997), and make recommendations to inform judicial decisions and probation orders (Barnett, 1997).

Effectiveness of Medication and Recommendations for Medication Measurement

The effectiveness of psychotropic drugs for clients with FAS has not been well established (IOM, 1996). Alternative medication trials are needed (Weinberg, 1997), as is research on the safety of the often-used strategy of combined psychopharmacology (given the higher frequency of alcohol-related birth defects and attendant medical risks in this population) (O'Malley, 1997a). According to the IOM report (1996), alcohol-affected children are often referred for treatment of ADHD (with methylphenidate the drug tried first), but anecdotally success with this agent is less frequent than in children with ADHD of non-teratogenic cause. There has been initial discussion in the psychiatric literature about the relation between ADHD and FAS/FAE (O'Malley, 1994); some have suggested there are different pathways by which a child can have both problems, and so subsets of children who respond differently to various intervention techniques (Osterheld & Wilson, 1997). Literature on medication use with mentally retarded and brain-injured populations, and research on behavioral pharmacology in animals prenatally exposed to alcohol, may be relevant (O'Malley, 1997b). Given the widely variable CNS dysfunction induced by alcohol, response to medication dosage and type will likely be highly individual and require monitoring through multiple trials. For children, medication is only one component of a treatment program to be used after behavior management and parent counseling have been well established, and there may be heightened parental concern about medication use with a child already affected by substance exposure (Snyder, Nanson, Snyder, & Block, 1997). For alcohol-affected adolescents and adults, medication (if any) will likely be part of multimodal treatment (Streissguth & O'Malley, 1997).

Effectiveness of Clinical Approaches

Clinical experience indicates that programmatic treatment, a 'one size fits all' approach, is unlikely to address the complex interplay between the wide-ranging primary and secondary disabilities of many alcohol-affected clients, so that individual treatment planning is needed. At this point there are almost no empirical data on the effectiveness of psychosocial interventions for this population. Findings from early pilot programs focused on younger children with FAS showed that symptoms could be altered (though not eliminated) over the short-term, using techniques designed for other handicapped children (Morse & Weiner, 1996). Techniques may differ for school-age or older alcohol-affected clients. A case analysis of an 18-year-old with FAS showed that even comprehensive residential, educational, and vocational support services for individuals with developmental disabilities and brain injury may need modification (or extensions in eligibility) (Dyer, Alberts, & Niemann, 1997).

There is increasing momentum in the search for best practices for intervention with alcohol-affected individuals and their families, with a 'standard of care' conference held in Atlanta in 2001. Systematic research is sorely needed to evaluate whether recommended methods and programs are effective, and what aspects of intervention are unique to and/or critical for this population (IOM, 1996). Pilot studies so far have explored several intervention models, and shown that treatment is feasible and can sometimes be tied to existing service systems.

For alcohol-affected individuals and families at the very highest risk, one approach to intervention takes the form of intensive advocacy services and home visiting/mentoring programs. Grant and colleagues (Grant, Ernst, Streissguth, & Porter, 1997) describe an advocacy model useful for 'mothers with FAS/FAE,' or for high-risk birth parents raising alcohol-affected children. The Parent-Child Assistance Program involves a mentoring, one-on-one relationship between the birth parent and a paraprofessional staff member who acts as an advocate, involves the client's larger family, carries out an intensive program of home visiting, and helps the client put into place protective factors and a partnership of services.

For birth, foster, and adoptive families not described as 'highest need,' ongoing behavioral consultation services are a promising model. One pilot project, called the Special Needs Adoption Program, offers specialized parent group and individualized counseling services to adoptive families raising alcohol-exposed preschool and school-aged children at the local community mental health center (Rathbun, 2001). Another pilot project was described by Quinby and Rabkin (1998). The FAS Follow-up Program was a pilot behavioral consultation tied to existing public health services, in which public health nurse/educational specialist teams worked for a 6-month period with families raising alcohol-affected children, aged 3 to 12. The nurse assigned to the family made weekly home visits to each family, while the assigned psychologist observed in the classroom and provided information to school staff during three to six visits. Nurse/psychologist team members also consulted with and supported each other. Both interventionists provided: (a) support; (b) education about alcohol effects; (c) advocacy with other service systems when needed; (d) ideas for caregivers on self-help, respite care, and self-care; and (e) guidance on child management and parenting for the caregivers. Advice on child management was wide-ranging, but included ideas for redesigning the home and school environment to help the alcohol-affected child modulate incoming stimuli, and guidance in responding to the children's problems in behavioral organization, social communication, and cause-effect reasoning.

At this time, however, most of the published information about psychosocial treatment approaches exists in the form of case studies, like that of Josie, and the collected experiences and recommendations of parents, teachers, therapists, and researchers who have worked directly with alcohol-affected individuals. Streissguth (1997) acknowledges that: ' In the present research void of effective treatment modalities, the experience of other parents represents almost the only source of help and understanding regarding what is needed and what isn't needed, what works and what doesn't, and who understands FAS in each community ...' (p. 180). A parent-led organization, the Washington State FAS Family Resource Institute, has published a monograph describing a 'standard of care' for FAS intervention based on the experiences of parents, from infancy through adulthood. There are also published collections of ideas from both parent and professional perspectives. Kleinfeld and colleagues have edited two books that present the 'wisdom of practice,' focusing on positive treatment outcomes (Kleinfeld, et al., 2000; Kleinfeld & Westcott, 1992). Streissguth and her coworkers have published books containing a wealth of intervention information (Streissguth, 1997; Streissguth & Kanter, 1997). In addition, there is valuable discussion of intervention in a variety of papers and books. Lists of resources are available on the internet (e.g., see http://depts.washington.edu/fasdpn or http://depts.washington.edu/fadu.)

Psychosocial Treatment Goals and Techniques

In the field of FAS, a move away from the mental retardation model is important, because it creates false assumptions (Streissguth, 1994; Weiner & Morse, 1994). Professionals reading the initial case studies of clients with FAS assumed that assessment techniques and treatment services made available by the field of mental retardation were appropriate for individuals with alcohol effects. Over time, however, it has become clear that many alcohol-affected individuals (such as Josie) are not mentally retarded. Instead, they have complex profiles of strengths and weaknesses in cognition, learning, and adaptive behavior—and an 'unsettling degree of recognizable psychopathology' (Streissguth, 1994; p. 79)—that does not often conform to the template of mental retardation. Continuing to use a mental retardation framework means that alcohol-affected individuals with real problems may not be identified or fully understood, and an illusion is created that services are available when they are not. Using an inappropriate template leads to frustration as interventions expected to be effective simply do not work, and the complexity of services required by alcohol-affected clients becomes obvious. For a more appropriate approach, Carmichael Olson and colleagues have made two recommendations: (a) using 'multiple templates' for FAS and related conditions, based on similarities and differences of this spectrum disorder with other developmental disabilities in which there is neurological compromise (such as specific learning disabilities, ADHD, autism, mental retardation, or traumatic brain injury); and (b) taking a diathesis-stress approach in which the alcohol-affected individual is seen as vulnerable and interventions are directed toward limiting stressors and increasing protective factors (Carmichael Olson, Morse, & Huffine, 1998). (The body of research on 'children of alcoholics' is a possible source of information when developing treatment ideas from a diathesis-stress perspective. See Chapter 7, this volume).

As seen in Josie's case history, and in research on many developmental disabilities, useful techniques for younger children include efforts to improve the caregiver-child attachment relationship (such as infant mental health services or parenting education), and efforts to keep the home environment safe, stable, nurturant, appropriately structured and developmentally stimulating, with clear expectations and predictable basic routines. Diagnosis of alcohol-related disabilities can itself be an important intervention strategy. Useful strategies for older clients include behavior management, skill-building, and relaxation techniques designed to remediate an ongoing cycle of dysfunctional behavior and negative emotions. For any age, positive behavioral management—bringing about behavioral change through systematic management of behavioral consequences—may be helpful (Connor & Streissguth, 1996). However, in using behavioral approaches with this population it is essential to remember that 'contingency management techniques' (such as time out, sticker charts, or contracts) may be less effective with individuals who have problems linking cause and effect, or trouble generalizing from one situation to another. Carmichael Olson (2001) points out that it is essential to target interventions toward improving adaptive function, and that there may be single-modality, high-yield interventions that can help this disabled population. For younger children, sensory integration therapies may help with concerns about how they handle incoming stimuli. For alcohol-affected children of school age, direct coaching on social communication and social skills may be crucial because they can improve peer relations (which is an important predictor of a child's later mental health). Coaching can be carried out in school settings, or in structured extracurricular activities (which has the extra benefit of providing alcohol-affected children with important leisure skills that are needed for adolescent and adult life success). A summer daycamp for alcohol-affected, school-aged children could be an effective approach to providing this kind of 'social coaching' or 'friendship group' intervention.

As with other disability groups, developmental issues should be considered in carrying out these intervention strategies and finding natural time-points for intervention. Clinical observations suggest that alcohol-affected children, who are not mentally retarded (and especially those who are not recognized because they lack the identifiable facial features of the full syndrome), often have problems at the following times: (a) around 2nd or 3rd grade when more abstract learning is expected; (b) at entry to middle school when more independent function is demanded and peer relations are of primary importance; and (c) at entry into adulthood when independent living is the norm expected by society. For younger children, as seen in Josie's story, a carefully constructed, protective environment is needed to facilitate the learning and the growth of independence. Treatment planning must support teen clients with FAS and related conditions in their normal developmental tasks (such as developing peer relations and emerging 'self-rule'), devising ways to keep them safe while allowing some experimentation and challenge to adult rules. Treatment planning with clients preparing for life after school should, in part, have practical aims, including assisting the client to learn how to act as a friend and behave in a socially appropriate manner, find constructive solitary activities, and work productively and enjoy working (Streissguth, 1997). In addition, one important treatment goal for alcohol-affected individuals is learning to value and seek help in structuring their lives.

Yet more than with many developmentally disabled groups, slow progress and frequent setbacks seem to characterize intervention with the

alcohol-affected population. Behavior change can be difficult and new problems may readily occur, so that treatments that are initially helpful can become
ineffective. In this way, they appear more like brain-injured clients in their
prognostic course. Indeed, like others with brain injury, individuals with FAS
and related conditions often have complex learning problems and multiple
secondary disabilities, with developmental prerogatives that can repeatedly
interrupt care and propel the family into crisis. But unlike most other brain-
injured groups, alcohol-affected clients bring with them the additional complexity of familial substance abuse. Their birth families typically have
complicated histories of chemical dependency and related problems (including high rates of family dissolution, and maternal disability and death). The
clients themselves, like young Josie, are at high risk for later substance abuse.

Although there are important differences between acquired and developmental brain damage, literature on traumatic brain injury can provide insight
into specific intervention goals and techniques for individuals with FAS and
related conditions (e.g., Kehle, Clark, & Jenson, 1996). As with other brain-
injured groups, treatment goals include improving functional skills and ameliorating problem behavior. Brain-injured individuals often have difficulty in
modulating incoming stimuli, and in regulating and organizing behavior, so
that external supports become important. This can be readily seen in Josie's
case. For such clients, a generally useful approach is to redesign environments
to limit harmful consequences and make the most of the client's skills (Malbin,
1997). As D'Amato and Rothlisberg (1996) suggest, for these clients the physical organization of the environment should be designed for maximal learning
and function, using methods such as reducing distracting stimuli or providing
close supervision. Teaching and caregiving methods should provide environmental cues to support new learning and retrieval of prior knowledge. As
Streissguth (1997) has proposed, this can be accomplished through techniques
such as highlighting and repeatedly practicing new skills, rewarding the client
for paying attention, or putting consistent (and even rigid) lifestyle routines
into place. The affected individual can also be instructed in planning and self-
monitoring strategies, such as the use of memory aids or regular 'check-in and
planning times' with a caregiver, so that he or she can learn new ways to organize the environment. According to Connor and Streissguth (1996), cognitive
rehabilitation approaches (the use of compensation strategies for areas of
deficit and attempts to ameliorate the deficit directly) are frequently used with
clients with traumatic brain injury and may benefit those with alcohol effects.

As discussed earlier, research is just beginning to shed light on the patterns of CNS dysfunction among those with FAS and related conditions, and to
find similarities and differences with other disability groups. As this research
progresses, the choice of specific intervention techniques can be empirically
guided. So far, for example, the work of Coles, Mattson and their respective
colleagues highlights the problems of those with FAS/ARND in encoding
information into memory, and suggests the importance of educational
approaches that teach encoding strategies (Coles, Platzman, Raskind-Hood,
et al., 1997; Mattson, et al., 1996). Research suggesting that children with FAS

and ARND perform differently on neuropsychological tasks than do those with ADHD, at least in the early school years, begins to explain why medication regimens and educational techniques useful for children with attention deficits may fail with some alcohol-affected children, despite surface similarities in their behavior (Coles, Platzman, Raskind-Hood, et al., 1997). Even so, many techniques prescribed for individuals with ADHD do have potential for those with FAS and related conditions (Barkley, 1995). As another example, evidence of deficits in executive functions and social communication suggests why clients with FAS and related conditions—even the notable proportion whose IQ is within the borderline or average range—may less likely benefit from therapies heavily dependent on group process, verbal exchange, and/or achieving generalized insight into the reasons behind behavior. More successful may be techniques that take these deficits into account, providing external support for planning, organization, and social interaction, such as experiential learning, mentoring and coaching, therapeutic roommates, apprenticeship with a supportive trainer, and (as discussed in more detail below) advocacy programs. Olswang and colleagues even propose that social communication skills, social problem-solving, mental state reasoning, and other social-cognitive skills be directly taught to children and adolescents with FAS, as they are to other disabled individuals with problems in similar domains (such as clients with autism) (Olswang, Coggins, Carmichael Olson, & Timler, 2001). This is being tried with Josie. In this same vein, older clients, who may not be successful in social and job situations, may need training in receiving and sending nonverbal messages and emotional signals (Duke, Nowicki, & Martin, 1996).

For intervention with alcohol-affected individuals across the lifespan, Streissguth (1997) proposes a general 'advocacy model.' She recommends this model to mental health professionals as an important adjunct to therapies initiated to treat symptoms of mental illness. An advocate is described as an active mediator between the person with FAS/FAE and the environment, who helps interpret the affected individual to herself and to the world. Effective advocates, who are characterized as creative, determined problem solvers with a genuine affection for the affected individual, can be parents, other family members, or community professionals (including those in mental health). Advocates understand the behavioral manifestations of FAS and related conditions and infer client needs from their behaviors, help clients to maintain emotional control, assist them in defining their cognitive and social limitations, teach compensatory methods, and help affected individuals (and their caregivers) to define and set realistic expectations and seek solutions that work. While Josie is young, her adoptive parents act as her advocates. When she is older, new advocates will be needed, depending on her level of need. One kind of advocacy program has been recommended by Schmucker (1997), a practitioner, who suggests that case managers and independent living instructors be considered in treatment for higher-need adults with FAS. These interventionists help to problem solve the practical needs of an adult with developmental disabilities, including guardianship, housing, and financial management. In addition, they directly teach social skills and practical techniques for overcoming common behavioral manifestations of alcohol effects (such as problems with impulse control or forgetfulness).

IN CLOSING

FAS prevention research and programs are always essential. But the need for more research on intervention with FAS and related conditions is increasingly urgent, as families raising these individuals state very clearly. For the field to more readily move forward, professionals must be educated about the value of making alcohol-related diagnoses, and a sufficient network of reliable and accessible diagnostic services put into place. Research on screening techniques and early indicators of problems in this population is essential in the effort to establish a diagnostic network that is comprehensive and able to identify children with problems early in life. With diagnostic services more available, children like Josie will increasingly come with alcohol-related diagnoses to medical, school, mental health, correctional, and other settings, which will have to respond with services. Now is the time to begin research to examine the lives of 'resilient' alcohol-affected individuals and learn what makes for successful outcomes. It is also time to look carefully at how current methods of early intervention, family support, social services, pharmacotherapy, and psychosocial intervention apply to those with FAS and related conditions. It is also time to systematically evaluate the effectiveness of specialized strategies designed for alcohol-affected clients, such as ongoing consultation, advocacy programs, and therapies for sensory integration and social communication. These children, and their families, need and deserve help.

ACKNOWLEDGMENTS

Portions of this chapter are reprinted with permission from: Carmichael Olson, H., Morse, B. A., & Huffine, C. (1998). Development and psychopathology: FAS and related conditions, *Seminars in Clinical Neuropsychiatry, 3*, 262–284. Address reprint requests to the author: Dr. Heather Carmichael Olson, FAS Diagnostic and Prevention Network, Box 359300, CH-47, University of Washington, Seattle, WA 98195. Phone: (206) 526-1995. FAX: (206) 527-3959.

REFERENCES

Aase, J. (1994). Clinical recognition of FAS: Difficulties of detection and diagnosis. *Alcohol Health & Research World, 18*(1), 5–9.

Aase, J. M., Jones, K. L., & Clarren, S. K. (1995). Do we need the term 'FAE'? *Pediatrics, 95*, 428–430.

Abel, E. L. & Hannigan, J. H. (1996). Risk factors and pathogenesis. In H. L. Spohr & H. C. Steinhausen (Eds.), *Alcohol, pregnancy, and the developing child* (pp. 63–76). New York: Cambridge University Press.

Aronson, M. & Hagberg, B. (1998). Neuropsychological disorders in children exposed to alcohol during pregnancy: A follow-up study of 24 children born to alcoholic mothers in Goteborg, Sweden. *Alcoholism: Clinical & Experimental Research, 22*, 321–324.

Astley, S. J. & Clarren, S. K. (1995). A fetal alcohol syndrome screening tool. *Alcoholism: Clinical & Experimental Research, 19*, 1565–1571.

Astley, S. J. & Clarren, S. K. (1999). *Diagnostic guide for fetal alcohol svndrome and related conditions: The 4-digit diagnostic code.* Seattle, WA: University of Washington Press.

Astley, S. J., Bailey, D., Talbot, C., & Clarren, S. K. (2000). Fetal alcohol syndrome (FAS) primary prevention through FAS diagnosis: II. A comprehensive profile of 80 birth mothers of children with FAS. *Alcohol & Alcoholism, 35*, 509–519.

Barkley, R. A. (1995). *Taking charge of ADHD.* New York: Guilford Press.

Barnett, C. C. (1997). A judicial perspective on FAS: Memories of the making of Nanook of the North. In A.P. Streissguth & J. Kanter (Eds.), *The challenge of fetal alcohol syndrome: Overcoming secondary disabilities* (pp. 134–145). Seattle, WA: University of Washington Press.

Cadoret, R. J. & Riggins-Caspers, K. (2000). Fetal alcohol exposure and adult psychopathology: Evidence from an adoption study. In R. P. Barth, M. Freundlich, & D. Brodzinsky (Eds.), *Adoption and prenatal alcohol and drug exposure: Research, policy, and practice* (pp. 83–114). Washington, DC: Child Welfare League.

Carmichael Olson, H. (1994). The effects of prenatal alcohol exposure on child development. *Infants & Young Children, 6*, 10–25.

Carmichael Olson, H. (2001, February 1). FAS intervention: Moving forward. *Centers for Disease Control Fact-finding Workshop.*

Carmichael Olson, H., Clarren, S. G., Beck, S., Lewis, G., & Jirikowic, T. (1998). *Washington State Diagnostic & Prevention Network: Psychometric training guide for brief assessment of CNS dysfunction as part of an FAS diagnostic clinic.* Seattle, WA: FAS Diagnostic and Prevention Network Technical Report 98-03-02.

Carmichael Olson, H., Feldman, J. J., Streissguth, A. P., Sampson, P. D., & Bookstein, F. L. (1998). Neuropsychological deficits in adolescents with fetal alcohol syndrome: Clinical findings. *Alcoholism: Clinical & Experimental Research, 22*, 1998–2012.

Carmichael Olson, H., Morse, B. A., & Huffine, C. (1998). Development and psychopathology: Fetal alcohol syndrome and related conditions. *Seminars in Clinical Neuropsychiatry, 3*, 262–284.

Church, M. W. & Kaltenbach. J. A. (1997). Hearing, speech, language, and vestibular disorders in fetal alcohol syndrome: A literature review. *Alcoholism: Clinical & Experimental Research, 21*, 495–512.

Church, M. W., Eldis, F., Blakley, B. W., & Bawle, E. V. (1997). Hearing, language, speech, vestibular, and dentofacial disorders in fetal alcohol syndrome. *Alcoholism: Clinical & Experimental Research, 21*, 227–237.

Clarren, S. K., Carmichael Olson, H., Clarren, S. G., & Astley, S. M. (2000). A child with fetal alcohol syndrome. In M. J. Guralnick (Ed.), *Interdisciplinary clinical assessment of young children with developmental disabilities* (pp. 306–327). Baltimore, MD: Brookes.

Coggins, T. E. (1998). *Washington State Diagnostic & Prevention Network: Communicative behavior assessment for individuals with FAS and related conditions.* Seattle, WA: FAS Diagnostic and Prevention Network Technical Report 98-03-01.

Coggins, T. E., Friet, T., & Morgan. T. (1997). Analyzing narrative productions in older school-age children and adolescents with fetal alcohol syndrome: An experimental tool for clinical applications. *Clinical Linguistics & Phonetics, 12*, 221–236.

Coles, C. D., Platzman, K. A., Brown, R. T., Smith, I. E., & Falek, A. (1997). Behavior and emotional problems at school age in alcohol-affected children. *Alcoholism: Clinical & Experimental Research, 21*, 116A (No. 677).

Coles, C. D., Platzman, K. A., Raskind-Hood, C. L.. Brown, R. T., Falek, A., & Smith, I. E. (1997). A comparison of children affected by prenatal alcohol exposure and Attention Deficit/ Hyperactivity Disorder. *Alcoholism: Clinical & Experimental Research 21*, 150–161.

Connor, P. D. & Streissguth, A. P. (1996). Effects of prenatal exposure to alcohol across the lifespan. *Alcohol Health & Research World, 20*, 170–174.

Connor, P. D., Streissguth, A. P., Sampson, P. D., Bookstein, F. L., & Barr, H. M. (1999). Individual differences in auditory and visual attention among fetal alcohol-affected adults. *Alcoholism: Clinical & Experimental Research, 23*, 1395–1402.

D'Amato, R. C. & Rothlisberg, B. A. (1996). How education should respond to students with traumatic brain injury. *Journal of Learning Disabilities, 29*, 670–683.

Driscoll, C. D., Streissguth, A. P., & Riley, E. P. (1990). Prenatal alcohol exposure: Comparability of effects in humans and animal models. *Neurotoxicology & Teratology, 12*, 231–237.

Duke, M. P., Nowicki, S., & Martin, E. A. (1996). *Teaching your child the language of social success.* Atlanta, GA: Peachtree Publishing.

Dyer, K., Alberts, G., & Niemann, G. (1997). Assessment and treatment of an adult with FAS: Neuropsychological and behavioral considerations. In A. P. Streissguth & J. Kanter (Eds), *The challenge of fetal alcohol syndrome: Overcoming secondary disabilities* (pp. 52–63). Seattle, WA: University of Washington Press.

Famy, C., Streissguth, A. P., & Unis, A. S. (1998). Mental illness in adult patients with fetal alcohol syndrome and fetal alcohol effects. *American Journal of Psychiatry, 155*, 552–554.

Fetal Alcohol Syndrome Diagnostic & Prevention Network (FAS DPN). (2000). *Summary of first 1,000 patients evaluated.* Seattle, WA: FAS DPN Tech. Report, 10-2000.

Fetal Alcohol Syndrome Diagnostic & Prevention Network (FAS DPN). (2001). *FAS magnetic resonance imaging.spectroscopy project.* FAS DPN Tech. Report, 01-2001.

Grant, T., Ernst, C., Streissguth, A., & Porter, J. (1997). An advocacy program for mothers with FAS/FAE. In A. P. Streissguth & J. Kanter (Eds.), *The challenge of fetal alcohol syndrome: Overcoming secondary disabilities* (pp. 102–112). Seattle, WA: University of Washington Press.

Hannigan, J. H., Berman, R. F., & Sajac, C. S. (1993). Environmental enrichment and the behavioral effects of prenatal exposure to alcohol in rats. *Neurotoxicology & Teratology, 15*, 261–266.

Institute of Medicine (U.S.), Division of Biobehavioral Sciences and Mental Disorders, Committee to Study Fetal Alcohol Syndrome. (1996). K. Stratton, C. Howe, & F. Battaglia (Eds.), *Fetal alcohol syndrome: Diagnosis, epidemiology, prevention, and treatment.* Washington, DC: National Academy Press.

Jacobson, J. L. & Jacobson, S. W. (1997, May 12–13). Prenatal exposure to alcohol: Is there a distinctive neurobehavioral profile? *Extramural Scientific Advisory Board Meeting on FAS.*

Jacobson, J. L., Jacobson, S. W., & Sokol, R. J. (1996). Increased vulnerability to alcohol-related birth defects in the offspring of mothers over 30. *Alcoholism: Clinical & Experimental Research, 20*, 359–363.

Jacobson, J. L., Jacobson, S. W., Sokol, R. J., & Ager, J. W. (1998). Relation of maternal age and pattern of pregnancy drinking to functionally significant cognitive deficits in infancy. *Alcoholism: Clinical & Experimental Research, 22*, 345–351.

Kehle, T. J., Clark, E., & Jenson, W. R. (1996). Interventions for students with traumatic brain injury: Managing behavioral disturbances. *Journal of Learning Disabilities, 29*, 633–642.

Kerns, K. A., Don, A., Mateer, C. A., & Streissguth, A. P. (1997). Cognitive deficits in nonretarded adults with fetal alcohol syndrome. *Journal of Learning Disabilities, 30*, 685–693.

Kleinfeld, J. & Westcott, S. (Eds.). (1992). *Fantastic Antone succeeds!: Experiences in educating children with fetal alcohol syndrome.* Anchorage. AK: University of Alaska Press.

Kleinfeld, J., Morse, B. A., & Westcott, S. (Eds.). (2000). *Fantastic Antone grows up: Assisting alcohol-affected adolescents and adults.* Anchorage, AK: University of Alaska Press.

Klintsova, A. Y., Matthews, J. T., Goodlett, C. R., Napper, R. M. A., & Greenough, W. T. (1997). Therapeutic motor training increases parallel fiber synapse number per Purkinje neuron in cerebellar cortex of rats given postnatal binge alcohol exposure: Preliminary report. *Alcoholism: Clinical & Experimental Research, 21*, 1257–1263.

Kodituwakku, P. W., Handmaker, N. S., Cutler, S. K., Weathersby, E. K., & Handmaker, S. D. (1995). Specific impairments in self-regulation in children exposed to alcohol prenatally. *Alcoholism: Clinical & Experimental Research, 19*, 1558–1564.

LaDue, R. & Dunne, T. (1997). Legal issues and FAS. In A.P. Streissguth & J. Kanter (Eds.), *The challenge of fetal alcohol syndrome: Overcoming secondary disabilities* (pp. 146–161). Seattle, WA: University of Washington Press.

Li, C. & Pearson, K. (1996). A clinical intervention for children exposed to alcohol in utero. *Alaska Medicine, 39,* 124–131, 147.

Malbin, D. (1997). A poor fit: Treating FAS with non-FAS methods. *Iceberg, 7*(2), 1–2, 5.

Mattson, S. N. & Riley, E. P. (1998). A review of the neurobehavioral deficits in children with fetal alcohol syndrome or prenatal exposure to alcohol. *Alcoholism: Clinical & Experimental Research, 22,* 279–294.

Mattson, S. N., Riley, E. P., Delis, D. C., Stern, C., & Jones, K. L. (1996). Verbal learning and memory in children with fetal alcohol syndrome. *Alcoholism: Clinical & Experimental Research, 20,* 810–816.

Mattson, S. N., Goodman, A. M., Caine, C., Delis, D. C., & Riley, E. P. (1999). Executive functioning in children with heavy prenatal alcohol exposure. *Alcoholism: Clinical & Experimental Research, 23,* 1808–1815.

Morse, B. A. & Barnwell, C. (2000). *Charting the future: Resource directory for the diagnosis, prevention, and treatment of fetal alcohol syndrome.* Vienna, VA: Maternal and Child Health Clearinghouse. (Phone number: (703) 356-1964.)

Morse, B. A. & Cermak, S. (1994). Sensory processing in children with FAS. *Alcoholism: Clinical & Experimental Research, 18* (Abstract No. 503).

Morse, B. A. & Weiner, L. (1996). Rehabilitation approaches for fetal alcohol syndrome. In H. L. Spohr & H. C. Steinhausen (Eds.), *Alcohol, pregnancy, and the developing child* (pp. 249–268). Cambridge, England: Cambridge University Press.

National Institute for Alcoholism & Alcohol Abuse (NIAAA). (1997). *Ninth special report to the U.S. Congress on alcohol and health,* NIH Publication No. 97-4017. Washington, DC: U.S. Department of Health & Human Services.

Nigg, J. T. (2000). On inhibition/disinhibition in developmental psychopathology: Views from cognitive and personality psychology and a working inhibition taxonomy. *Psychological Bulletin, 126,* 220–246.

Nigg, J. T., Quamma, J. P., Greenberg, M. T., & Kusche, C. A. (1999). A two-year longitudinal study of neuropsychological and cognitive performance in relation to behavioral problems and competencies in elementary school children. *Journal of Abnormal Child Psychology, 27,* 51–63.

O'Connor, M. J. (1996). Attachment behavior of infants prenatally exposed to alcohol: Mother-infant interaction. In H. C. Steinhausen & H. L. Spohr (Eds.), *Alcohol, pregnancy, and the developing child* (pp. 183–206). Cambridge, England: Cambridge University Press.

O'Connor, M. J. & Kasari, C. (2000). Prenatal alcohol exposure and depressive features in children. *Alcoholism: Clinical and Experimental Research, 24,* 1084–1092.

Olswang, L. B., Coggins, T., Carmichael Olson, H., & Timler, G. (2001). Understanding social communication deficits in children with FAS and related conditions. *Speech & Hearing Sciences Tech. Report, 00-011.*

O'Malley, K. D. (1994). Fetal alcohol effects and ADHD (letter). *Journal of the American Academy of Child and Adolescent Psychiatry, 33,* 1059–1060.

O'Malley, K. D. (1997a). Safety of combined pharmacotherapy (letter). *Journal of the American Academy of Child and Adolescent Psychiatry, 36,* 1489–1490.

O'Malley, K. D. (1997b). Medication's therapy role for FAS. *Iceberg, 7*(4), 1–4.

Osterheld, J. R. & Wilson, A. (1997). ADHD and FAS (letter). *Journal of the American Academy of Child & Adolescent Psychiatry, 36,* 1163.

Price, K. J. (2000). *The ecological validity of neuropsychological tests of attention in a pediatric sample.* Unpublished master's thesis, University of Victoria. Victoria, BC, Canada.

Quinby, R. & Rabkin, J. (1998). *Report to the Centers for Disease Control: FAS follow-up project. Unpublished manuscript.* (Contact R. Quinby, Casey Family Program, 1300 Dexter Avenue. N., Floor #3, Seattle, Washington, 98109, for details about this program.)

Rathbun, A. R. (2001). *Report to the Administration of Children, Youth, and Families: Special Needs Adoption Program.* Unpublished manuscript. (Contact A. Rathbun, Children's Center, P.O. Box 484, Vancouver, Washington, 98666, for details about this program.)

Riikonen, R. S. (1994). Difference in susceptibility to teratogenic effects of alcohol in discordant twins exposed to alcohol during the second half of gestation. *Pediatric Neurology, 11,* 332–336.

Riley, E. P. (1990). The long-term behavioral effects of prenatal alcohol exposure in rats. *Alcoholism: Clinical & Experimental Research, 14*, 670–673.

Riley, E. P. & Mattson, S. N. (1997, May 12–13). Behavioral deficits and brain alterations following prenatal alcohol exposure. *Extramural Scientific Advisory Board Meeting on FAS.*

Roebuck, T. M., Mattson, S. N., & Riley, E. P. (1999). Behavioral and psychosocial profiles of alcohol-exposed children. *Alcoholism: Clinical & Experimental Research, 23*, 1070–1076.

Rosett, H. L. & Weiner, L. (1984). *Alcohol and the fetus: A clinical perspective.* New York: Oxford University Press.

Schmucker, C. A. (1997). Case managers and independent living instructors: Practical hints and suggestions for adults with FAS. In A. P. Streissguth & J. Kanter (Eds.), *The challenge of fetal alcohol syndrome: Overcoming secondary disabilities* (pp. 96–101). Seattle, WA: University of Washington Press.

Smith, I. E. & Coles, C. D. (1991). Multilevel intervention for prevention of fetal alcohol syndrome and effects of prenatal alcohol exposure. In M. Galanter (Ed.), *Children of alcoholics* (pp. 165–180). New York: Plenum Press.

Snyder, J., Nanson, J., Snyder, R., & Block, G. (1997). A study of stimulant medication in children with FAS. In A. P. Streissguth & J. Kanter (Eds.), *The challenge of fetal alcohol syndrome: Overcoming secondary disabilities* (pp. 64–77). Seattle, WA: University of Washington Press.

Spohr, H. L. (1996). Psychopathology and cognitive functioning children with fetal alcohol syndrome. In H. L. Spohr & H. C. Steinhausen (Eds.), *Alcohol, pregnancy, and the developing child* (pp. 207–226). Cambridge, England: Cambridge University Press.

Steinhausen, H. C. & Spohr, H. L. (1998). Long-term outcome of children with fetal alcohol syndrome: Psychopathology, behavior, and intelligence. *Alcoholism: Clinical & Experimental Research, 22*, 334–338.

Streissguth, A. P. (1994). A long-term perspective of FAS. *Alcohol Health & Research World, 18*, 74–81.

Streissguth, A. P. (1997). *Fetal alcohol syndrome: A guide for families and communities.* Baltimore, MD: Brookes.

Streissguth, A. P. & Kanter, J. (Eds.) (1997). *The challenge of fetal alcohol syndrome: Overcoming secondary disabilities.* Seattle, WA: University of Washington Press.

Streissguth, A. P. & O'Malley, K. D. (1997, Spring). Fetal alcohol syndrome/fetal alcohol effects: Secondary disabilities and mental health approaches. *Treatment Today, 9*, 16–17.

Streissguth, A. P., Aase, J. M., Clarren, S. K., LaDue, R. A., Randels, S. P., & Smith, D. F. (1991). Fetal alcohol syndrome in adolescents and adults. *Journal of the American Medical Association, 265*, 1961–1967.

Streissguth, A. P., Barr, H. M., Kogan, J., & Bookstein, F. L. (1996). *Understanding the occurrence of secondary disabilities in clients with fetal alcohol syndrome and fetal alcohol effects.* Seattle, WA: University of Washington.

Streissguth, A. P., Bookstein, F. L., Barr, H. M., Press, S., & Sampson, P. D. (1998). A fetal alcohol behavior scale. *Alcoholism: Clinical & Experimental Research, 22*, 325–333.

Thomas, S. E., Kelly, S. J., Mattson, S. N., & Riley, E. P. (1998). Comparison of social abilities of children with fetal alcohol syndrome to those of children with similar IQ scores and normal controls. *Alcoholism: Clinical & Experimental Research, 22*, 528–533.

Weinberg, J., Kim, C. K., & Ju, W. (1995). Early handling can attenuate adverse effects of fetal ethanol exposure. *Alcohol, 12*, 317–327.

Weinberg, N. Z. (1997). Cognitive and behavioral deficits associated with prenatal alcohol use. *Journal of the American Academy of Child & Adolescent Psychiatry, 36*, 1177–1186.

Weiner, L. & Morse, B. A. (1994). Intervention and the child with FAS. *Alcohol Health & Research World, 18*, 67–72.

Whitty, J. E. & Sokol, R. J. (1996). Alcohol teratogenicity in humans: Critical period, threshold, specificity, and vulnerability. In H. L. Spohr & H. C. Steinhausen (Eds.), *Alcohol, pregnancy, and the developing child* (pp. 3–14). Cambridge, England: Cambridge University Press.

CHAPTER 9

Children of Substance-Abusing Parents

Current Findings from the Focus on Families Project

RICHARD F. CATALANO, KEVIN P. HAGGERTY, CHARLES
B. FLEMING, DEVON D. BREWER, & RANDY R. GAINEY

Research into risk factors for problem behavior among children has established clear links between family characteristics and the likelihood that children will become involved in drug abuse, delinquency and other forms of problem behavior (Hawkins, Catalano, & Miller, 1992; Jessor, 1998; Simcha-Fagan, Gersten, & Langner, 1986). Family risk factors that increase risk of substance abuse include parental substance abuse, poor family management practices, family conflict, parental attitudes favorable toward drug use, and parents' involving their children in their drug use. Family characteristics that protect or buffer children from risk include parent-child attachment and warmth (Brook, Brook, Gordon, Whiteman, & Cohen, 1990; Werner & Smith, 1992), parent support of child competencies (Coie, et al., 1993; Rutter, 1990), and positive parent-child interaction and communications (Shedler & Block, 1990).

Children of drug-abusing parents are frequently exposed to elevated levels of multiple risk factors (Kolar, Brown, Haertzen, & Michaelson, 1994; Kumpfer & DeMarsh, 1986; Mays, 1995). In addition to possibly having a physiological predisposition toward drug abuse (Griffith, Azuma, & Chasnoff, 1994), these children are likely to receive inadequate parental supervision and support (Kumpfer & DeMarsh, 1986) and be exposed to the modeling of drug use and other illegal behavior by their parents (Catalano & Hawkins, 1996).

Selective prevention programs (Institute of Medicine, 1994) intervene with children who are exposed to multiple risk factors or are highly exposed to a single risk factor. This chapter reviews the findings of a selective intervention, Focus on Families (FOF), an experimental evaluation of an intervention with substance abusers and their children. The following four reports are based on data from the sample of methadone clients and their children used in the FOF study and illustrate unique problems and family processes of this population.

(1) Bonding in parent, peer, and school domains was compared in a general population sample of children and the FOF sample (Hoppe, et al., 1998). Consistent with the work of Bernardi, Jones, and Tennant (1989) and Johnson and Pandina (1991), attachment to parents was weaker in the FOF sample than in the general population sample. However, attachment to peers and school was stronger in the FOF sample. Multivariate analyses indicated that the FOF children were more likely to smoke than children in the general sample, even after accounting for the effects of demographic and attachment variables.

(2) The influence of family management practices, maternal attachment, and deviant peers on early problem behavior among FOF children was investigated (Gainey, Catalano, Haggerty, & Hoppe, 1997). Age and contact with deviant peers were significant predictors of delinquency and initiation of drug use. Consistent with other studies focusing on children whose parents use drugs (Dembo, Grandon, LaVoie, Shmeidler, & Burgos, 1986; Jenson & Brownfield, 1983), no relationship was found between maternal attachment and substance use among children whose parents are substance abusers. Negative relationships were found between maternal attachment and association with deviant peers and self-reported delinquency, although the relationships were relatively weak and varied with age. Further investigation revealed that, although older children of substance abusers tended to be less attached to their mothers than the younger ones, older children who maintained close maternal relationships were less actively involved in delinquent behaviors than older children who did not maintain close relationships with their mothers.

(3) The extent to which parent use of illicit drugs moderates the relationship between bonding to parents and child substance use was examined (Fleming, Brewer, Gainey, Haggerty, & Catalano, 1997). Bonding to parents and child substance use were negatively correlated among FOF children whose parents ceased using drugs but were positively correlated among FOF children whose parents continued using drugs. The results are consistent with the social development model (Catalano & Hawkins, 1996) hypothesis that the valence of bonding to parents is contingent on whether parents model pro-social or anti-social behavior.

(4) The use of specific drugs as longitudinal predictors of violence between domestic partners in the FOF sample was investigated (Brewer, Fleming, Haggerty, & Catalano, 1998). Use of crack cocaine, other forms of cocaine, and tranquilizers were each positively associated with partner violence victimization. Women who were heavy users of these drugs were more likely to be hit, slapped, or shoved by their partners than light users or nonusers of these drugs.

Prevention of parent relapse to drug use should be a major focus of preventive interventions for children of drug-addicted parents. Multiple studies have identified factors that contribute to relapse, including family conflict, lack of family support, drug use among other family and network members, lack of involvement in non-drug leisure activities, skill deficits, high life stress, and lack of needed services (Marlatt & Gordon, 1985; Surgeon General, 1988). As part of the FOF study, a meta-analysis was conducted of 69 published studies (Brewer, Catalano, Haggerty, Gainey, & Fleming, 1998) on predictors of continued drug use among opiate users. The following ten variables showed statistically significant and longitudinally predictive relationships with continued use: (a) high level of pretreatment opiate/drug use, (b) prior treatment for opiate addiction, (c) no prior abstinence from opiates, (d) abstinence from/light use of alcohol, (e) depression, (f) high stress, (g) unemployment/employment problems, (h) association with substance abusing peers, (i) short length of treatment, and (j) leaving treatment prior to completion. As with primary prevention, a promising approach to prevent relapse is for interventions to address these longitudinal predictors of drug use during and after treatment. Given the overlap of several predictors of children's substance abuse and parent relapse, family interventions based on reducing risk and relapse factors and enhancing protective factors may be particularly effective.

The FOF intervention was designed as a multi-pronged intervention to address both family related risk factors for children's substance abuse and risk factors for parents' relapse, and to enhance family-related protective factors. A primary goal of the intervention was to reduce parents' illicit drug use by teaching them relapse prevention and coping skills. Parents were also taught how to manage their families better by increasing child involvement in problem solving, providing opportunities for involvement, giving consistent consequences for both positive and negative behavior, setting clear expectations for their children, and addressing conflict. Although a number of programs have been developed to reduce children's risk of drug abuse when one or both parents have a substance abuse problem (Falco, 1992; Gross & McCaul, 1992; Haskett, Miller, Whitworth, & Huffman, 1992; Russel & Free, 1991; Springer, Phillips, Phillips, Cannady, & Derst-Harris, 1992), few rigorous experimental evaluations of these programs have been published (Catalano, Haggerty, Gainey, Hoppe, & Brewer, 1998; Kumpfer & DeMarsh, 1986). Thus, the FOF project represents one of the first randomized experimental evaluations of a preventive intervention with this population.

Prior reports on the effect of the intervention compared study participants assigned to the experimental condition with participants assigned to the control condition. The first (Catalano, Haggerty, Gainey, & Hoppe, 1997) used data on parents collected immediately after the intervention period and found positive intervention effects on improving coping skills and reducing heroin use. The second (Catalano, Gainey, Fleming, Haggerty, & Johnson, 1999) used data from parent and child surveys 6 and 12 months after the intervention and again found differences in coping skills and drug use favoring parents in the experimental group. Overall, few differences were found in family processes in either of these two reports, although at the 12-month follow-up, experimental parents reported they had experienced less domestic conflict with their spouse or partner and had established more household rules for their children. The data on children at 6- and 12-month follow-ups showed few statistically significant differences by experimental condition, although the direction of differences in problem behavior did tend to favor the children in the experimental group. Finally, a benefit-cost analysis of the FOF program was developed (Plotnick, 1994) to compare benefits and costs that could be assessed monetarily. Using data from the 6-month follow-up time point, no statistically significant monetary effects of the project were found (Plotnick, Young, Catalano, & Haggerty, 1998).

This chapter summarizes results of the first two outcome analyses mentioned above. In addition, comparisons between experimental and control participants are included here, which are based on 24-month follow-up surveys of both parents and children. Also, a larger sample of children are included in these analyses than in earlier reports, since data are used from children who were not old enough to complete baseline surveys but who were old enough to be surveyed at the time of the follow-up surveys.

SUMMARY OF INTERVENTION OUTCOMES

Method

Participants

Over a period of $2\frac{1}{2}$ years, 144 parents from 130 families were recruited from two Seattle-area methadone clinics. To be eligible to participate, parents had to have been in methadone treatment for a minimum of 90 days and have one or more children between the ages of 3 and 14 years old living with them at least 50% of the week. Families were randomly assigned to the experimental or control condition after blocking on parents' race, parents' age at first drug use, whether parents lived with a spouse or partner, and ages of children. Because of anticipated attrition from the experimental program, a higher proportion of eligible families were assigned to the experimental ($n = 75$) than control ($n = 55$) condition. Of the 144 parents who enrolled in the project, 94% were interviewed immediately after the completion of the family training sessions of the intervention, 94% were interviewed 6 months later, 92% completed a 12-month follow-up interview, and 92% completed the 24-month follow-up interview. Attrition did not vary by condition at any of the time points.

Seventy-five percent of the parents in the sample were female, 77% were white, 18% were African-American, and 5% were of mixed or other ethnicity. Parents' mean age was 35.36 ($SD = 5.67$) and their mean age of first use of opiates was 19.14 ($SD = 5.00$). Although only 20% were married, 60% lived with a spouse or partner. Seventy-four percent had graduated from high school, 4% had graduated from college, and 66% were unemployed in the 3 months prior to enrolling in methadone treatment. Sixty-eight percent had been incarcerated at some point prior to enrollment. The mean length of time in methadone treatment prior to enrolling in the FOF project was 14.96 months ($SD = 15.98$). Although all participants were receiving methadone treatment at baseline, 54% used illicit drugs in the prior month: 24% used marijuana, 38% used opiates, 23% used cocaine, and 14% used other illegal drugs.

The 130 families in the project included 178 children (97 experimental, 81 control), between the ages of 3 and 14 at baseline. Children age 6 and older were interviewed at baseline and at 6, 12, and 24 months after the completion of the skills training portion of the intervention. Attrition over time was slightly higher for children (86% of youth completed the 24 month follow-up interview) but did not vary by treatment condition.

In order to gauge the degree of children's problem behavior in this sample, data from FOF children were compared to data collected by the Seattle Social Development Project (SSDP) (see Hawkins, Catalano, Morrison, et al., 1992, for a more detailed description of this sample). Collection of the SSDP sample data began in 1985 with a sample of 808 fifth-grade students from 18 Seattle public elementary schools. These students were interviewed annually for 5 years. Because there is considerable variation in the range of ages among the FOF children, for these comparisons the FOF sample was divided into those aged 9 to 11 and those aged 12 to 14 and compared to the sample of Seattle public school children in fifth grade (ages 10 to 11) and seventh grade (ages 12 to 13). As indicated in Table 9-1, there is a higher prevalence of problem behavior and sanctioning for problem behavior in the FOF sample.

Development of FOF Parent Training Component

Three major challenges in working with parents exposed to multiple risk factors have been noted in tests of parent training interventions. The first is difficulty recruiting these parents (Grady, Gersick, & Boratynski, 1986; Hawkins,

Table 9-1 Descriptive comparison of FOF (ages 9–11 and 12–14) and SSDP children (5th and 7th grades)

	SSDP (Ages 10–11) %	FOF (Ages 9–11) %	SSDP (Ages 12–13) %	FOF (Ages 12–14) %
Drug Use				
Drank alcohol	27.3	19.2	51.8	53.1
Smoked cigarettes	12.8	26.9*	28.0	51.0*
Used marijuana	3.1	1.9	8.6	22.4*
Delinquency				
Picked fights[a]	40.9	51.9	38.7	28.6
Threw objects[a]	14.9	15.4	15.8	34.7*
Break and enter[a]	3.3	5.8	2.9	4.1
Official Reaction				
Picked up by police	3.2	15.7*	19.3	46.9*
Suspended or expelled[b]	10.0	21.2*		

Note: SSDP sample sizes range from 633 to 662 for the 11–12 age group and 474 to 490 for the 13–14 age group. FOF sample sizes are 51 or 52 for the 9–11 age group and 49 for the 12–14 age group.
[a] Older children were asked about the prior year.
[b] This item was not comparable across samples for the oldest children.
*$p < .05$.

Catalano, Jones, & Fine, 1987). Second, studies of families exposed to multiple risks have made it clear that short-term programs (8–10 sessions) are unlikely to succeed because of the multiplicity of these families' problems (Patterson & Reid, 1973). Clinical reports suggest that these parents may require twice as many hours of training as parents from the general population to achieve the same level of change in their own and their children's behavior (Patterson & Fleishman, 1979). Third, parent training alone may not be potent enough to produce substantial, lasting changes in parents' and children's behaviors among families exposed to multiple risk factors (Serketich & Dumas, 1996; Tremblay, et al., 1992). The FOF intervention attempts to address each of these issues.

Parents in methadone treatment are good candidates for such a program because they have already made a commitment to examine their drug use and have begun to work on making changes in their lives. Their regular attendance at the clinic provides ready availability for parent training sessions. The FOF program was of long duration, paid particular attention to recruitment and retention mechanisms, and offered other support services. The Focus on Family intervention lasted 9 months (4 months of parent training groups, 9 months of home-based services). The program also linked clients with other treatment services (housing, child welfare services, employment services, etc.) when appropriate.

FOF Parent Training Program

The FOF parent training curriculum consisted of a 5-hour family retreat and 32 1.5 hour parent training sessions. Data reported here are from seven 'waves' or cohorts of parent training conducted from December 1990 to June 1993. Sessions were conducted twice a week over a 16-week period. Children attended 12 of the sessions to practice developmentally appropriate skills with their parents. Session topics focused on specific developmental risk and protective factors and included the following:

Family Goal Setting. A 5-hour kick-off retreat focused on goal-setting and brought families together to share a common trust-building experience. This session sought to empower families to work together to develop goals for their participation in the family sessions. Case managers later worked with individual families to identify small steps to take in order to reach their identified goals.

Relapse Prevention. These four sessions included (a) identification of relapse signals or triggers, (b) anger and stress control, and (c) creating and practicing a plan to follow in case a relapse occurred. The impact of relapse on the client's children was emphasized, and skills were taught to prevent and cope with relapse and relapse-inducing situations (Marlatt & Gordon, 1985). Parents were taught to identify the cognitive, behavioral, and situational antecedents (signals) of relapse, and to use self-talk to anticipate the consequences of their drug-using behavior (Hawkins, Catalano, & Wells, 1986).

Family Communication Skills. The skills of paraphrasing, asking open-ended questions, and 'I' messages were taught during these sessions. Families practiced using the skills during two practice sessions. All subsequent groups reinforced the use of the communication skills taught in these early sessions. Families then used these skills to develop family expectations, conduct regular family meetings, and make family play and fun time successful.

Family Management Skills. Parents learned and practiced setting clear and specific expectations, monitoring expectations, rewarding positive behavior, and providing appropriate consequences for negative behaviors. Parents practiced implementing 'the law of least intervention,' using the smallest intervention to get the desired behavior from their child. A variety of discipline skills were learned and practiced by parents including praise, ignoring, expressing feelings, using 'if-then' messages, time outs, and privilege restrictions. The advantages and disadvantages of using spanking as a discipline technique were discussed and parents reviewed tips for reducing spanking. Parents charted both their own behavior (for consistency) and their children's behavior, to aid in recognizing and reinforcing the desired behaviors. Parents were referred to outside resources for children's behavioral problems, if needed.

Creating Family Expectations About Drugs and Alcohol. Families worked together to define and clarify expectations about drug and alcohol use in their families. Parents were taught how to involve their children in creating clear and specific expectations, monitor compliance with these expectations, and provide appropriate consequences. Families also worked together to establish written family policies for tobacco, alcohol, and other drug use.

Teaching Children Skills. Parents learned how to teach their children refusal and problem-solving skills. Parents taught and practiced the skills with their children during sessions so that trainers could guide parent teaching practices. Teaching skills provided parents with additional reinforcement of techniques for avoiding relapse.

Helping Children Succeed in School. Parents built on the previously learned skills to create, monitor and provide appropriate consequences in a home learning routine for their children. Parents identified times, places, and rewards for homework completion. Strategies to assist children with homework were taught and practiced. Parents reviewed communication skills and practiced using the skills to communicate with school personnel. The group sessions ended with a family 'graduation' ceremony and potluck event.

Parent sessions were conducted with groups of six to eight families by a team that included one male and one female master's level social worker. Both had extensive backgrounds in parenting, addiction, and mental health issues. The parent training format combined a peer support and skill training model. The training curriculum taught skills using 'guided participant modeling' (Rosenthal & Bandura, 1978), in which skills were modeled by trainers and other group members, discussed by participants, and then practiced. Videotape was frequently used in modeling the skills or giving feedback after skill practice. To maximize effectiveness, the training focused on affective and cognitive, as well as behavioral, aspects of performance (W. T. Grant Consortium on School-Based Promotion of Social Competence, 1992).

The curriculum allowed participants to practice in situations they frequently confronted with their own children. Parents completed home extension exercises after each session to generalize the skills from the training setting to the home setting (Goldstein & Kanfer, 1979). After parents learned and practiced skills, parents and children practiced using their new skills together in family sessions with their home-based services case manager.

Following their graduation from the parent training group, families were invited to a monthly potluck. The potluck acted as a booster session for families and helped them maintain behavior changes learned in parent training sessions. At each potluck, families reviewed their progress toward their goals, went over skill steps, and discussed their use of skills at home.

The FOF intervention used several incentives to address the anticipated problems with recruitment and retention. Monetary reinforcers were given for session attendance ($3) and completion of homework assignments ($2), and transportation and child care at sessions were provided as needed. Food was provided at all sessions. Children received small toys for their participation, and a variety of other family incentives were offered, such as tickets to the zoo, aquarium, and baseball games.

FOF Home-Based Case Management

In addition to the parenting curriculum, the program also included home-based case management to help parents and children generalize and maintain the skills learned in the group sessions. Two master's level home-based service providers, one male and one female, worked individually with families for approximately 9 months, beginning 1 month before the start of the parent training sessions, continuing through the group training period (4 months), and 4 months afterward. Following a standardized manual, case managers helped families identify goals, monitored progress toward these goals, and reinforced the skills parents learned in training sessions at home. They helped families hold regular family meetings, increased each member's opportunities for family involvement, and promoted children's opportunities for involvement in positive activities outside of the family. Case managers also worked with parents to reduce their risk for relapse through reinforcing training in relapse prevention and coping skills, assisted parents to be productively engaged in school or employment, and helped to structure a supportive and drug-free social network for parents. Weekly supervision was conducted by the project director to ensure that case managers were following the case management protocols. Case managers helped to secure community services for families as needed. Case managers attempted to have one home visit (about 90 minutes' duration) and two phone calls per week. Thus, during the parent training phase, each family received up to 5 hours of direct service per week, including 3 hours of group sessions and 2 hours of case management (Catalano, Haggerty, Gainey, & Hoppe, 1997).

The FOF case management system used a six-step model.

Step 1: Joining and engaging with families. Case managers sought to build a trusting relationship not only with the addicted parent but with all family members. Although initially the addicted parent was the client, after the first meeting the case manager shifted the focus from the client as addict to the client as parent, and then from the addict-parent as client to the family as identified client.

Step 2: Risk and relapse assessment. A structured assessment form was used to identify a family's strengths and weaknesses and their risk profile. Assessments were organized into six sections: parenting skills, social skills/relationships, community services, employment/education, school support, and life support. The case manager conducted this assessment informally with the family and used it to develop a service plan.

Step 3: Service plan agreement. Case managers worked with families to identify goals for priority areas identified in the assessment. Families were encouraged to create and develop goals *they* wanted for their family, and these goals became the center of the case management service plan.

Step 4: Service plan implementation. Case managers possessed the knowledge and ability to apply a variety of therapeutic interventions to broad areas of assessment and client goal areas. These interventions included couples' therapy, strategic family therapy, skills training, problem solving, and crisis intervention.

Step 5: Monitoring, evaluating, and revising service plans. Case managers were responsible for monitoring the outcomes of their clients' progress toward their goals. Monitoring service plans kept both case managers and clients accountable to the family's goals. Each month, case managers reviewed progress toward goals with their clients.

Step 6: Terminating with clients. Termination included providing clients with alternate resources they could access on their own, assisting them to develop at least one strong prosocial relationship, and modeling how to terminate a relationship in a healthy, non-aggressive manner. Case managers evaluated minimum outcomes expected with each family. These included: (a) parents refrained from using illegal drugs in front of their children, (b) no physical abuse took place in the family, (c) the family carried out a successful family meeting without case managers present, (d) the family had a written family drug policy, (e) all school-age youth regularly attended school, (f) the family had an established home learning routine, (g) families used communication skills of 'I' messages, paraphrasing, and asking open-ended questions, (h) each family had one new resource in their network, and (i) each family attended at least two follow-up groups.

Evaluation Issues

Evaluations of preventive interventions with substance-using parents must address two major issues. First, since such programs are designed for families exposed to multiple risk factors, the success of recruitment and participation in such programs must be assessed. The questions to be addressed here are: Can families be recruited into an intensive prevention program? If recruited, what will be the level of participation? The second issue is the effectiveness of the program. The questions here concern the immediate, proximal goals of the intervention, as well as more distal goals. Does the program reduce targeted relapse and risk factors and/or enhance protective factors? Does it achieve the ultimate goal of reducing substance abuse by parents and reducing later problem behaviors, including substance abuse, by children?

Engagement and Participation

Seventy-five percent of eligible parents consented to be involved in the study. Of those assigned to the program condition ($n = 82$), 87% initiated participation in the parenting groups. These relatively high rates of consent and initiation for this high-risk sample suggest that parents in treatment for opiate addiction are willing to enroll in an intensive family prevention program.

Treatment exposure measures were rated at the end of each skill session by the parent skill group leaders. There was tremendous variation in participation in the skills training sessions across the measures of treatment exposure (Table 9-2). When all those assigned to the experimental condition are included, families attended 45% of the sessions on average. However, when the 11 persons (14.5%) who never attended a single session are excluded, families attended about 52% of the sessions. On average, those attending at least one session were rated as paying close attention in about 57% (range 0–100%), and participating actively in about 38% (range 0–94%) of the sessions they attended.

Among those attending at least half of the sessions, more active participation and less distraction were found. These persons were rated by session

Table 9-2 Levels of program participation: means and standard deviations for all clients, initiators, and high attenders

		Percentage of Sessions							
		Attended		Paid Attention		Actively Participated		Children Attended	
	N	M	(SD)	M	(SD)	M	(SD)	M	(SD)
Total assigned	82	45.0	(34.5)						
Total initiating	71	51.9	(31.8)	56.7	(30.3)	38.4	(27.0)	32.2	(29.7)
Completed 16+ sessions	42	75.0	(15.8)	69.2	(20.8)	46.1	(22.8)	46.2	(27.9)

		% Homework Completed		# Role Plays		Mean Rating of Role Plays (1–5 Scale)	
	N	M	(SD)	M	(SD)	M	(SD)
Total initiating	71	45.7	(30.0)	10.0	(6.4)	3.0	(1.2)
Completed 16+ sessions	42	64.3	(20.4)	14.1	(4.2)	3.5	(4.2)

From Catalano, R. F., Gainey, R. R., Fleming, C., Haggerty, K. P., & Johnson, N. O. (1999), An experimental intervention with families of substance abusers: 1-year follow-up of the Focus on Families project. *Addiction, 94,* 241–254, Taylor & Francis, Ltd., London, United Kingdom. http://www.tandf.co.uk/journals

leaders as paying attention in an average of 69% (range 6–100%) and actively participating in 46% (range 0–94%) of the sessions they attended. These high attenders brought their children to an average of 46% (0–100%) of the 12 child-attended sessions and completed an average of 64% (13–100%) of their home-work assignments. High attenders came to an average of 64% (range 18–100%) of the 22 sessions in which role-plays were practiced. Session leader ratings of these parents' skill levels in the role-play situations averaged 3.5 (range 2.6–4.5) on a scale from 1 to 5. (For a more detailed description of these results see Gainey, Catalano, Haggerty, & Hoppe, 1995). In sum, clients attended about half of the sessions and actively participated in about 40% of the sessions they attended. This pattern of participation indicates that programs need to contain mechanisms for reviewing missed content and personally engaging clients both in and out of training sessions. FOF had both mechanisms in place through the active use of case managers in reviewing and reinforcing content and motivat-ing client participation. The average number of contacts with parents who par-ticipated in the program was 63 over the 9-month period and ranged from 4 to 291. Case managers also conducted 16.7 home visits on average, ranging from 0 to 39, again depending on the needs and cooperation of the family.

Assessment Procedures for Evaluating Intervention Effects

Parents were interviewed in person prior to the intervention, immediately after the end of the parent training component, and at 6, 12, and 24 months following parent training. Children age 6 and older were interviewed at baseline and 6-, 12-, and 24-month follow-up. For children, three different developmentally appropriate interviews were used for the age groups 6 to 8, 9 to 10, and 11 and older. The interviews for older children included more items and gave respondents more complex and specific response options. The inter-view a child completed was based on the age of the child at the time of the interview.

Descriptions of the measures used to assess intervention effects are pre-sented in Table 9-3. These measures were derived from prior work with both general and high-risk populations (Hawkins, Catalano, Gillmore, & Wells, 1989; Hawkins, Catalano, Morrison, et al., 1992; Jenson, Wells, Plotnick, Hawkins, & Catalano, 1993; O'Donnell, Hawkins, Catalano, Abbott, & Day, 1995). They measure problem behavior among parents and children as well as risk and pro-tective factors for drug abuse and other problem behaviors among children.

All measures were based on responses to survey questions with the excep-tion of the two measures of problem-solving skills. The skills measures were derived from the Problem Situation Inventory (PSI; Hall, et al., 1983), an audio-taped role-play instrument. The PSI has demonstrated reliability and validity and discrimination of intervention related changes in general, drug refusal, and relapse prevention skills (Hawkins, et al., 1986, 1989; Wells, Hawkins, & Catalano, 1988a,b). Periodic interrater reliability was assessed by re-rating 25% of all tapes. Pearson's correlations were used to compare ratings. The ratings were reliable with correlations ranging from .73 to .91.

Table 9-3 Description of scales and indices

Problem-Solving Skills (PSI)	No. of Items	Components	Cronbach's α (Range)	Source
PARENT MEASURES				
Relapse/refusal	6	Example situation: Co-worker offers you drugs. What would you do?	.74–.81	(Hall, et al., 1983)
General situations	6	Example situation: You are home alone and bored. What would you do?	.52–.62	(Hall, et al., 1983)
		Family Factors		
# family meetings	4	Frequency of family meetings regarding (1) fun activities, (2) family problems, (3) drug use, and (4) household chores.		
Household rules	9	Whether household has rules regarding television, household chores, drug use, etc.		
Domestic conflict	6	How often yelled at, threatened to hit, and hit partner and how often victim of these behaviors.	.72–.81	(Strauss, 1979)
Family bonding	9	Example: 'Do family members have a feeling of togetherness?'	.63–.72	(Moos, 1974)
Family conflict	3	Example: 'How often do family members argue?'	.75–.86	(Moos, 1974)
		Deviant Peer Network		
Deviant peer network	3	Proportion of parent's four best friends who used heroin, used other illegal drugs, and engaged in other illegal activities.	.86–.87	
		Drug Use		
Marijuana use	1	Times used marijuana in the prior month.		
Heroin use	1	Times used heroin in the prior month.		
Cocaine	1	Times used cocaine in the prior month.		

CHILD MEASURES

Measure	Items	Description	Reliability
Family Factors			
Rules index	6	Whether household has rules regarding television, etc.	
Parental recognition	4	Example: 'Do your parents praise you when you do something good?'	.78–82
Bonding to family	12	Example: 'Do you share your thoughts and feelings with your mother?'	.82–89
Involvement index	7	In the past week did child, e.g, read or do craft projects with parent, etc.	
Peer Factors			
Negative peers	4	Proportion of 3 best friends who get into serious trouble or use drugs or alcohol, etc.	.62–68
School			
School attachment	4	Example: 'Do you look forward to going to school in the morning?'	
Grades	1	'What grade did you most commonly receive in in school during the past year?'	.70–75
Problem Behaviors			
% used cigarettes	1	Smoked in the prior month.	
% used alcohol	1	Drank alcohol (more than sip) in prior 6 months.	
% used marijuana	1	Used marijuana in the prior month.	
Delinquency scale	6	Frequency in prior 6 months respondent cheated on test, stole, destroyed other person's property, picked a fight, hit teacher, and threw objects at cars or people.	.70–74

Reprinted from *Addictive Behaviors, 20,* Gainey, R. R., Catalano, R. F., Haggerty, K. P., & Hoppe, M. J. (1995). Participation in a parent training program for methadone clients, pp. 117–125, Copyright (1995), with permission from Elsevier Science.

Measures based on parent and child surveys overlapped in the areas of household rules and family attachment/bonding. Correlations between parent and child reports were only moderately positive. For the household rule indices, the correlation (Pearson's r) between parent and child reports was .22 at 6-month, .38 at 12-month, and .25 at 24-month follow-up. For the family bonding and attachment scales the correlations were .13 at 6-month, .22 at 12-month, and .08 at 24-month follow-up. The lack of correspondence between parent and child reports is consistent with prior research (Jessop, 1981) and argues for the inclusion of both sets of measures in the analyses.

In order to examine and enhance the validity of parent self-reported drug use, all participants were informed that a different random sample of participants at each data collection point would be asked for a urine sample. This 'bogus pipeline' procedure has been found to enhance the validity of self-reports for all participants, both those providing urine samples and those who do not (Roese & Jamieson, 1993). Twenty-five percent of the participants were randomly selected at each follow-up data collection point to provide a urine specimen and answer a set of questions with time periods corresponding to the ability to detect the particular drug in the toxicology screen. Overall, few false negatives were found across substances (from 4.5% to 6.1% depending on the substance) and no statistically significant differences were found in false negatives across the experimental and control groups. This suggests that self-reports are largely valid, with no difference in reporting veracity by condition.

Results

Outcomes for Parents and Children

Analysis of covariance and logistic regression were used to assess differences between the experimental and control group at follow-up time points. For analyses of parent outcomes, a baseline measure corresponding to the given outcome measure was included as a control variable. Baseline controls were not included in the analyses of children's outcomes reported here since many of the children who completed interviews at follow-up time points were too young to be interviewed at baseline or were interviewed with a more limited questionnaire. Age was included as a control variable for child outcomes and the interaction between experimental assignment, age, and each outcome variable was examined to test whether the effectiveness of the intervention was contingent on the age of the child.

Parent Outcomes. Table 9-4 displays the results of parent outcomes at immediate post-parent training and the 6-, 12-, and 24-month follow-ups. Differences consistently favored the experimental group.

Experimental parents received higher scores on the PSI in both general and drug related situations at all time points. Differences did not diminish over time and were statistically significant at the 24-month follow-up. Few statistically significant differences between experimental and control parents were found in parent reports of family involvement, management, conflict, or

Table 9-4 Parent outcomes: ANCOVA with baseline measures as covariates

	Immediate Post Adj. M (SD)			6-Month Follow-up Adj. M (SD)			12-Month Follow-up Adj. M (SD)			24-Month Follow-up Adj. M (SD)		
	Control	Exper.	n	Control	Exper.	n	Control	Exper.	n	Control	Exper.	n
Problem Solving Skills (PSI)												
Relapse/refusal	3.77 (1.85)	4.49* (1.94)	125	3.54 (1.81)	4.10[+] (1.75)	129	3.38 (1.97)	4.06* (1.89)	122	3.23 (1.85)	3.91* (1.81)	116
General situations	4.06 (1.07)	4.45[+] (1.32)	127	3.97 (1.23)	4.06 (1.19)	130	4.00 (1.13)	4.11 (1.12)	124	3.79 (1.03)	4.32** (1.08)	116
Peer Network[a]												
Deviant peers				0.20 (0.27)	0.18 (0.24)	133	0.26 (0.30)	0.17[+] (0.26)	132	0.27 (0.34)	0.19 (0.26)	125
Family Factors												
# family meetings	1.55 (1.23)	1.94 (1.49)	134	1.13 (0.62)	1.44[+] (1.16)	133	1.18 (0.67)	1.46 (1.14)	131	1.27 (0.92)	1.30 (0.85)	126
Household rules	7.37 (1.60)	7.35 (1.55)	93	7.50 (1.40)	7.55 (1.36)	88	6.89 (2.00)	7.74* (1.31)	83	6.98 (1.92)	7.15 (1.88)	123
Family bonding	7.30 (2.00)	7.21 (2.19)	135	7.21 (1.76)	7.02 (1.88)	134	7.15 (1.59)	6.91 (2.23)	130	6.98 (1.92)	7.15 (1.88)	123

Table 9-4 *Continued*

	Immediate Post Adj. M (SD)			6-Month Follow-up Adj. M (SD)			12-month Follow-up Adj. M (SD)			24-Month Follow-up Adj. M (SD)		
	Control	Exper.	n	Control	Exper.	n	Control	Exper.	n	Control	Exper.	n
Family conflict	2.98	2.95	135	2.99	3.09	134	3.01	2.95	131	3.02	3.03	127
	(0.86)	(0.90)		(0.61)	(0.67)		(0.76)	(0.89)		(0.74)	(0.79)	
Domestic conflict	2.00	2.04	78	1.96	2.11	73	2.05	1.79*	67	1.87	1.87	59
	(0.70)	(0.75)		(0.68)	(0.93)		(0.66)	(0.66)		(0.51)	(0.70)	
Drug Use												
Marijuana use[b]	1.61	2.17	135	1.54	4.11	135	3.90	1.79	132	4.39	3.08	127
	(11.27)	(6.18)		(10.97)	(12.74)		(18.98)	(4.56)		(22.77)	(10.90)	
Heroin use[b]	8.64	3.30*	135	6.78	9.08	135	19.68	6.89**	132	17.14	14.59	126
	(22.14)	(5.46)		(19.69)	(25.78)		(36.82)	(15.81)		(36.95)	(43.35)	
Cocaine use[b]	1.09	1.36	135	10.0	9.29	135	12.16	1.78+	132	10.22	9.92	126
	(4.30)	(3.56)		(36.72)	(63.34)		(45.72)	(7.35)		(37.25)	(48.98)	

+ $p < .10$; * $p < .05$; ** $p < .01$.
[a] Peer network variables were not measured at baseline or immediate post test time points.
[b] At immediate posttest, drug use was measured by the average number of times used per month since baseline; at 6- and 12-month follow-ups, it was measured by times used in the month prior to the follow-up interview.

Adapted from *Addictive Behaviors, 20,* Gainey, R. R., Catalano, R. F., Haggerty, K. P., & Hoppe, M. J. (1995). Participation in a parent training program for methadone clients, pp. 117–125, Copyright (1995), with permission from Elsevier Science.

bonding until later follow-up periods. At the 6-month follow-up, there were small differences ($p < .10$) in the number of family meetings favoring experimental families. At the 12-month follow-up, trend level differences were found in reports of domestic conflict and the number of household rules, both favoring the experimental group. These differences were not sustained at the 24-month follow-up.

Overall, experimental parents reported less drug use than control parents. Experimental parents used significantly less heroin at the end of parent training and at the 12-month follow-up, and less cocaine at the 12-month follow-up. No significant differences were found at the 24-month follow-up. At the 12-month follow-up, there was a trend level difference indicating that experimental participants had fewer deviant peers than controls. Although the difference on this measure favored experimental participants at 24-month follow-up, it was not statistically significant.

Child Outcomes. The results of comparisons between experimental and control children are presented in Table 9-5. There were few significant main effects of the intervention. Fourteen measures were examined at three time points and only one significant difference at the $p < .05$ level was found, and five trend level differences were found at the $p < .10$ level.

In the family domain, overall differences appeared to favor the control group. At 6 months, the scale of parental recognition favored the control group at the $p < .10$ level. The one significant age by experimental condition interaction indicated that the relationships between experimental condition and parent-child involvement was contingent on the child's age. At the 6-month follow-up, older experimental children reported engaging in fewer activities with their parents than did older control children, while among the youngest children, the experimental children reported more involvement in activities with their parents. This is illustrated in Figure 9-1 with respect to the involvement index item concerning whether parents read with their child.

Although no statistically significant differences between experimental and control children were found in the areas of drug use or delinquency at 6- and 12-month follow-ups, the direction of differences favored the experimental group in all but one of the comparisons made in these two areas. At the 24-month follow-up, the difference in the prevalence of marijuana use in the prior month was significant at the $p < .10$ level. Analysis of individual items in the delinquency scale found a significant difference in child reports of stealing at the 6 month follow-up and trend level differences in reports of stealing at the 12-month follow-up and picking fights at the 24-month follow-up.

Discussion

FOF is one of few experimental tests of a prevention intervention with children of substance abusers. The program was delivered to parents in methadone treatment and their children. The goal of the intervention was to prevent parents' relapse, help them cope with relapse if it occurred, and reduce

Table 9-5 Child outcomes: ANCOVA and logistic regression analyses with age and gender as covariates

	6-Month Follow-up Adj. M (SD) or %			12-Month Follow-up Adj. M (SD) or %			24-Month Follow-up Adj. M (SD) or %		
	Control	Exper.	n	Control	Exper.	n	Control	Exper.	n
Family Factors									
• Rules index	4.39 (1.04)	4.14 (1.35)	80	4.21 (1.24)	4.31 (1.25)	83	3.80 (1.47)	4.07 (1.27)	91
• Parental recognition scale	2.57 (0.57)	2.33[+] (0.66)	80	2.55 (0.54)	2.32 (0.65)	88	2.44 (0.76)	2.43 (0.69)	97
• Bonding scale	0.09 (0.53)	−0.07 (0.60)	80	0.13 (0.68)	−0.11 (0.69)	88	−0.01 (0.67)	0.00 (0.65)	97
Problem Behaviors									
• % smoked cigs in prior month	22	7	80	19	12	88	33	26	98
• % drank alcohol in last 6 mos.	22	21	80	39	21	88	42	33	98
• % used marijuana in prior month	8	2	80	8	6	88	16	7[+]	98
• Delinquency scale	1.27 (0.47)	1.13[+] (0.23)	80	1.23 (0.49)	1.20 (0.32)	88	1.28 (0.42)	1.21 (0.44)	98

• Stole in last 6 months	24	10*	79	31	14+	88	30	23	98
• Picked fights in last 6 months	30	36	80	25	29	88	37	26+	98
School									
• School attachment scale	1.93 (0.70)	1.96 (0.98)	80	1.99 (0.73)	1.92 (0.69)	86	2.08 (0.76)	2.21 (0.65)	98
• Grades	2.78 (0.87)	3.00 (0.93)	80	2.66 (1.03)	2.73 (0.87)	88	2.55 (0.95)	2.70 (0.86)	98
• % sent from classroom	57	54	80	58	54	88	47	55	98
• % expelled or suspended	17	16	79	14	14	88	26	15	98
Peers Factors									
• Negative peers scale	0.61 (0.84)	0.54 (0.78)	79	0.64 (0.82)	0.75 (0.84)	88	0.89 (0.79)	0.81 (0.91)	96

+ $p < .10$; * $p < .05$; ** $p < .01$.

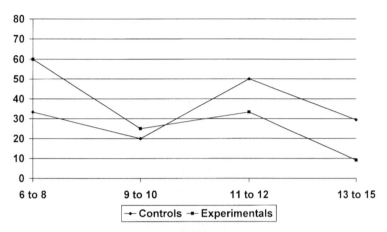

Figure 9-1 Percentage with parent in prior week by age of child. Reprinted from *Addictive Behaviors, 20*, Gainey, R. R., Catalano, R. F., Haggerty, K. P., & Hoppe, M. J. (1995). Participation in a parent training program for methadone clients, pp. 117–125, Copyright (1995), with permission from Elsevier Science.

the likelihood of substance abuse among their children. The FOF project has documented several key findings. First, children of recipients of methadone treatment displayed higher levels of problem behavior than similarly aged children in a general population sample. Second, parents in methadone treatment can be successfully engaged, and will participate in intensive family interventions, as indicated by the high level of consent to participate and attendance at parent training sessions. Third, the risk- and protective-focused intervention increased parent relapse prevention skills. Fourth, the intervention had effects on reducing parents' drug use, domestic conflict, and deviant peer networks, and increased the number of family rules at the 1-year follow-up time point. Fifth, the intervention had few impacts on children's reports of risk factors, although 24-month follow-up data revealed trend level lower rates of drug use and delinquent behaviors.

The most impressive results for the FOF intervention appear to be among parents. Parents in the experimental group improved their skill levels for avoiding drug use and sustained these skills over a 2-year period. At the 12-month follow-up, parents in the experimental group had fewer deviant peers in their networks, better family management, and less domestic conflict. Further, their frequency of heroin use was almost one third of the comparison group on average, and experimental participants had lower prevalence of cocaine use, and used cocaine less frequently on average. The curriculum only devoted 4 of the 32 sessions to relapse prevention and coping skills. However, considerable time was spent discussing and building family management and involvement skills of parents and children. Further, the training constantly reinforced the point that reducing their drug use was the most important change parents could make to improve family life. This suggests the critical role that family plays in the life of parents in drug treatment. Programs like

FOF may be an important adjunct to treatment programs to aid in reducing participants' drug use.

As a preventive intervention for children of substance abusers, there is some promise of effectiveness. Reductions in family risk factors, including parents' skill levels, family management, domestic conflict, and parents' drug use, were strongest at 12-month follow-up. Theoretically, changes in parent behavior are expected prior to changes in child behavior, and changes in parent behavior are expected to precede changes in children's perceptions of parent behavior. Further, child reports of drug use and delinquent behavior favored the experimental group most strongly at the 24-month time point. The FOF intervention may have more salutary effects on younger children. Post hoc analysis demonstrated that younger children in the experimental group were not reporting the negative effects reported by older children in the experimental group. Older children in the experimental group were less likely to have a father figure, less likely to live with an FOF parent, and less likely to be involved in activities with their parents than children in the control condition. These differences were not observed for younger children. In fact, younger children reported more involvement with their parents than younger control children. It may be that changes introduced by parents in the experimental condition who were not setting rules and limits prior to intervention are perceived by older children as restricting their freedom and lead to less positive perceptions of family involvement, while for younger children this parental involvement was welcomed. Thus, the intervention may be better suited for parents with younger children.

The analyses presented are a conservative test of the effects of the intervention. Several parents and their children in the intervention condition never received the program and only about half attended more than half of the sessions. Despite this underexposure there were still condition differences, suggesting a robust effect. However, since a fairly high proportion of the participants in the experimental group had little or no exposure to the intervention, we re-ran our analyses excluding 43 experimental parents who left methadone treatment prior to the end of the parent training portion of the intervention, or attended fewer than half of the parent training sessions. To control for the potential bias of only including highly exposed parents, we also excluded 16 control parents who left methadone treatment prior to when they would have finished the parent training portion of the intervention if they had been in the experimental group. In general, the comparison between the more highly exposed experimental group and the matched control group revealed a pattern of results similar to those found in the larger sample. For example, differences at 6 months favoring the experimental group in the number of family meetings and relapse/refusal skills became significant at the $p < .05$ level, while no loss of significance at the $p < .05$ level occurred for any variable. We also re-ran our analyses for children, limiting the sample to children of the more highly exposed experimental parents or matched control parents. This eliminated approximately 25% of the children in the control group and approximately 50% of the children in the experimental group. Again, the pattern of results remained similar to that found when looking at the larger sample.

Limitations of the Study

Several caveats should be made. First, analysis of covariance was used at each follow-up point to increase the absolute numbers of participants available at each time point. Repeated measures analysis of variance, which in some cases provides a more sensitive examination of trends over time, was not used. Second, although a sample of parents' reports of drug use were verified by biochemical assays, children's self-reports of drug use were not verified. This may produce some experimentwise error and caution must be applied to these results. Finally, 25% of parents approached by project staff refused to participate. It is unknown how these parents differed from the participants who agreed to participate. Further, this program is a Seattle program and may differ from methadone programs in other areas of the country. Caution should be made in generalizing the results achieved with this sample of parents attending Seattle methadone clinics.

Implications for Future Research

These findings suggest that interventions to prevent relapse among parents and substance abuse among their children may produce immediate, as well as delayed, or 'sleeper,' effects on targeted risk and protective factors and substance use. While studies such as FOF can report on molar changes in risk and protective factors and substance use, molecular process measures may be needed to study the mechanisms of family change that produce such findings. Such measures could include structured observations, (Conger, et al., 1992; Hops, Tildesley, Lichtenstein, Ary, & Sherman, 1990; & Szapocznik, et al., 1991), in vivo observations (Hops, Davis, & Longoria, 1995), structured daily or weekly debriefing interviews with parents and their children on activities and significant incidents (Catalano & Hawkins, 1985), or subject logs or checklists of daily activities of family life (Dishion, Patterson, Stoolmiller, & Skinner, 1991). Ideally, to study these processes of change, the measurement should be more frequent than the 6-month intervals usually reported in follow-up studies. Finally, longitudinal measurement over multiple years to examine patterns of decay (Schinke & Gilchrist, 1984), maintenance (Perry, Killen, Telch, Slinkard, & Danaher, 1980), or delayed effects (Spoth, Redmond, & Shin, 2001) should be incorporated.

ACKNOWLEDGMENTS

Preparation of this report was supported by NIDA grant # R01 DA05824-02. Focus on Families was conducted by the Social Development Research Group, University of Washington, in cooperation with Therapeutic Health Services of Seattle, WA. The authors gratefully acknowledge the assistance of

Norman O. Johnson and all the staff of Therapeutic Health Services. We thank
Ed Lorah, Linda Kamerrer, Liz Mills, Susan Anderson, and David Hawkins for
contributions to program development and implementation; Marilyn Hoppe,
Lindsay Dobrzynski, Lisa Sherry, Tom Keller, and Tony Wilsdon for data collection and data management; and Cynthia Shaw for editorial assistance.

REFERENCES

Bernardi, E., Jones, M., & Tennant, C. (1989). Quality of parenting in alcoholics and narcotic
    addicts. *British Journal of Psychiatry, 154,* 677–682.
Brewer, D. D., Catalano, R. F., Haggerty, K. P., Gainey, R. R., & Fleming, C. B. (1998). A meta-analysis
    of predictors of continued drug use during and after treatment for opiate addiction. *Addiction,
    93,* 73–92.
Brewer, D. D., Fleming, C. B., Haggerty, K. P., & Catalano, R. F. (1998). Drug use predictors of
    partner violence in opiate dependent women. *Violence and Victims, 13,* 107–115.
Brook, J. S., Brook, D. W., Gordon, A. S., Whiteman, M., & Cohen, P. (1990). The psychosocial
    etiology of adolescent drug use: A family interactional approach. *Genetic, Social, and General
    Psychology Monographs, 116,* 111–267.
Catalano, R. F. & Hawkins, J. D. (1985). Project Skills: Preliminary results from a theoretically based
    aftercare experiment. In R. S. Ashery (Ed.), *Progress in the development of cost-effective treat-
    ment for drug abusers* (pp. 157–181). (NIDA Publication No. ADM 85-1401). Washington, DC:
    U.S. Government Printing Office.
Catalano, R. F. & Hawkins, J. D. (1996). The Social Development Model: A theory of antisocial
    behavior. In J. D. Hawkins (Ed.), *Delinquency and crime: Current theories* (pp. 149–197). New
    York: Cambridge University Press.
Catalano R. F., Haggerty, K. P., Gainey, R. R., & Hoppe, M. J. (1997). Reducing parental risk factors
    for children's substance abuse: Preliminary outcomes with opiate-addicted parents. *Substance
    Use and Misuse, 32,* 699–721.
Catalano, R. F., Haggerty, K. P., Gainey, R. R., Hoppe, M. J., & Brewer, D. D. (1998). Effectiveness of
    primary prevention interventions with high-risk youth. In W. J. Bukoski & R. I. Evans (Eds.),
    *NIDA Research Monograph: 176. Cost benefit/cost effectiveness research on drug abuse
    prevention: Implications for programming and policy* (pp. 83–110). Rockville, MD: National
    Institute on Drug Abuse.
Catalano R. F., Gainey, R. R., Fleming, C., Haggerty, K. P., & Johnson, N. O. (1999). An experimen-
    tal intervention with families of substance abusers: 1-year follow-up of the Focus on Families
    project. *Addiction, 94,* 241–254.
Coie, J. D., Watt, N. F., West, S. G., Hawkins, J. D., Asarnow, J. R., Markman, H. J., Ramey, S. L.,
    Shure, M. B., & Long, B. (1993). The science of prevention: A conceptual framework and some
    directions for a national research program. *American Psychologist, 48,* 1013–1022.
Conger, R. D., Conger, K. J., Elder, G. H., Lorenz, F. O., Simons, R. L., & Whitbeck, L. B. (1992).
    A family process model of economic hardship and adjustment of early adolescent boys. *Child
    Development, 63,* 526–541.
Dembo, R., Grandon, G., LaVoie, L., Schmeidler, J., & Burgos, W. (1986). Parents and drugs revis-
    ited: Some further evidence in support of social learning theory. *Criminology, 24,* 85–103.
Dishion, T. J., Patterson, G. R., Stoolmiller, M., & Skinner, M. L. (1991). Family, school, and behav-
    ioral antecedents to early adolescent involvement with antisocial peers. *Developmental
    Psychology, 27,* 172–180.
Falco, M. (1992). *The making of a drug-free America: Programs that work.* New York: Times Books.
Fleming, C. B., Brewer, D. D., Gainey, R. R., Haggerty, K. P., & Catalano, R. F. (1997). Parent drug
    use and bonding to parents as predictors of substance use in children of substance abusers.
    Journal of Child and Adolescent Substance Abuse, 6(4), 75–86.
Gainey, R. R., Catalano, R. F., Haggerty, K. P., & Hoppe, M. J. (1995). Participation in a parent train-
    ing program for methadone clients. *Addictive Behaviors, 20,* 117–125.

Gainey, R. R., Catalano, R. F., Haggerty, K. P., & Hoppe, M. J. (1997). Deviance among the children of heroin addicts in treatment: Impact of parents and peers. *Deviant Behavior, 18,* 143–159.

Goldstein, A. P. & Kanfer, F. H. (1979). *Maximizing treatment gains: Transfer enhancement in psychotherapy.* New York: Academic Press.

Grady, K., Gersick, K., & Boratynski, M. (1986). Preparing parents for teenagers: A step in prevention of substance abuse. *Journal of Drug Education, 16,* 203–220.

Griffith, D. R., Azuma, S. D., & Chasnoff, I. J. (1994). Three-year outcome of children exposed prenatally to drugs. *Journal of the American Academy of Child and Adolescent Psychiatry, 33,* 20–27.

Gross, J. & McCaul, M. E. (1992). An evaluation of a psychoeducational and substance abuse risk reduction intervention for children of substance abusers. *Journal of Community Psychology, (OSAP Special Issue), 20,* 75–87.

Hall, J. A., Vaughan, J. E., Gross, G., Catalano, R. F., Hawkins, J. D., & Farber, J. (1983). *Project Skills Problem Situation Inventory.* Seattle: University of Washington, Social Development Research Group.

Haskett, M. E., Miller, J. W., Whitworth, J. M., & Huffman, J. M. (1992). Intervention with cocaine-abusing mothers. *Families in Society, 73,* 451–61.

Hawkins, J. D., Catalano, R. F., & Wells, E. A. (1986). Measuring effects of skills training intervention for drug abusers. *Journal of Consulting and Clinical Psychology, 54,* 661–664.

Hawkins, J. D., Catalano, R. F., Jones, G., & Fine, D. N. (1987). Delinquency prevention through parent training: Results and issues from work in progress. In J. G. Wilson & G. C. Loury (Eds.), *From children to citizens: Families, schools, and delinquency prevention: Vol. 3* (pp. 186–204). New York: Springer-Verlag.

Hawkins, J. D., Catalano, R. F., Gillmore, M. R., & Wells, E. A. (1989). Skills training for drug abusers: Generalization, maintenance and effects on drug use. *Journal of Consulting and Clinical Psychology, 57,* 559–563.

Hawkins, J. D., Catalano, R. F., & Miller, J. Y. (1992). Risk and protective factors for alcohol and other drug problems in adolescence and early adulthood: Implications for substance abuse prevention. *Psychological Bulletin, 112,* 64–105.

Hawkins, J. D., Catalano, R. F., Morrison, J. D., O'Donnell, J., Abbott, R. D., & Day, L. E. (1992). The Seattle Social Development Project: Effects of the first four years on protective factors and problem behaviors. In J. McCord & R. Tremblay (Eds.), *The prevention of antisocial behaviors in children* (pp. 139–161). New York: Guilford Press.

Hoppe M. J., Wells, E. A., Haggerty, K. P., Simpson, E., Gainey, R. R., & Catalano, R. F. (1998). Bonding in a high risk and a general sample of children: Comparison of measures of attachment and their relationship to smoking and drinking. *Journal of Youth and Adolescence, 27,* 59–82.

Hops, H., Tildesley, E., Lichtenstein, E., Ary, D., & Sherman, L. (1990). Parent-adolescent problem-solving interactions and drug use. *American Journal of Drug and Alcohol Abuse, 16,* 239–258.

Hops, H., Davis, B., & Longoria, N. (1995). Methodological issues in direct observation: Illustrations with the Living in Familial Environments (LIFE) coding system. *Journal of Clinical and Consulting Psychology, 24,* 193–203.

Institute of Medicine, Committee on Prevention of Mental Disorders. (1994). *Reducing risks for mental disorders: Frontiers for preventive intervention research.* Washington: National Academy Press.

Jenson, G. R. & Brownfield, D. (1983). Parents and drugs. *Criminology, 21,* 543–554.

Jenson, J. M., Wells, E. A., Plotnick, R. D., Hawkins, J. D., & Catalano, R. F. (1993). The effects of skills and intentions to use drugs on posttreatment drug use of juvenile delinquents. *American Journal of Drug and Alcohol Abuse, 19,* 1–18.

Jessop, D. J. (1981). Family relationships as viewed by parents and adolescents: A specification. *Journal of Marriage and the Family, 43,* 95–107.

Jessor, R. (1998). *New perspectives on adolescent risk behavior.* New York: Cambridge University Press.

Johnson V. & Pandina R. J. (1991). Effects of the family environment on adolescent substance use, delinquency, and coping styles. *American Journal of Drug and Alcohol Abuse, 17,* 71–88.

Kolar, A. F., Brown, B. S., Haertzen, C. A., & Michaelson, M. A. (1994). Children of substance abusers: The life experiences of children of opiate addicts in methadone maintenance. *American Journal of Drug and Alcohol Abuse, 202*, 159–171.

Kumpfer, K. L. & DeMarsh, J. P. (1986). Family environmental and genetic influences on children's future chemical dependency. In S. Ezekoye, K. Kumpfer, & W. Bukoski, (Eds.), *Childhood and chemical abuse: Prevention and intervention* (pp. 49–91). New York: Haworth.

Marlatt, G. A. & Gordon, J. R. (1985). *Relapse prevention: Maintenance strategies in the treatment of addictive behaviors.* New York: Guilford Press.

Mays, L. C. (1995). Substance abuse and parenting. In M. H. Bornstein (Ed.), *Handbook of parenting: Vol. 4. Applied and practical parenting* (pp. 101–123). Mahwah, NJ: Lawrence Erlbaum Associates.

Moos, R. H. (1974). *Family Environment Scale.* Palo Alto, CA: Consulting Psychology Press.

O'Donnell, J., Hawkins, J. D., Catalano, R. C., Abbott, R. D., & Day, L. E. (1995). Preventing school failure, drug use, and delinquency among low-income children: Long-term intervention in elementary schools. *American Journal of Orthopsychiatry, 65*, 87–100.

Patterson, G. R. & Fleishman, M. J. (1979). Maintenance of treatment effects: Some considerations concerning family systems and follow-up data. *Behavior Therapy, 10*, 168–185.

Patterson, G. R. & Reid, J. B. (1973). Intervention for families of aggressive boys: A replication study. *Behaviour Research and Therapy, 11*, 383–394.

Perry, C., Killen, J., Telch, M., Slinkard, L. A., & Danaher, B. G. (1980). Modifying smoking behavior of teenagers: A school-based intervention. *American Journal of Public Health, 70*, 722–7250.

Plotnick, R. D. (1994). Applying benefit-cost analysis to substance use prevention programs. *The International Journal of the Addictions, 29*, 339–359.

Plotnick, R. D., Young, D. S., Catalano, R. F., & Haggerty, K. P. (1998). Benefits and costs of a family-focused methadone treatment and drug abuse prevention program: Preliminary findings. In W. J. Bukoski & R. I. Evans (Eds.), *NIDA Research Monograph: 176. Cost benefit/cost effectiveness research of drug abuse prevention: Implications for programming and policy* (pp. 161–183). Rockville, MD: National Institute on Drug Abuse.

Roese, N. J. & Jamieson, D. W. (1993). Twenty years of bogus pipeline research: A critical review and meta-analysis. *Psychological Bulletin, 114*, 363–375.

Rosenthal, T. & Bandura, A. (1978). Psychological modeling: Theory and practice. In S. Garfield & A. E. Bergin (Eds.), *Handbook of psychotherapy and behavior change: An empirical analysis* (pp. 621–658). New York: Wiley.

Russel, F. F. & Free, T. A. (1991). Early intervention for infants and toddlers with prenatal drug exposure. *Infants and Young Children, 3*, 78–85.

Rutter, M. (1990). Psychosocial resilience and protective mechanisms. In J. Rolf, A. S. Masten, D. Cicchetti, K. H. Nuechterlein, & S. Weintraub (Eds.), *Risk and protective factors in the development of psychopathology* (pp. 181–214). Cambridge, England: Cambridge University Press.

Schinke, S. P. & Gilchrist, L. D. (1984). Preventing cigarette smoking with youth. *Journal of Primary Prevention, 5*, 48–56.

Serketich, W. J. & Dumas, J. E. (1996). The effectiveness of behavioral parent training to modify antisocial behavior in children: A meta-analysis. *Behavior Therapy, 27*, 171–186.

Shedler, J. & Block, J. (1990). Adolescent drug use and psychological health: A longitudinal inquiry. *American Psychologist, 45*, 612–630.

Simcha-Fagan, O., Gersten, J. C., & Langner, T. S. (1986). Early precursors and concurrent correlates of patterns of illicit drug use in adolescence. *Journal of Drug Issues, 16*, 7–28.

Spoth, R. L., Redmond, C., & Shin, C. (2001) Randomized trial of brief family interventions for general populations: Adolescent substance use outcomes 4 years following baseline. *Journal of Consulting and Clinical Psychology, 69*, 627–642.

Springer, F., Phillips, J., Phillips, L., Cannady, L. P., & Derst-Harris, E. (1992). CODA: A creative therapy program for children in families affected by abuse of alcohol or other drugs. *Journal of Community Psychology (OSAP Special Issue), 20*, 55–74.

Straus, M. A. (1979). Measuring intrafamily conflict and violence: The Conflict Tactics (CT) scales. *Journal of Marriage and the Family, 41*, 75–88.

Surgeon General. (1988). *The health consequences of smoking: Nicotine addiction. A report of the Surgeon General.* Rockville, MD: U.S. Department of Health and Human Services.

Szapocznik, J., Rio, A. T., Hervis, O., Mitrani, V. B., Kurtines, W., & Faraci, A. M. (1991). Assessing change in family functioning as a result of treatment: The Structural Family Rating Scale (SFSR). *Journal of Marital and Family Therapy, 17*, 295–310.

Tremblay, R. E., Vitaro, F., Bertrand, L., LeBlanc, M., Beauchesne, H., Boileau, H., & David, L. (1992). Parent and child training to prevent early onset of delinquency: The Montreal Longitudinal-Experimental Study. In J. McCord & R. Tremblay (Eds.), *Preventing antisocial behavior: Interventions from birth through adolescence* (pp. 117–138). New York: Guilford Press.

Wells, E. A., Hawkins, J. D., & Catalano, R. F. (1988a). Choosing drug use measures for treatment outcome studies: I. The influence of measurement approach on treatment results. *The International Journal of the Addictions, 23*, 851–873.

Wells, E. A., Hawkins, J. D., & Catalano, R. F. (1988b). Choosing drug use measures for treatment outcome studies: II. Timing baseline and follow-up measurement. *The International Journal of the Addictions, 23*, 875–885.

W. T. Grant Consortium on School-Based Promotion of Social Competence. Drug and Alcohol Prevention Curricula. (1992). In J. D. Hawkins, R. F. Catalano, & Associates (Eds.), *Communities that care: Action for drug abuse prevention* (pp. 129–148). San Francisco: Jossey-Bass Publishers.

Werner, E. E. & Smith, R. S. (1992). *Overcoming the odds: High risk children from birth to adulthood.* Ithaca, NY: Cornell University Press.

CHAPTER 10

Children of Parents with Intellectual Disabilities

Maurice A. Feldman

My mother loved me. I know that emphatically, down in the deepest recesses of my being. I do not always give her love the respect it deserves—she is retarded—a priori for me, it devalues most of what she gave me (Ronai, 1997, p. 420).

As society moves towards supporting full inclusion of people with disabilities, questions are raised about parenting rights and competencies, and the impact of parental disabilities on offspring. This chapter reviews the current state of knowledge on the development of children raised by parents with intellectual disabilities and the efficacy of child- and parent-focused interventions. First, a description of parents with intellectual disabilities is provided.

PARENTS WITH INTELLECTUAL DISABILITIES

In this chapter, 'intellectual disabilities' refers to adult IQ scores of less than 80. Most parents with intellectual disabilities have a diagnosis of mental retardation (typically obtained when they were in school), but many of them would no longer meet two crucial diagnostic criteria of having an IQ score below 75 and deficits in adaptive functioning (American Psychiatric Association, 1994; Luckasson, et al., 1992). Nevertheless, once so labelled, these parents are treated differently than other parents (Hayman, 1990; Tymchuk & Feldman, 1991). A presumption of inevitable parental inadequacy due to cognitive limitations (as evidenced by low IQ) persists; consequently, parents with intellectual disabilities frequently are not given the opportunity to parent or have their parenting rights terminated even when there is no prima facie evidence of child maltreatment (Booth & Booth, 1997; Hayman, 1990; Schilling, Schinke, Blythe, & Barth, 1982; Seagull & Scheurer, 1986; Taylor, et al., 1991; Vogel, 1987). Usually the concern is not physical or sexual abuse per se, but rather the potential risk of neglect due to perceived or demonstrable parental incompetence.

Although it is difficult to verify incidence with precision, it has been estimated that there are 120,000 births each year to parents with intellectual disabilities in the U.S. (Keltner, 1992). More and more families with parents who have intellectual disabilities are being referred to child protection, family, and early intervention services across North America, Europe, and Australia (Llewellyn, 1996; McGaw, 1996; Pixa-Kettner, 1996; Ray, Rubinstein, & Russo, 1994).

The rise in the number of these families can be traced to several recent developments. With the deinsitutionalization and community living movements in full force for over 20 years, many more people with intellectual disabilities than ever before have experienced and internalized conventional family values and norms. Perhaps, an inevitable consequence of greater acceptance and integration of people with disabilities is their fundamental desire to do what most adults do—marry and raise a family. Furthermore, many people with mild intellectual disabilities are aware of, and hire lawyers to defend, their legal rights. Discriminatory sterilization and marriage laws have been repealed in many jurisdictions and family legislation makes child removal a last resort (e.g., P.L. 96-272—Adoption Assistance and Child Welfare Act, 1980; Child and Family Services Act of Ontario, 1987). Judges now ask the state what services have been, or could be, offered to keep the child at home and rulings favoring family preservation are more common (Hayman, 1990; Vogel, 1987). Nevertheless, current field and popular knowledge still is tainted by prejudices and misconceptions. For example, it is not clear to what extent research findings are representative of all families with parents who have intellectual disabilities because most studies involve mothers with intellectual disabilities who have already been identified by the child welfare and family services systems. There is growing realization, however, that many parents with intellectual disabilities may be (or can become) competent parents, especially when provided appropriate supports and services (Feldman, 1994).

Parents with intellectual disabilities who come to the attention of child protection and social service agencies have characteristics and experiences, in addition to low IQ, that may lead to inadequate parenting. Thus, while it is tempting to blame parenting problems on parental cognitive limitations, an interactional model is most applicable (Belsky, 1984). Various vulnerability factors that typically are present include: a history of abuse, inadequate parental role models, stigmatization, victimization, parental physical and mental health problems, child disability and behavior disorders, poverty, substandard housing, and unemployment (Tymchuk & Keltner, 1991). Many of these parents are highly stressed (Feldman, Léger, & Walton-Allen, 1997), socially isolated (Feldman & Walton-Allen, 1997), and depressed (Walton-Allen, 1993).

Families with parents who have intellectual disabilities need and receive many services related to child-care, child protection monitoring, early intervention, child behavior management, public health, community living and vocational skills training, advocacy, and individual and couples counselling (Walton-Allen & Feldman, 1991). Objective evaluations of parenting knowledge and skills (before training) revealed varied deficiencies in basic child-care routines such as handling a newborn, bathing, diapering, feeding, nutrition, childhood illnesses, first aid, safety, and knowing when to call the doctor or 911 (Feldman, 1998; Feldman & Case, 1997, 1999; Feldman, Case, Garrick, et al., 1992; Feldman, Case, & Sparks, 1992; Feldman, Ducharme, & Case, 1999; Feldman, Garrick, & Case, 1997). Some parents may have only one or two problem areas, while others have numerous skill deficits that must be rectified before the child can safely be at home. Home environments consistently are unstimulating (Feldman & Walton-Allen, 1997; Keltner, 1994) and parental interactions generally are devoid of warmth, sensitivity, responsiveness, and reinforcement (Crittenden & Bonvillian, 1984; Feldman, Case, Towns, & Betel, 1985; Feldman, Case, Rincover, Towns, & Betel, 1989; Feldman, Sparks, & Case, 1993; Feldman, et al., 1986; Slater, 1986). Clearly, families with parents who have intellectual disabilities have many risk factors associated with negative parental and child outcomes.

CHILDREN OF PARENTS WITH INTELLECTUAL DISABILITIES

There is increasing evidence that offspring of parents with intellectual disabilities are at risk for developmental and adjustment problems across the lifespan.

Infants and Young Children

Language, cognitive, and physical delays are apparent in infancy. A preliminary study found significant mental (but not physical) delay in 5 of 12, 2 year olds raised by Caucasian mothers with intellectual disabilities (Feldman, et al., 1985). The mean Bayley Scales of Infant Development Mental Development Index (Bayley, 1969) was 84 and these scores were highly correlated with the quality of home environment as measured by the Caldwell Home Observation for the Measurement of the Environment (HOME) Inventory (Caldwell & Bradley, 1984). Child language delay was particularly evident in this, and other infant studies (Feldman, et al., 1986, 1989, 1993).

A more recent cross-sectional study (Feldman, unpublished data) with a larger sample ($n = 86$) and broader age-range of young children (age range: 2 to 35 months) of parents with intellectual disabilities (mean IQ = 71) found significant delays in both the 6-month Bayley mental and psychomotor scales (means = 86 and 87, respectively). Bayley mental (but not physical) development scores significantly declined to a mean of 78 at a mean of 22 months of age. A longitudinal analysis of 33 children replicated the cross-sectional findings.

School-Age Children

Several studies have examined the intellectual status of older children of parents with intellectual disabilities. Reed and Reed (1965) studied 7,778 children who were genetically related to 289 probands with IQs less than 69 who had lived in a Minnesota institution for people with mental retardation. Reed and Reed found that when both parents had mental retardation, 40% of the children had IQs below 70; 80% had IQs lower than 90 and the mean IQ for this group was 74. When only one parent had mental retardation, 15% of the children had IQs below 70 and only 54% scored above 90; the mean score was 90. Child IQ scores were lower when the mother rather than the father had mental retardation. These findings compared to 1% with IQs below 70, 91% above 90, and a mean score of 107 for children with two parents without mental retardation.

Increased risk of developmental delay and mental retardation in children of parents with intellectual disabilities also has been seen in England (Mickleson, 1947), Northern Ireland (Scally, 1973), Sweden (Gillberg & Geijer-Karlsson, 1983), the U.S. (Garber, 1988; Ramey & Ramey, 1992), and Canada (Feldman & Walton-Allen, 1997). Only one published study (in England), failed to detect lowered IQ in offspring of parents with mental retardation (Brandon, 1957). While it is conceivable that increased risk may be related to poverty because virtually all parents with intellectual disabilities are poor (Fotheringham, 1971), Feldman and Walton-Allen (1997) found that the mean IQs of children with mothers who had adult IQ scores of less than 70 were significantly lower than that of impoverished children of parents without intellectual disabilities.

Several studies have examined other child outcome measures in addition to IQ. Children of parents with intellectual disabilities are at risk for cerebral palsy (Nelson & Ellenberg, 1986). Feldman and Walton-Allen (1997) found that academic achievement of school-age children (especially the boys) of mothers with intellectual disabilities was significantly below that of a low-income comparison group; 36% of the children in the maternal intellectual disabilities group met the diagnostic criteria for learning disabilities and 59% were receiving special education services. Children of parents with intellectual disabilities are at risk for behavioral and psychiatric problems (Feldman & Walton-Allen, 1997; Gillberg & Geijer-Karlsson, 1983; O'Neill, 1985). Feldman and Walton-Allen (1997) found that over 40% of the children of mothers with intellectual disabilities had clinically significant conduct disorders (as measured by the Ontario Child Behaviour Checklist; Offord et al., 1987). In the maternal intellectual disabilities group, boys had more behavior problems than girls, and children with IQs $\geq$ 85 were more likely to have multiple behavior problems. Similarly, O'Neill (1985) reported that 50% of 'normal' or 'bright' children of parents with mental retardation had behavior problems such as noncompliance and pseudo-retardation. A retrospective study in Sweden found that 58%

of children of parents with intellectual disabilities had accessed psychiatric services (Gillberg & Geijer-Karlsson, 1983). Although more research is needed, existing studies of school-age children of parents with intellectual disabilities indicate that the children are at risk for intellectual, academic, and behavioral problems. Boys may be affected more than girls, and the children with average or above-average IQs may demonstrate greater social and emotional maladjustment than children with below-average IQs.

Adolescents and Adults

Very little is known about adolescent and adult offspring of parents with intellectual disabilities. Quantitative data are not available and only ethnographic and personal accounts exist (Booth & Booth, 1997; Ronai, 1997). These qualitative studies suggest a common theme of ambivalence of the adult offspring to their childhood and their affected parent—'I both love and hate my mentally retarded mother' (Ronai, 1997, p. 431). Booth and Booth (1997) interviewed 30 adolescent and adult offspring (age range: 16 to 42 years) and reported that about half had ongoing learning problems. Although this finding is consistent with the child studies noted above, the authors suggested that their high prevalence rate may have been a result of sampling bias (it was easier to find adult offspring with intellectual disabilities because of their continuing involvement with the social service system). About 23% of the entire sample reported serious mental health issues (two had attempted suicide). Consistent with the findings of Feldman and Walton-Allen (1997), Booth and Booth (1997) reported that adolescent and adult offspring who did not have learning problems were more likely to report social adjustment problems as children and adults. The majority of those interviewed (as well as Ronai, 1997) were abused as children, but usually not by the parent with intellectual disabilities. As parents themselves, none of the offspring without intellectual disabilities had lost their children compared to eight who had intellectual disabilities. Booth and Booth (1997) and Ronai (1997) highlighted the importance of the extended family and positive social support in fostering resiliency in the offspring. Much more research is needed to substantiate these preliminary qualitative findings of the long-term impact of being raised by parents with intellectual disabilities. For example, it is not known whether placing children in foster care ultimately is a better or worse alternative than providing supports and services to parents with intellectual disabilities so that they can keep their children at home.

EARLY CHILDHOOD EDUCATION INTERVENTIONS FOR CHILDREN OF PARENTS WITH INTELLECTUAL DISABILITIES

This section will review the limited literature on child-focused early intervention in which the children are placed in specialized daycares. The next section will review parent education programs that presented child outcome results.

The Milwaukee Project

This controversial program was started in the 1960s and targeted inner-city, impoverished, African-American families with mothers who had IQs of less than 75. Its purpose was to prevent mild mental retardation in the children of these mothers by placing the infants in a specialized daycare environment designed to replicate the type of stimulation, activities, and adult-child inter-actions typically provided in a 'middle-class' home. The children spent week-days in this setting until they started school when they were 6 years old. In addition, the mothers were visited at home by a paraprofessional who offered advice on child-care, nutrition, and community living skills. The mothers also received vocational training and academic remediation.

The evaluation of the daycare component consisted of 17 experimental and 18 (nonrandomized) control children who were followed for 14 years (Garber, 1988). There were numerous outcome measures of child development, academic achievement, and mother-child interactions. Results indicated that upon entering school, the project children had significantly higher IQs than the control group. Over the school years, the IQs of the experimental children declined and the differences between groups decreased (but still remained sta-tistically significant). At the conclusion of the study, Garber and his associates (Garber, Hodge, Rynders, Dever, & Velu, 1991) estimated that the overall inter-vention effect was an increase in 22 IQ points—enough to move the children into the average range of intelligence. Despite this IQ advantage, no significant differences were found on academic achievement measures; however, twice as many control children repeated a grade (Garber, et al., 1991). Direct observa-tions of mother-child interactions indicated that although the experimental and control mothers' interaction modes were similar, the project children were better able to solicit positive and verbal interactions from their mothers (in effect, the children created a more stimulating environment at home).

The Milwaukee Project has been criticized on several methodological and other grounds, including the small sample size, nonrandom group assignment, teaching to the (developmental) test, few peer-reviewed publications, and inconsistent reporting of methods and results (Jensen, 1989; Page, 1986; Sommer & Sommer, 1983; Spitz, 1991; Weinberg, 1991). The project's consid-erable cost, the drop in the experimental children's IQ, and unimpressive school achievement results raise concerns about the cost-benefit of such a large-scale intervention.

The Carolina Abecedarian Project and the Infant Health and Development Program (IHDP)

Over the past 30 years, Craig Ramey and his associates have conducted several long-term early intervention studies. The Carolina Abecedarian Project was directed at rural, impoverished African-American children while the IHDP focused on premature, low birth weight (<2,500 g), mostly poor children across the U.S. Like the Milwaukee Project, a specialized stimulating daycare curriculum was provided starting in infancy until school-age (Sparling & Lewis, 1979, 1984). Importantly, unlike the Milwaukee Project, children in Ramey's studies were *randomly* assigned to experimental and control groups.

Both the Abecedarian Project and the IHDP included families where mothers had IQ or verbal competency scores of less than 70. Ramey and his colleagues (Martin, Ramey, & Ramey, 1990; Ramey & Ramey, 1992) have provided separate analyses of the children of these parents. Both studies found that early intervention reduced the extent of decline of IQ scores in these children. In the Abecedarian Project, the spread between experimental and control IQs after 4 years was the same as in the Milwaukee Project—22 points. All of the Abecedarian children of parents with intellectual disabilities had IQs in the average range ($M = 95$) compared to only 14% of the control children ($M = 73$).

While the Abecedarian results are based on a sample size of 13 African-Americans (6 intervention and 7 control children of parents with intellectual disabilities), the IHDP involved a mixed race subsample of 288 low birthweight children (116 intervention and 172 control children) whose parents had verbal competence scores below 70 on the Peabody Picture Vocabulary Test. Although the IQ scores of both groups declined, at 3 years of age, the experimental children leveled off at a mean IQ of 85 while the control children's mean IQ was 77 (see Ramey & Ramey, 1992, Figure 5). Only 23% of the intervention children had IQs less than 75 compared to almost 50% in the control group. A subsample of 207 IHDP children whose mothers scored between 71 and 85 on the Peabody revealed similar trends. At 3 years of age, the mean IQs of the intervention and control children of these 'borderline' parents were approximately 95 and 83, respectively (Ramey & Ramey, 1992).

Taken together, the findings of the Milwaukee Project, Carolina Abecedarian Project, and the IHDP revealed that declines in IQ in children of parents with intellectual disabilities may be diminished by early, intensive, ongoing specialized daycare involvement. Interestingly, Ramey and Ramey (1992) presented some suggestive data from the control groups that even enrollment in a regular daycare may have beneficial effects on these children (but not to the extent of specialized daycare). Because of loss of IQ gains and weak school achievement results observed in the Milwaukee Project, further follow-up data are needed to ascertain the breath, scope, and long-term cost-benefits of the Abecedarian Project and IHDP.

PARENT EDUCATION INTERVENTIONS

Although specialized daycare interventions for children of parents with intellectual disabilities have shown promising results, they are expensive and may not be cost-beneficial. Furthermore, they focus on child intellectual development and do not address the real risk of in-home physical and psychological neglect due to parental child-care skill deficits. Several programs have attempted to improve child welfare and development by teaching child-care and interactional skills to parents with intellectual disabilities (e.g., Feldman, 1996, 1998; Greene, Norman, Searle, Daniels, & Lubeck, 1995; Madsen, 1979; McGaw, 1996; Tymchuk & Andron, 1992; Whitman & Accardo, 1990). Few programs have provided objective parent training data, and fewer still have documented child outcomes (Feldman, 1994). This section will describe characteristics of effective parent-focused interventions and review studies that evaluated the effects of parent training on the child and family.

Characteristics of Effective Parent Education Interventions

The more effective intervention strategies are home-based, skill-focused, and use behavioral teaching strategies (Feldman, 1994). Although several studies have provided instruction in classroom settings (e.g., Fantuzzo, Wray, Hall, Goins, & Azar, 1986; Tymchuk, 1991; Tymchuk, Andron, & Hagelstein, 1992), consistently better results were obtained with in-home training (e.g., Bakken, Miltenberger, & Schauss, 1993; Feldman, Case, & Sparks, 1992; Feldman, et al., 1993). When training cannot be conducted in the home, then an alternative home-like setting may be necessary to achieve generalization back to the home (Bakken, et al., 1993; Feldman, et al., 1986).

Effective training programs break child-care skills down to component steps and teach them individually (e.g., Feldman, et al., 1986; Feldman, Case, Garrick, et al., 1992). Programs that rely on behavioral instructional strategies such as task analysis, modelling, roleplaying, performance feedback, and social and tangible reinforcement tend to get better results than those using didactic instruction (Feldman, 1994). Generalization and maintenance strategies need to be incorporated into training (e.g., Feldman, et al., 1989). Picture books and audiocassettes that present basic child-care, health, and safety skills in a simple step-by-step format (Case & Feldman, 1993) can be used as self-learning aids (Feldman & Case, 1997, 1999; Feldman, et al., 1999). Parent education is not seen as a panacea; it frequently is combined with other services and supports (e.g., child protection monitoring, subsidized daycare, visiting nurse, community living skills training, individual and marital counselling, help from extended family, legal and advocacy services).

Review of Child and Family Outcomes of Parent Education Interventions

Over the past 15 years there has been a dramatic increase in empirical evaluations of parent training for parents with intellectual disabilities (see reviews by Feldman, 1994, 1997). Most of these studies presented data on changes in parenting skills, but few have demonstrated the impact of parent education on child and family outcomes. This section will focus on those studies that provided child and family results.

Infant and Child Health and Safety

Children of parents with intellectual disabilities are at risk for physical neglect due to parental child-care knowledge and skill deficiencies (Feldman, 1998; Feldman, Case, Garrick, et al., 1992; Feldman, Case, & Sparks, 1992). Several studies have provided child outcome results related to improvements in child health, safety, and physical development when their parents received training in basic child-care skills.

Over the past 15 years, Feldman and his associates have developed a model for the assessment and training of parenting skills to parents with intellectual disabilities (Feldman, 1996, 1998). This model incorporates the features and training techniques of effective in-home intervention noted above. Feldman's studies have demonstrated the efficacy of both full training (Feldman, Case, Garrick, et al., 1992; Feldman, Case, & Sparks, 1992) and self-instruction (Feldman & Case, 1997, 1999; Feldman, et al., 1999) in improving basic child-care skills in parents with intellectual disabilities. Several of these studies also presented anecdotal reports (substantiated by other health and social service professionals) suggesting improvements in child weight gain, diaper rash, and toileting when parents received training in related skills such as nutrition and feeding, treating diaper rash, and toilet training (Feldman, Case, Garrick, et al., 1992; Feldman, Case, & Sparks, 1992; Feldman, et al., 1999).

In a recent study, Feldman, Garrick, and Case (1997) taught feeding and nutrition skills to two mothers with intellectual disabilities (one mother's IQ was 70 and the other's was not known) who had children (ages: 7 months and 10.5 months) independently diagnosed as nonorganic-failure-to-thrive. Before and during parent training, one family was involved with a hospital-based failure-to-thrive clinic while the other child was monitored by her pediatrician. A multiple-baseline design across children revealed an increase in rate of weight gain related to the addition of the parent training component. Both children's weights started below the third percentile. After parent training, the children's weights were at the 15th and 25th percentiles, respectively. Substantial follow-up periods of 28.5 and 59 months, respectively, confirmed the durability of parent training effects on the children.

Using similar training methods as in the Feldman studies, Greene, et al. (1995) taught a single mother with an IQ of 71 a wide-range of child-care skills, including diapering, bathing, recognizing illnesses, home safety, feeding, and nutrition. Her infant son, who was diagnosed as failure-to-thrive, remained in foster care and training was conducted during supervised visits. Although an experimental design was not used and unstable baselines partially obscured the time series effects, training was associated with an increase in the amount of nutritious foods that the mother served. The child's weight increased from below the 5th percentile at 7 weeks of age to approximately the 50th percentile when he was 17 months old. Note that the child was in foster care over most of this period and that could have contributed substantially to child weight gain.

Tymchuk, Hamada, Andron, and Anderson (1990) evaluated home safety training in four mothers with intellectual disabilities (IQs ranged from 69 to 71) and found that reports of child accidents increased from three to six from base-line to training, but then dropped to zero over the 1-month follow-up period. Certainly, an experimental design, confirmations of reports, and a longer follow-up period would be required to ascertain whether parent training had indeed reduced child accidents.

Parent–Child Interactions and Child Development Data

A lack of a stimulating home environment, sensitivity, responsivity, affection, limit-setting, and consistent discipline places children of parents with intellec-tual disabilities at risk for developmental and behavioral problems (Crittenden & Bonvillian, 1984; Feldman, et al., 1985, 1986, 1993; Feldman & Walton-Allen, 1997; Garber, 1988; Keltner, 1994; O'Neill, 1985). Thus, several studies have evalu-ated parent-child interaction training and have presented child outcome data.

Slater (1986) used a between-groups design with random assignment and an attention-control group to demonstrate that when parents with intellectual disabilities (mean IQ was approximately 75) were taught how to promote the cognitive development of their preschoolers (mean age was approximately 4 years), increases were noted on the Caldwell HOME Inventory total scores and some scales of the McCarthy Scales of Children's Abilities. In addition, the children in the training groups improved the accuracy and complexity of their responses to comprehension questions about a recent field trip. The more sophisticated the interactional skills that were taught to the parents (e.g., ask-ing the child more complex questions; providing more detailed information to the child), the better their children did. Because follow-up was limited to 1 month, the long-term impact of this training was not evaluated.

Tymchuk and Andron (1988) provided clinic and home behavior manage-ment training to an overly punitive mother (IQ = 74) with three children (ages 1.5, 5.3, and 7.8 years) who exhibited various problem behaviors such as cry-ing, temper tantrums, soiling, and noncompliance. Training focused on deliv-ery of positive reinforcement for appropriate child behaviors and the mother viewed videotapes of her interactions with her children to identify child behaviors that should be reinforced. Training was only partially effective in improving the mother's positive interactions. Observations made at the clinic revealed that the two older children showed greater increases in appropriate behaviors (e.g., attending, cooperation, positive vocalizations) than the youngest child when they were alone with their mother, but the youngest and oldest children generally improved more than the middle child when the three children were together with their mother. Observations at home suggested that the youngest and oldest children, but not the middle child increased their pos-itive vocalizations. A clear interpretation of the findings is marred by several methodological weaknesses including: having only one participating family, high baseline scores, absence of interobserver agreement scores and normative comparison data, and very short (2-min) observation sessions.

Feldman, et al. (1986) showed that mothers with intellectual disabilities (IQs ranged from 64 to 77) had fewer positive stimulating interactions with their infants and toddlers (ages ranged from 4 to 22 months), who in turn had significantly fewer vocalizations, as compared to parents without intellectual disabilities and their age-matched children. In particular, the former mothers did not praise or imitate/expand child vocalizations as often as did the mothers without intellectual disabilities. Feldman, et al. (1986) showed that not only was training effective in rapidly increasing maternal interactional skills, but also that child vocalizations increased substantially in four of the seven children (including the two language delayed children). In a subsequent study (Feldman, et al., 1989), two other children with language delays not only showed more vocalizations, but also improved their performance on the language items of standardized developmental tests after their mothers had received interaction training.

Because the single-subject time series designs used in Feldman, et al. (1986, 1989) could not factor out maturational effects, Feldman, et al. (1993) employed a between-groups design with random assignment of 28 mothers with intellectual disabilities (mean IQ = 71.5) to either interaction training or attention-placebo groups. The latter group of mothers participated in the same parenting program as the interaction group, but they received (and needed) training in home safety rather than interactions. At the start of the study, the children ranged in age from 4 to 28 months and the training phase lasted a mean of 45 weeks (scheduled weekly visits lasted approximately 1 hour). Parent interaction training resulted in significant improvements in several child language measures (frequency of vocalizations, verbalizations, initiation of first words, quality of speech, performance on language items of standardized developmental tests). Whereas the interaction group children's vocalizations and verbalizations started significantly below age-matched children whose parents did not have intellectual disabilities (comparison group), after training there was no longer a difference. These improvements maintained in the 55 week follow-up period. Over the period of time that the interaction group received training, an increase in child vocalizations and verbalizations also was seen in the attention-control group. However, their scores were significantly below both the interaction training and comparison children on the posttest. The increase in language behaviors in the control children probably reflected nonprogrammatic maturational and experiential factors. When the control mothers subsequently received interaction training, their children showed a significant increase in language performance and reached levels seen in the original interaction training and comparison groups.

Tymchuk and Andron (1992) used a multiple-baseline design across participants and systematically replicated the Feldman, et al. interaction training with nine mothers with intellectual disabilities (IQs ranged from 63 to 74) and their preschool children (ages not reported). Neither the parental nor child outcomes were as impressive as in Feldman's studies; only 17% of appropriate child behaviors such as compliance, attending to task, and positive speech improved. Although Tymchuk and Andron (1992) worked with similar parents and used similar training strategies as did Feldman and his associates, the varying results of these two programs may be attributable to several methodological differences. Tymchuk and Andron's children were older than those in Feldman, et al. (preschoolers versus infants and toddlers) and they measured several behaviors not reported by Feldman, et al. (1986, 1989, 1993). Feldman, et al. (1989, 1993) used tangible reinforcement for attendance, acquisition, and maintenance of skills, but Tymchuk and Andron did not. Tymchuk and Andron claimed that multiple risk factors (e.g., parental history of abuse, physical and mental illness) may have impeded parental responsiveness to training, while Feldman, et al. (1993) found that similar risk factors were present in their participating mothers but were not correlated with outcomes.

In the case study described above, Greene, et al. (1995) reported that the mother did not know how to properly calm and stimulate her baby and instead she engaged in aversive behaviors such as yelling and rough handling. Interaction training, which started with roleplaying (using a doll) before moving to direct instruction (with the child in the mother's arms), increased the mother's positive, and decreased her negative, handling of her infant. Time series observations showed corresponding increases in child positive behaviors (babbling, cooing) and decreases in child negative behaviors (crying, grimacing).

Keltner, Finn, and Shearer (1995) randomly assigned 40 impoverished mothers with intellectual disabilities (mean IQ was approximately 61), who had children from 23 to 36 months old, either to an intervention consisting of case management, weekly group meetings, and individual home visits or a control condition involving monthly telephone contacts and service referrals. The focus of training was to teach the mothers how to play with and teach their children. Keltner, et al. (1995) found that the intervention group has significantly more positive parent-child interactions than the control group after 1 year. Interaction scores in both groups, however, remained below the normative group on the standardized observational measure (Nursing Child Assessment Teaching Scale; Barnard & Kelly, 1990). The results suggested that the mothers in the intervention group had become more sensitive and responsive to the child's cues, were more positive in their feedback, and promoted social-emotional and cognitive development. The intervention children showed improvements in the interpretability of their cues and their responsiveness to their mothers. Contingent interactions between mothers and children increased in the training group, but their post-training scores were similar to the control group. The findings are difficult to interpret because the statistical tests employed were not described.

In the sole data-based study investigating the combination of psychotherapy and parent training in parents with intellectual disabilities, Leifer and Smith (1990) worked with a single 30 year old depressed mother with 'mild to moderate' mental retardation who had a 4 month old son. They found improvements in mother-child interactions (only after directive parent training was initiated), but no increases in Caldwell HOME Inventory scores; the child's development remained low-average. The potential facilitative role of long-term psychotherapy could not be determined in this case study.

Family Preservation

Few studies have provided family preservation outcomes related to participation in parent education. Feldman, Case, and Sparks (1992) reported a child removal rate prior to intervention of 82% in Toronto that was remarkably consistent with previous citations of family court statistics in the U.S. (e.g., Seagull & Scheurer (1986) reported 83%). After involvement in parent education, however, only 19% of the children were removed from the home in the 1 year following training. Similar results were obtained by Feldman, et al. (1993): 78% of families lost their previous child(ren) before participating in parent training, whereas only 20% had their child removed in the 3 years following their involvement. In both studies, those parents who lost their children tended to be the ones who had dropped out of the program prematurely. Although these findings are encouraging, they should be interpreted cautiously because an experimental design was not used to ascertain that improvements in the trained skills were responsible for the reduced rate of children removed by child protection agencies. It is possible that if a parent with intellectual disabilities simply remains involved in a parenting program, regardless of benefit, then child protection is less likely to place the child in protective custody or seek permanent termination of parenting rights.

Greene, et al. (1995) investigated the relationship between the parent's progress and return of the child in two families with parents who had intellectual disabilities. Verbal agreements or written contracts were established with the child protection agency that stipulated increased child access (and eventual restoration of parental custody) contingent on improvements in trained parenting skills and accomplishment of various tasks (e.g., keeping the house clean and safe; preparing nutritious meals). For the 22-year-old single mother (IQ = 71), whose training results were presented above, improvements in parenting skills resulted in more and longer visits and the subsequent return of her son after 15 months of training.

The second family consisted of two parents who both had intellectual disabilities (mother's IQ = 75; father's IQ was not known, but he was eligible for services for people with mental retardation). An ABA design was used to evaluate a written contract that explicitly tied the parents' completion of tasks to increased access to their two children (ages: 2 and 8 years) who had been in foster care for 18 months when this study started. The implementation of the contract resulted in an immediate, but inconsistent, increase in tasks accomplished and a gradual increase in unsupervised visits with the children. A series of events such as the birth of a third child, a family move, the father's arrest, and the mother's bout of depression were related to reduced task completions. Interestingly, services were terminated by child protection when the father became verbally abusive to a staff member, and the parents never regained custody of their children. Explicit arrangements that make child access contingent on *objective* measures of cooperation and skill improvements have the potential to bring greater impartiality to what are often subjective and biased custody decisions that, nevertheless, have profound implications for families where the parents have intellectual disabilities. The Greene, et al. (1995) methods and findings are intriguing and should encourage further evaluation of these access-for-results contracts.

Summary of Parent Education Interventions

Evidence is accumulating that parent education, together with other services and supports, is a viable alternative to removing the child from the home (Feldman, 1994). Based on current knowledge, ongoing intervention from birth to (at least) 6 years of age likely is necessary to increase the chances that children of parents with intellectual disabilities will be able to stay at home; be raised in a sufficiently safe, nurturing, and stimulating environment; and succeed in school. For most families, such long-term intervention should include (at least) the following components: (a) parent education in child health, safety, nutrition, and other child-care skills (e.g., Feldman, Case, & Sparks, 1992) with ongoing training as the child ages, as needed; (b) daycare placement; (c) parent interaction training to promote child language development during infancy (e.g., Feldman, et al., 1993); and (d) continuing training during the preschool and early school-age years in parenting strategies that foster parent-child rapport, the child's cognitive development (Slater, 1986), and the child's social, emotional, and behavioral adjustment.

FUTURE RESEARCH

Although major strides have been made in understanding the impact of being raised by parents with intellectual disabilities and in the establishment of effective interventions for children of these parents, much work remains to be done. Even basic questions remain unanswered. For example, accurate statistics on the incidence and prevalence of children growing up with parents who have intellectual disabilities are unavailable; existing information primarily is limited to families that have come to the attention of the social service and child welfare systems. Quantitative studies across the age-span of the offspring of parents with intellectual disabilities are needed to determine short- and long-term developmental outcomes and identify risk and protective factors. At present, our knowledge of infant development is limited, and only two qualitative studies inform us about the lives of adolescent and adult offspring (Booth & Booth, 1997; Ronai, 1997).

Much of the research on parenting problems has yet to look beyond intellectual capacity and skill competency to other factors that may negatively impact on parenting abilities. Certainly, a multivariate, transactional or interactional model of parenting (Belsky, 1984; Sameroff & Chandler, 1975) should be applied to better understand the role of pre-, peri-, and postnatal parent, child, and family ecological variables in predicting parenting competency and child outcomes. Further research is required to clarify how parent, child, and family outcomes are affected by the multitude of adversities that (unfortunately) define the lives of many parents with intellectual disabilities.

The ameliorating potential of social support and effective services demands further inquiry. Many more studies are needed to answer basic questions about interventions. Research with parents who have children with developmental disabilities have found that social support protects the family against the negative effects of stress (Dunst, Trivette, & Cross, 1985). Are parents with intellectual disabilities better able to handle adversity if they have satisfactory social support networks? Further study is needed to verify Ramey and Ramey's (1992) preliminary finding that regular daycare may be an important protective experience for children of parents with intellectual disabilities. With about 80% of these children being placed in custody (Feldman, Case, & Sparks, 1992; Feldman, et al., 1993; Seagull & Scheurer, 1986; Taylor, et al., 1991), the lack of suitable foster homes (Keltner, et al., 1995), and the negative effects of foster care (Finklestein, 1980), it is essential to determine if early intervention is more beneficial (and less costly) than foster care. More data are needed on the long-term effects and relative cost-benefits of specialized daycare and parent education interventions on child, parent, and family outcomes. Perhaps a combination of these two strategies will be most effective in protecting children of parents with intellectual disabilities.

Although children of parents with intellectual disabilities are at-risk for behavioral and psychiatric disorders (Feldman & Walton-Allen, 1997; Gillberg & Geijer-Karlsson, 1983; O'Neill, 1985), little effort has been made to develop and evaluate relevant interventions. Finally, further research should examine extensions of the parent education technology developed for parents with intellectual disabilities to other at-risk parents and their children (teenage parents, parents with other disabilities such as acquired brain injury or learning disabilities).

CONCLUSION

Families in which parents have intellectual disabilities probably are increasing in number. Many of these parents have knowledge and skill deficiencies and other characteristics and experiences that impede adequate parenting. Their children clearly are at risk for developmental, academic, behavioral, and social adjustment problems. The more we learn about variables that affect parenting competencies, the impact of being raised by these parents, risk and protective factors, and the provision of effective supports and interventions, the greater the likelihood that the children will be able to remain with their natural families and grow up in safe, nurturing environments that foster positive outcomes. With increasing knowledge, humane custody decisions, and creative solutions, perhaps the cycle of intergenerational transmission of intellectual and parental challenges can be halted.

ACKNOWLEDGMENTS

My research that is cited in this chapter was funded primarily by the Ontario Mental Health Foundation and Ontario Ministry of Community and Social Services. I would like to thank the staff and families of the Parent

Education Program in Toronto (circa 1981–1994) for their contributions to the development and evaluation of the parent education model described herein. Correspondence concerning this chapter should be addressed to Maurice Feldman, Dept. of Psychology, Queen's University, Kingston, Ontario, Canada K7L 3N6; email: feldman@psyc.queensu.ca.

REFERENCES

Adoption Assistance and Child Welfare Act (1980), P.L. 96-272, 94 Stat. 500.

American Psychiatric Association (1994). *Diagnostic and statistical manual of mental disorders* (4th ed.). Washington, DC: Author.

Bakken, J., Miltenberger, R. G., & Schauss, S. (1993). Teaching parents with mental retardation: Knowledge vs. skills. *American Journal on Mental Retardation, 97*, 405–417.

Barnard, K. E. & Kelly, J. F. (1990). Assessment of parent-child interaction. In S. J. Meisels & J. P. Shonkoff (Eds.), *Handbook of early childhood intervention* (pp. 278–302). New York: Cambridge University Press.

Bayley, N. (1969). *Bayley Scales of Infant Development: Birth to two years.* New York: Psychological Corporation.

Belsky, J. (1984). The determinants of parenting: A process model. *Child Development, 55*, 83–96.

Booth, T. & Booth, W. (1997). *Exceptional childhoods, unexceptional children. Growing up with parents who have learning difficulties.* London, UK: Family Policies Studies Centre.

Brandon, M. W. G. (1957). The intellectual and social status of children of mental defectives. *Journal of Mental Science, 103*, 710–738.

Caldwell, B. & Bradley, R. (1984). *Home Observation for Measurement of the Environment.* Unpublished manuscript. Little Rock: University of Arkansas.

Case, L. & Feldman, M. A. (1993). *Step-by-step child-care: A pictorial manual for parents, child-care workers, and babysitters.* Toronto: Authors.

Child and Family Services Act of Ontario (1987). Toronto: Government Printers.

Crittenden, P. M. & Bonvillian, J. D. (1984). The relationship between maternal risk status and maternal sensitivity. *American Journal of Orthopsychiatry, 54*, 250–262.

Dunst, C. J., Trivette, C. M., & Cross, A. H. (1986). Mediating influences of social support: Personal, family, and child outcomes. *American Journal of Mental Deficiency, 90*, 403–417.

Fantuzzo, J. W., Wray, L., Hall, R., Goins, C., & Azar, S. (1986). Parent and social-skills training for mentally retarded mothers identified as child maltreaters. *American Journal of Mental Deficiency, 91*, 135–140.

Feldman, M. A. (1994). Parenting education for parents with intellectual disabilities: A review of outcome studies. *Research in Developmental Disabilities, 15*, 299–332.

Feldman, M. A. (1996). Courses for parents with intellectual disabilities and their children. In Danish Ministry of Social Affairs (Ed.). *Parenting with intellectual disabilities* (pp. 107–121). Copenhagen: Author.

Feldman, M. A. (1997). The effectiveness of early intervention for children of parents with mental retardation. In M. J. Guralnick, (Ed.). *The effectiveness of early intervention: Directions for second generation research* (pp. 171–191). Baltimore: Paul H. Brookes.

Feldman, M. A. (1998). Parents with intellectual disabilities: Implications and interventions. In J. Lutzker (Ed.). *Child abuse: A handbook of theory, research, and treatment* (pp. 401–419). New York: Plenum Press.

Feldman, M. A. & Case, L. (1997). Effectiveness of self-instructional audiovisual materials in teaching child-care skills to parents with intellectual disabilities. *Journal of Behavioral Education, 7*, 235–257.

Feldman, M.A. & Case, L. (1999). Teaching child-care and safety skills to parents with intellectual disabilities through self-learning. *Journal of Intellectual and Developmental Disability, 24*, 27–44.

Feldman, M. A. & Walton-Allen, N. (1997). Effects of maternal mental retardation and poverty on intellectual, academic, and behavioral status of school-age children. *American Journal on Mental Retardation, 101*, 352–364.

Feldman, M. A., Case, L., Towns, F., & Betel, J. (1985). Parent education project I: The development and nurturance of children of mentally retarded parents. *American Journal of Mental Deficiency, 90*, 253–258.

Feldman, M. A., Towns, F., Betel, J., Case, L., Rincover, A., & Rubino, C. A. (1986). Parent Education Project II: Increasing stimulating interactions of developmentally handicapped mothers. *Journal of Applied Behavior Analysis, 19*, 23–37.

Feldman, M. A., Case, L., Rincover, A., Towns, F., & Betel, J. (1989). Parent Education Project III. Increasing affection and responsivity in developmentally handicapped mothers: Component analysis, generalization, and effects on child language. *Journal of Applied Behavior Analysis, 22*, 211–222.

Feldman, M. A., Case, L., Garrick, M., MacIntyre-Grande, W., Carnwell, J., & Sparks, B. (1992). Teaching child-care skills to parents with developmental disabilities. *Journal of Applied Behavior Analysis, 25*, 205–215.

Feldman, M. A., Case, L., & Sparks, B. (1992). Effectiveness of a child-care training program for parents at-risk for child neglect. *Canadian Journal of Behavioural Science, 24*, 14–28.

Feldman, M. A., Sparks, B., & Case, L. (1993). Effectiveness of home-based early intervention on the language development of children of mothers with mental retardation. *Research in Developmental Disabilities, 14*, 387–408.

Feldman, M. A., Garrick, M., & Case, L. (1997). The effects of parent training on weight gain of nonorganic-failure-to-thrive children of parents with intellectual disabilities. *Journal on Developmental Disabilities, 5*, 47–61.

Feldman, M. A., Léger, M., & Walton-Allen, N. (1997). Stress in mothers with intellectual disabilities. *Journal of Child and Family Studies, 6*, 471–485

Feldman, M. A., Ducharme, J. M., & Case, L. (1999). Using self-instructional pictorial manuals to teach child-care skills to mothers with intellectual disabilities. *Behavior Modification, 23*, 480–497.

Finklestein, N. E. (1980). Children in limbo. *Social Work, 25*, 100–105.

Fotheringham, J. B. (1971). The concept of social competence as applied to marriage and child care in those classified as mentally retarded. *Canadian Medical Association Journal, 104*, 813–816.

Garber, H. L. (1988). *The Milwaukee Project: Preventing mental retardation in children at risk.* Washington, DC: American Association on Mental Retardation.

Garber, H. L., Hodge, J. D., Rynders, J., Dever, R., & Velu, R. (1991). The Milwaukee Project: Setting the record straight. *American Journal on Mental Retardation, 95*, 493–525.

Gillberg, C. & Geijer-Karlsson, M. (1983). Children born to mentally retarded women: A 1–21 year follow-up study of 41 cases. *Psychological Medicine, 13*, 891–894.

Greene, B. F., Norman, K. R., Searle, M. S., Daniels, M., & Lubeck, R. C. (1995). Child abuse and neglect by parents with disabilities: A tale of two families. *Journal of Applied Behavior Analysis, 28*, 417–434.

Hayman, R. L. (1990). Presumptions of justice: Law, politics, and the mentally retarded parent. *Harvard Law Review, 103*, 1201–1271.

Jensen, A. R. (1989). Raising IQ without increasing *g*? A review of the Milwaukee Project: Preventing mental retardation in children at risk. *Developmental Review, 9*, 234–258.

Keltner, B. R. (1992). Caregiving by mothers with mental retardation. *Family & Community Health, 15*(2), 10–18.

Keltner, B. R. (1994). Home environments of mothers with mental retardation. *Mental Retardation, 32*, 123–127.

Keltner, B. R., Finn, D., & Shearer, D. (1995). Effects of family intervention on mother-child interaction for mothers with developmental disabilities. *Family & Community Health, 17*, 35–49.

Leifer, M. & Scott, S. (1990). Preventive intervention with a depressed mother with mental retardation and her infant: A quantitative case study. *Infant Mental Health Journal, 11*, 301–314.

Llewellyn, G. (1996). Support and services needs of parents with intellectual disabilities: Parent perspectives. Danish Ministry of Social Affairs (Ed.), *Parenting with intellectual disabilities*, (pp. 7–24). Copenhagen: Author.

Luckasson, R., Coulter, D. L., Polloway, E. A., Reiss, S., Schalock, R. L., Snell, M. E., Spitalnik, D. M., & Stark, J. A. (1992). *Mental retardation: Definition, classification, and systems of supports* (9th ed.). Washington, DC: American Association on Mental Retardation.

Madsen, M. (1979). Parenting classes for the mentally retarded. *Mental Retardation, 17*, 195–196.

Martin, S. M., Ramey, C. T., & Ramey, S. (1990). The prevention of intellectual impairment in children of impoverished families: Findings of a randomized trial of educational day care. *American Journal of Public Health, 80*, 844–847.

McGaw, S. (1996). Development of parent capabilities. In Danish Ministry of Social Affairs (Ed.), *Parenting with intellectual disabilities* (pp. 123–126). Copenhagen: Author.

Mickelson, P. (1947). The feebleminded parent: A study of 90 family cases. *American Journal of Mental Deficiency, 51*, 644–653.

Nelson, K. B. & Ellenberg, J. H. (1986). Antecedents of cerebral palsy: Multivariate analysis of risk. *New England Journal of Medicine, 315*, 81–86.

Offord, D. R., Boyle, M. H., Szatmari, P., Rae-Grant, N. I., Links, P. S., Cadman, D. T., Byles, J. A., Crawford, J. W., Blum, H. M., Byrne, C., Thomas, H., & Woodward, C. A. (1987). Ontario Child Health Study: II. Six month prevalence of disorder and rates of service utilization. *Archives of General Psychiatry, 44*, 832–836.

O'Neill, A. M. (1985). Normal and bright children of mentally retarded parents: The Huck Finn syndrome. *Child Psychiatry and Human Development, 15*, 255–268.

Page, E. B. (1986). The disturbing case of the Milwaukee Project. In H. H. Spitz (Ed.), *The raising of intelligence: A selected history of attempts to raise retarded intelligence* (pp. 115–140). Hillsdale, NJ: Lawrence Erlbaum Associates.

Pixa-Kettner, U. (1996). Can we, or shall we prevent intellectually disabled people from becoming parents? In Danish Ministry of Social Affairs (Ed.), *Parenting with intellectual disabilities* (pp. 93–105). Copenhagen: Author.

Ramey, C. T. & Ramey, S. L. (1992). Effective early intervention. *Mental Retardation, 30*, 337–345.

Ray, N. K., Rubinstein, H., & Russo, N. J. (1994). Understanding the parents who are mentally retarded: Guidelines for family preservation programs. *Child Welfare, 73*, 725–742.

Reed, R. & Reed, S. (1965). *Mental retardation: A family study*. New York: Saunders.

Ronai, C. R. (1997). On loving and hating my mentally retarded mother. *Mental Retardation, 35*, 417–432.

Sameroff, A. J. & Chandler, M. (1975). Reproductive risk and the continuum of caretaker causality. In F. Horowitz (Ed.), *Review of child development research* (Vol. 4, pp. 157–243). Chicago: University of Chicago Press.

Scally, B. G. (1973). Marriage and mental handicap: Some observations in Northern Ireland. In F. F. de la Cruz & G. D. La Veck (Eds.), *Human sexuality and the mentally retarded* (pp. 186–194). New York: Brunner/Mazel.

Schilling, R., Schinke, P., Blythe, B., & Barth, R. (1982). Child maltreatment and mentally retarded parents: Is there a relationship? *Mental Retardation, 20*, 201–209.

Seagull, E. A. & Scheurer, S. L. (1986). Neglected and abused children of mentally retarded parents. *Child Abuse and Neglect, 10*, 493–500.

Slater, M. A. (1986). Modification of mother-child interaction processes in families with children at-risk for mental retardation. *American Journal of Mental Deficiency, 91*, 257–267.

Sommer, R. & Sommer, B. A. (1983). Mystery in Milwaukee: Early intervention, IQ, and psychology textbooks. *American Psychologist, 38*, 982–985.

Sparling, J. & Lewis, I. (1979). *Learningames for the first three years: A guide to parent/child play*. New York: Walker & Co.

Sparling, J. & Lewis, I. (1984). *Learningames for threes and fours: A guide to adult/child play*. New York: Walker & Co.

Spitz, H. H. (1991). Review of the Milwaukee Project: Preventing mental retardation in children at risk. *American Journal on Mental Retardation, 95*, 482–490.

Taylor, C. G., Norman, D. K., Murphy, J. M., Jellinek, M., Quinn, D., Poitrast, F. G., & Goshko, M. (1991). Diagnosed intellectual and emotional impairment among parents who seriously mistreat their children: Prevalence, type, and outcome in a court sample. *Child Abuse and Neglect, 15*, 389–401.

Tymchuk, A. J. (1991). Training mothers with mental retardation to understand general rules in the use of high-risk household products. *Journal of Practical Approaches to Developmental Handicaps, 15*, 15–19.

Tymchuk, A. J. & Andron, L. (1988). Clinic and home parent training of a mother with mental handicap caring for three children with developmental delay. *Mental Handicap Research, 1*, 24–38.

Tymchuk, A. J. & Andron, L. (1992). Project Parenting: Child interactional training with mothers who are mentally handicapped. *Mental Handicap Research, 5*, 4–32.

Tymchuk, A. J. & Feldman, M. A. (1991). Parents with mental retardation and their children: A review of research relevant to professional practice. *Canadian Psychology/Psychologie Canadienne, 32*, 486–496.

Tymchuk, A. J. & Keltner, B. (1991). Advantage profiles: A tool for health care professionals working with parents with mental retardation. *Pediatric Nursing, 14*, 155–161.

Tymchuk, A. J., Hamada, D., Andron, L., & Anderson, S. (1990). Home safety training with mothers who are mentally retarded. *Education and Training in Mental Retardation, 25*, 142–149.

Tymchuk, A. J., Andron, L., & Hagelstein, M. (1992). Training mothers with mental retardation to discuss home safety and emergencies with their children. *Journal of Developmental and Physical Disabilities, 4*, 151–165.

Vogel, P. (1987). The right to parent. *Entourage, 2*, 33–39.

Walton-Allen, N. (1993). *Psychological distress and parenting by mothers with mental retardation* (Doctoral dissertation, University of Toronto).

Walton-Allen, N. & Feldman, M. A. (1991). Perception of service needs by parents with mental retardation and their workers. *Comprehensive Mental Health Care, 1*, 137–147.

Weinberg, R. A. (1991). Review of the Milwaukee Project: Preventing mental retardation in children at risk. *American Journal on Mental Retardation, 95*, 490–492.

Whitman, B. & Accardo, P. (1990). *When the parent is mentally retarded.* Baltimore: Paul H. Brookes.

Index